The Dialogues

of

A COURSE OF

LOVE

Coming to Voice

THE COURSE OF LOVE SERIES

Book One: A Course of Love
Book Two: The Treatises of A Course of Love
Book Three: The Dialogues of A Course of Love

The Dialogues

of

A COURSE OF

LOVE

Coming to Voice

COURSE OF LOVE PUBLICATIONS
ST. PAUL, MINNESOTA

Course of Love Publications
432 Rehnberg Place
W. St. Paul, Minnesota 55118
www.acourseoflove.com
acol@thedialogues.com

First Course of Love Publications Edition
Printed in the United States of America
Formerly printed as The Dialogues: Coming to Voice

ISBN 0-9728668-4-1

This edition is printed on 60 lb. Vellum natural recycled paper.

Distributed in the United States by Itasca Books
Prism Publishing Center
5120 Cedar Lake Road
Minneapolis, MN 55416
www.ItascaBooks.com

CONTENTS

FOREWORD

After the Course of Love series was complete, Jesus provided "Learning in the Time of Christ" as an aid to those questioning how to work with the material of this Course. It has been edited here to serve as an introduction to The Dialogues. The full text is available from: www.acourseoflove.com.

Beyond the coursework of the treatises lies direct relationship...direct relationship with me. Entering the dialogue is the way this is expressed, yet this is not merely about entering spoken dialogue. As was said in *A Treatise on the Art of Thought*, "Creation is but a dialogue to which you have not responded."

Creation is a dialogue.

Creation is an unending act of giving and receiving as one. So too is dialogue.

"Listen and you will hear." But to what are you listening? Entering the dialogue is akin to residing in the present moment and to hearing all that is being spoken in all the ways it is being spoken. Now is the time to truly begin to "hear" my voice in every aspect of creation and to respond with your own voice in all of your own acts of creation. It is time to realize that you are a creator.

This is a time of great intimacy. This is a time that is between you and I more so that has been the coursework up to this point. It is a time of realizing that "I" am speaking to "you" directly in every moment of everyday, in all that you encounter, in all that you feel. It is a time of true revelation in which you are revealed to your Self. This is what dialogue, particularly the dialogue that is an exchange between "two or more gathered together" reveals. It reveals Who You Are.

This relationship between Self and Other, Self and Life, Self and God, Humanity and Divinity, is the dialogue of which we speak.

It may seem to suggest duality but it suggests relationship. The idea of unity and relationship must fully enter you now.

You are not a "student" of *The Dialogues* but a full participant in *The Dialogues*. You have entered the final stages of revelation of Who You Are. When Who You Are is fully revealed you will realize that it is time to leave the classroom and live as Who You Are in the world. You will realize that your participation in the world as Who You Are is part of an on-going dialogue, and that it is an on-going aspect of creation by which the new will be created.

What now will be your relationship to this work that has returned you to Who You Are? Your relationship to this work continues as you live and express Who You Are being in the world. For some of you this may mean continued involvement with this coursework and a direct sharing of it with others. For many more of you it will not.

For each, being Who You Are will be an expression of unity and oneness that only you are able to express. As each expresses who she/he is being in unity and relationship, creation of the new will proceed and wholeness and healing renew the world in which you live. This Course becomes a beloved alma mater, honored and returned to as a giver of new life. It offers no walls to confine you. It becomes not dogma to restrict you. It is new life come to extend the way of creation, the way of love, the way of life, the new way. It will be with you in every dialogue and will not leave you comfortless. It has no end point in its benefits and associations.

What continues of this Course is its dialogue. It is on-going.

Gather still with those with whom you learned and grew and became new, but gather in ever wider configurations. This dialogue is going on all around you. I am with you and will never leave you comfortless. Call on me, for I am here. Talk to me, and I will hear you. Listen, and I will respond. I am in each voice that responds to you and your voice is mine as you respond to others.

Go forth not as completed works of art but as permeable energy, ever changing, ever creating, ever new. Go forth with openness for revelation to happen through you and through all you encounter. Go forth joyously on this adventure of discovery. Be ever new, ever one, ever the beloved.

Bring your voice to this continuing dialogue. This is all that is asked of you. This is the gift you have been given and the gift you bring the world: your own voice, the voice of Who You Are. This is a voice not of separation or of the separated self but a voice of union and of the One Self. It is how union is expressed and made recognizable in form. It is what will usher in the new and change the world. It cannot be accomplished without you - without your ability to stand in unity and relationship as The Accomplished. Beloved brothers and sisters, You are The Accomplished.

Acceptance

chapter 1

Acceptance of the State of Grace of the Newly Identified Child of God

Dear Brothers and Sisters in Christ,

I come to you today as co-creator of the Self you are and the Self you hope to represent with your physical form. I come to you today not as a personal self who is "other" than you, but as a divine Self who is the same as you. In our union we bear the sameness of the Son of God. In going forth with the vision of unity you become as I was during life. You receive and you give from the well of the spirit. You need not prepare or plan, you need only to claim your inheritance, your gifts, your Self.

What this means in practical terms is that you let the personal self step back and the true Self step forward. Realize that all of your concerns are still for the personal self, a self whom you continue to believe can fail to fulfill or live your mission and your purpose. You "see" this failure occurring through ineptness of speech, through inappropriateness of attire, through lack of physical stamina, through lack of intelligence — through lack, in other words, of abilities of the personal self. As long as you "see" such visions, you see the pattern of the personal self going forth much as it did before. You do not see the new, the new Self of elevated form or the true Self of divine union.

You "see" the separated self still trying, still struggling, still fumbling along. You do not see the natural grace and order of the universe extending into the realm of the elevated Self, the space

3

of the elevated Self. As long as you see in this way, you keep the personal self in the forefront rather than allowing and aiding the personal self in the stepping back that is required in order for the true Self to step forward.

All of this confusion and struggle is occurring because you do not know what to do to prepare. You have not been convinced that you are done preparing as you are done with learning. You still want to figure out what to do, what comes next, what you need to learn, how to better "prepare" for what is ahead.

And yet you know that you have been prepared by me, and that in union with me you cannot fail. You cannot fail to be prepared, for you are already accomplished. What will it now take for your mind to accept this truth? For the mind's acceptance of this truth is what is needed.

Your heart knows the reality of this truth, knows that this new reality is real and different from the reality of old. Ideally, mind and heart in union together accept this new reality and, with this acceptance, the heart is freed to dwell in the house of the Lord, the new world, the Kingdom that has *already* been prepared and so needs no preparation.

This acceptance is crucial to the elevation of the personal self. Without this acceptance the personal self must still struggle and try, prepare and plan. It does not know how to do otherwise. *You* do not think you know how to do otherwise. This is the final surrender. The surrender of the control of the personal self. Even with the ego gone, the personal self can continue to move about within the world, a faceless and nameless entity, a being without an identity, humble and selfless and ineffective. For there must be cause to engender effect.

These anti-ego tendencies are a real danger in this time. You are not called to selflessness but to *Self!*

4

This is the transition you have felt yourself to be in. The ego is gone but the true Self has not been allowed as yet to dwell within the personal self, thus elevating the personal self. You have thus been self-less for a time and the personal self has floundered from this lack of identity. A person could literally die during this time from lack of identity, lack of cause. To die to the personal self is not what is required any longer as we work instead to elevate the personal self. This elevation occurs through the acceptance of your true identity, not through being identity-less. The reign of the ego began during just such a time of identity-less-ness. You cannot go on in such a way.

Help is here.

Be what you have been called to be. Open your dwelling place to your true Self, your true identity. Imagine this opening and this replacement occurring with every fiber of your being. Imagine the separate self being enfolded, embraced, and finally consumed — taken into the Self of union. The body of Christ becomes real through this indwelling of Christ in form.

This thought makes you worry about the identity of the one you have called yourself. This has been the purpose of many renaming ceremonies that symbolize the release of the old and the acceptance of the *new*. This occurs in one form or another in the sacraments you have known as Baptism, Confirmation, and Marriage. Each of these invite a new *identity*. So, too, do we invite a new identity now. While these sacraments have largely lost their meaning, the sacrament I now call you to restores meaning. Since new names are only symbols of new identities, renaming is not required or expected here. We go beyond what can be symbolized to what can only be known within. It is to this state of grace that I call you now, today: the state of grace of the newly identified child of God.

Open your heart, for the one who dwells there in union with all will emerge from this opening. What was once a tiny pinprick of

light becomes a beacon as you open your heart and allow your
true identity to be what *is,* even within your form. You *are* in
grace and union with the Source and Cause of unity. Be no longer
causeless. You and your Source are one.

I am no longer the personal self
who was separate and alone.
I am my Christ Self.
I dwell in unity.
My identity is certain.
This is the truth.
I am not less than I once was, but more.
Where once I was empty, I now am full.
Where once I dwelt in darkness
I now dwell in the light.
Where once I had forgotten
Now I remember
Who I Am.
Now I go forth
To live as who I Am within the world
To make cause and effect as one, and
Union with the Source of love
and all creation the reality.

These dialogues are for everyone because we exist in unity with everyone. No one will be forced to join our conversation. Only those listening will be ready to hear. Only those ready to hear will listen. Remember that you cannot be taught what unity would freely give. The goal is no longer learning. The goal is accepting the identity that has always been yours and that has newly been revealed and returned to your remembrance. To "know" and not accept what you "know" to be the truth is a continuation of the pattern of insanity that must be replaced with a pattern of sanity.

Insanity is acting as if the truth is not the truth. Sanity is accepting the truth as your reality and acting from that truth. Once the truth has been learned, the nature of untruth remains only as an acceptance of insanity. What I will help you now to do is to reject this insanity and to accept the perfect sanity of the truth.

This cannot be done through learning, for as you have been told, learning was the means of the separated self's return to unity. These lessons have been given. They can be reviewed and reviewed again. They can be used as continuing lessons until you feel that learning is fully accomplished. They can serve as reminders as you continue to become the Self you have learned that you are. But further learning is not what will complete the transformation of the personal self to the elevated self. Learning will not sustain Christ-consciousness.

So what is it that we will now do? If I do not teach, and you do not learn, what is our continuing means for completing this transformation? As you have been shown, this will not occur by means of preparation but by means of acceptance. This will not occur by means of trying but by means of surrender.

As you begin this dialogue, questions naturally arise. You might think that for the receiver of this dialogue, this dialogue may, in truth, feel like a dialogue, an exchange, a conversation, and wonder how you, as a reader of these words, can feel that same way. You can feel that same way by realizing that you are, as you read these words, as much a "receiver" of this dialogue as she who first hears these words and transfers them to paper.

Is a piece of music not received by you even when you may be one of thousands or millions who hear it? Does it matter who is first to hear the music? This is, in truth, a dialogue between me and you. Wish not that the "way" of the transcriber of these words were the way for everyone, and think not that to hear "directly" from the Source is different than what you do here. This is thinking with the mindset of separation rather than the mindset of unity. What I say to you here, I say to you. It matters not that I say these same words to many, for you and the many who join you in receiving these words are one.

These dialogues begin with prayer to remind you of what you have learned in unity, a learning that has been different from all learning you but thought you accomplished as a separated self. You have achieved an incredible feat by allowing and accepting the state of unity even though you could not learn how to do so. This has been the difficulty with every curriculum that has sought to teach the truth. In order for the truth to be truly learned, you first had to enter a state in which this learning could occur, a state that could not be taught but only accessed through your longing and desire.

You who have joined mind and heart in unity have returned to a natural state of knowing in which learning is no longer needed. You have now come upon a curriculum that is impossible to learn. No teacher is available for none is needed. And yet many of you still feel what you would describe as a need for continued learning and a continuing relationship with a teacher who will guide you through the application of what you have learned. You dare not, as yet, turn to your own heart, and trust the knowing that has been returned to you as you begin to live in the reality of the truth.

This is akin to thinking of a god who exists outside or apart from yourself. If you fully accepted your true identity, you would no longer look outside of yourself for guidance for you would realize that your Self is all there is. We are one body, one Christ.

We are one Self.

Your Self is not the person you have been since birth. Your body does not contain you. What you are going to find happening, as you accept your true identity, is a transference of purpose concerning your body. What once you saw as yourself, you now must come to see only as a *representation* of your Self. You *are* everything and everyone. All that you see *is* you. You stand not separate and apart from anything.

We are one body.

Learning accepts that there are those separate from you who know things that you know not. This is not the case. When you fully accept this, you will see that it is true. Like the acceptance of unity that could not be taught, but was the condition for true learning, acceptance of your true identity cannot be taught but is the condition necessary for being who you are and the realization that learning is no longer necessary.

Thus we work now toward acceptance of what you have learned in unity. We work toward your acceptance of sanity and your rejection of insanity. We work together in love and unity for what can only be received in the love and unity in which we truly exist together, as one body, one Christ, one Self.

chapter 2

Acceptance and Denial

You are now asked to do two things simultaneously: To accept the new and to deny the old. Acceptance is a willingness to receive. Obviously, when you consider this definition of acceptance, you will see that this is not the way of the old. Willingness to receive is quite contrary to the attitudes and actions with which you have led your life thus far.

You were told within *A Course of Love* (the Course) that willingness was all that was necessary for you to be able to take the Course into your heart and let it return you to your true identity. Those of you who found within this willingness an ability to receive and left behind your effort to "learn" the Course, began the work that is being continued here, the work of replacing the old patterns of learning with the new pattern of acceptance.

To deny is to *refuse* to accept as true or right that which you know is not true or right. This is the denial of insanity in favor of the acceptance of sanity, the denial of the false for the acceptance of the true. Although you are called to these two actions simultaneously — the action of acceptance and the action of denial — it can be seen that they are, in truth, one and the same action, just as means and end, cause and effect are one. You are asked to accept or receive the truth of who you are and the revelations that will show you how to live as who you are within the world — and you are asked to *refuse* to accept who you are

10

not and the ways of life that allowed you to live within the world as a false self.

The patterns of the new will begin to arise naturally when you deny the patterns of the old. As you have been told, you now "know what you do" and are no longer a victim to the circumstance of a split mind that allowed the confusion that led me to once say, "They know not what they do." You must understand that you do know, and you will know, as soon as the patterns of old have been denied. Denial is the correct word here, for I do not want you combating or resisting the old patterns. Patterns are not in quite the same category as the false remembering you were able to purge through unlearning.

Patterns are both learned systems and systems of design. The pattern of learning was a pattern of divine design, created in unity and cooperation to enable the return to unity. This pattern has achieved its desired end and so is no longer needed nor appropriate. While it was once a pattern whose design was perfect for the desired end, continuation of this pattern will now but interfere with your full acceptance of who you are in truth.

An example of a pattern whose design was perfect for the desired end is that of formal education. Education has a natural endpoint. When the education of a doctor, teacher, scientist, priest, or engineer is completed, it is time for the student to claim a new *identity* — that of doctor, teacher, scientist, priest or engineer — and to begin to live that new identity. To continue to feel a need to learn rather than realizing that the time of learning has come to an end, would be to not realize *completion*.

In the example used here, an example that illustrates only one aspect of the learner's life, an inability to claim the new identity could at times be acceptable and even appropriate. In regard to the learning that you have now completed, learning that has revealed the true nature of who you are, your inability to realize

11

your *completion* and claim your new identity cannot be seen as acceptable or appropriate.

This is not a judgment but simply the truth. To learn the truth and not accept it is different from learning what is necessary for a career. To learn the truth and not accept the truth is insane. To learn the truth and not accept the *completion* of your learning is insane.

If you do not realize that you have learned all that you need to learn, you will retain the consciousness of the separated self rather than sustaining Christ-consciousness.

It is because the patterns of old have at times provided you with a false certainty that they are difficult to deny. When we speak of denying here, we speak of denying yourself the *use* of the old so that the new can *serve* you. We speak of denying modes of learning in favor of simple acceptance of what *is*.

It is proper now to deny the modes of learning, even when they seemed to work for you in the past. That they seemed to work is the illusion that will give way as you deny yourself access to the old so that the *new* can come.

If you will examine this pattern of what you have believed "works for you," you will find that you believe that each and every pattern will work in one instance and not in another and that you make this judgment based upon the outcome. You make this judgment "after the fact" when the outcome has occurred. For example, study habit that allowed the learner to achieve a successful grade or outcome in one instance would tend to be seen as a "successful pattern," and would be repeated until such a time as the pattern failed to achieve the successful grade or outcome in another instance. What you have believed "works for you" is really like a game of chance. You give it a try, and if the outcome is as you desired it to be you call it a success. If the outcome is not as you desired it to be you call it a failure. You admit that what you thought would work did not work.

This will not often prevent you from trying the same thing again although at times it will. No matter what you try, however, it is based on this concept of trial and error. No sure results are counted on. When a pattern of thought or behavior has been found to work in more cases than not, it is clung to as a "sure thing" — a proven pattern or way.

What is seen as not "working for you" are often those matters that are beyond your personal control. Patterns of personal control have become particularly entrenched. Thus have you learned ideas such as *when all else fails, plain old hard work will see you through,* or that *safety is the absence of risk taking,* or that *information is power.*

Many of you have believed that the more details of life you have within your control, the more likely you are to control outcome. Others of you have believed that the more details of your life that are kept under the control of a benevolent system, such as that of government, the more likely you are to experience desired outcomes. Either way, control is seen as a powerful pattern.

Although they may not have seemed so, all patterns have had to do with learning because you were, as a separated self, a being whose only function was learning. The function of all learning was to return you to your true identity. Because we are working now for the integration of your true identity into the self of form, or the elevation of the personal self, new patterns are needed.

Systems are the result of your attempts to externalize patterns. Patterns are contained within. Looking at the patterns you have attempted to externalize can help you to understand the nature of patterns.

The justice system is a good example, an example of a system which you believe works most of the time, and are happy to use to acquire a desired end, but which, when it does not provide the solution you might have desired, becomes a system you would rail against.

You might consider that no "system" is foolproof, and still be willing to accept the bad with the good; but you would freely admit that your belief in any system "working for you" is not total.

Any system that is not foolproof is based on a faulty design, a faulty pattern. Your misperceptions of the world have allowed for the development of no foolproof systems because these systems are based upon misperceptions or illusion. Your desire to cling to systems that are not foolproof is insane, for their creation is based on the workings of a split mind and a split mind does not think clearly.

All systems have been based upon your desire to understand the world *around* you rather than the world *within* you. If you were to understand the world *within,* you would need no systems to understand or manage the world *without*. These systems were attempts to learn the nature of who you are through external means — the means of learning the nature of the world around you. In the example used earlier of the justice system, you looked at the world and people around you and found the nature of both to be hostile. From this faulty conclusion you developed a faulty system based upon faulty judgment.

This system was meant to help you learn to deal fairly with a hostile environment and then to develop a pattern based on what was learned so that learning would not need to be endlessly repeated. Now these systems and patterns have become so entrenched that no new learning is seen as possible or desirable even though the systems and patterns are known not to work. In truth, no new learning or new systems based on the learning patterns of old will work.

Thus we begin anew.

The seeming difficulty with this new beginning stems from your desire to learn anew. You would say, "If the justice system doesn't work, let's fix it." You would say, "If the old way doesn't work, teach me a new way." You would say, "I will work hard to learn and to implement the new if you will just tell me what that new way is!" You would say, "Teach me the new pattern and I will put it into effect."

What this points out is a pattern in itself. It is a pattern of reaction rather than cause. It is a pattern of looking without and wondering what to do about what you see rather than a pattern of changing what you see by looking within. Within is where the real world and all your brothers and sisters exist in the unity of Christ-consciousness. Change within effects change without, not the other way around! Within is where you look to your own heart, rather than to any other authority, for advice or guidance. Within is where you find the knowing of Christ-consciousness, the consciousness of unity. Within is where you find the power of creation, the power to create the patterns of the new. Looking within is not an attempt to find the answers of the personal self of old, the separated self who depended on learned wisdom for answers. Looking within is turning to the real Self and the consciousness shared by all for the creation of a new answer, the answer to the only remaining question; that of how to sustain Christ-consciousness in form.

This is the agreement God asks of you, your part of the shared agreement that will fulfill the promises of your inheritance. This is the Covenant of the New in which you honor your agreement to bring heaven to earth and to usher in the reign of Christ. To *usher in* is to show the way, to cast your palms upon the path of

The Dialogues

your brothers and sisters. Do you not see that your acceptance of this promise is the acceptance of your own? Do you not see that acceptance of the new and denial of the old is the necessary forerunner of our work together in establishing the Covenant of the New?

chapter 3

the Covenant of the New

The Covenant of the New is simply our agreement to proceed together on the palm-strewn path of Christ-consciousness. It is a path upon which joy triumphs over sorrow and victory triumphs over defeat. All that it requires is the acceptance of the new and the denial of the old that will allow for the sustainability of Christ-consciousness in form.

My dear brothers and sisters in Christ, this is the call you have heard for as long as you can remember, the call you have heard as often as you have grown still and listened. It is the one beautiful note, the tolling of the bell of the Lord, your invitation to return home. This call has always sounded. It is not a death knell but a call to life. It is not of the past or the future but of the eternal now. It is within you as we speak, the tone and timber of this dialogue.

It calls to you and asks you to invest your life with the very purpose you have always desired. You are not purposeless now. Your life is not meaningless. You are the ushers, the pioneers of the new. Your work, as will be often repeated, is to accept the new, and deny or refuse to accept the old. Only in this way will the new triumph over the old.

I have purposefully used words such as *victory* and *triumph* — words unusual to the body of this work. I use them as I use together the words *accept* and *deny*. As the old must be denied for

17

the new to come into being, the old must be vanquished in order for the truth to triumph over illusion.

As the wholehearted, you have it within your ability to do what those who live their lives with a split mind could never do. You have it within your ability to mend the rift of duality, a state that was necessary for the learning of the separated self but that is no longer necessary. The mending of the rift between heart and mind returned you to your Self. In the same way, the mending of the rift of duality will return the world to its Self. The mending of the rift of duality was accomplished in you when you joined mind and heart and returned to the oneness and unity of Christ-consciousness. Sustaining Christ-consciousness will accomplish the same thing in your world.

Duality and contrast are synonymous. In the time of the Holy Spirit, you learned through contrast. You learned from the contrast of good and evil, weak and strong, right and wrong. You learned from the contrast of love and fear, sickness and health, life and death. In this time of Christ, such learning is no longer necessary, and so these conditions of learning are no longer necessary. Thus one of your first acts of acceptance is the acceptance of the end of the conditions of learning. Yet this does not mean that you accept goodness and deny evil or even that you accept love and deny fear. How can this be?

Our first action in understanding what we are called together to do is to begin to declassify all the various aspects of life that were needed in the time of learning. This is why we began quite truthfully and simply with an acceptance of the new and denial of the old. This is as far as acceptance and denial need go. For if you give credence to the ideas of contrast, you bring those ideas forward with you into the new. We let the old go, and with it all ideas of contrast and opposites, of conflict and opposing forces. This is all that is needed for the new to triumph over the old. There are no battles needed, no victories hard won through might and struggle. This is what is meant by surrender. We

18

achieve victory now through surrender, an active and total acceptance of what is given.

Let us talk again for a moment of the idea of giving and receiving as one that was introduced within *A Course of Love* and taught quite thoroughly in *A Treatise on Unity and Its Recognition*. Let's talk of this now as an idea rather than as something learned, and as an idea for you to carry forward with you into the new. This is the first of many ideas that were previously taught that I would like to talk of in a new way. These are ideas that address your true nature as a being existing in union, and this is why we call them ideas to carry forward. These are new ideas to you because you have recently learned them and through the art of thought begun to integrate them into the elevated Self of form. Yet these are really not new ideas. Rather, they are ideas of who you truly are birthed within the self. They allow the Self, and the elevated Self of form, to work with ideas birthed from the same source.

Ideas of who you truly are, birthed by the wholehearted self in union with all, are the ideas that will allow new patterns to emerge and the design of the future to be created. These are the ideas that replace the learned concepts we leave behind.

You will notice that all of these ideas have in common a quality of oneness. Oneness replaces duality or contrast. You will be seeking now for replacements for that which formerly ordered your life. Thus we will speak of these replacements.

That giving and receiving are one in truth is best understood by taking away the idea of one who gives and one who receives. If all are one, such ideas make no sense. This would seem to make the idea of giving and receiving as one senseless as well. In a way, this is true. Giving and receiving as one is senseless in terms related to a shared consciousness. Giving and receiving as one is not senseless when that shared consciousness is occupying form.

All ideas leave not their source. Giving and receiving is an idea.

19

The Dialogues

All ideas exist apart from form. Giving and receiving are one within the shared consciousness of unity, which is the same as saying giving and receiving are one in truth. A shared consciousness is the truth of who you are.

The elevation of the personal self requires that this giving and receiving as one be shared in form. Yet the elevated form, which now represents the shared consciousness of the Self, is not separate from the shared consciousness. Thus giving and receiving as one is now the nature of the elevated Self of form, and what we work toward through this dialogue is your full awareness of what this means.

Helping you to achieve full awareness of who you are is different than helping you to learn. You know what you need to know. What we seek to achieve through this dialogue is acceptance and awareness of what you know. Acceptance is easily achieved through willingness. Full awareness *in form* of what has previously been hidden by the mists of illusion is the more challenging task.

Giving and receiving as one have become one in form as well as one in idea. What this means, simply stated once again, is that giving and receiving occur in unison, or in union. There is no "time" in which giving and receiving seem to be separate actions. There is no "time" in which giving and receiving is not occurring. Giving and receiving as one simply describes the nature of the new, the nature of shared consciousness.

What might this mean to the elevated Self of form? Using this dialogue as an example will serve to explain. This dialogue is continuous and ongoing. It *is* giving and receiving as one. It is merely represented by the words on this page and the words on this page are but a representation of what is continuously being shared. So too is it with you. You, as the elevated Self of form, are a continual representation of what is continuously being given and received, what is continuously being shared. You are a representation, for instance, of this dialogue. You are a representation of all of your brothers and sisters in Christ. You are a representation of the truth. You are a representation of all that is given and received in truth. You are a representation of creation. A representation of union. You are a representation of the Self.

As the Self, you are giver and receiver. Your Self is a full participant in this dialogue. You as the Self *are* the truth. You as the Self *are* the creator and the created. You as the Self are union itself. This is what awareness is about. Consciousness has to do with that which you are aware of. To know what you now know, and remain aware only of the reality of the separated self, would not sustain Christ-consciousness in form.

This is why I will often repeat that I am no longer your teacher. You must realize your oneness with me and all that was created and you cannot do so while you think of me as teacher and yourself as student. While you think of yourself as a learning being you will still be looking to something or someone "other" than your Self rather than seeking the awareness that exists within.

This is not meant to convey any division between the Self and the elevated Self of form, but to demonstrate that there is a difference *in form* between the Self and the elevated Self of form. The Self was and will always remain more than the body. Yet the body is also newly the Self. The body is also, newly, one body, one Christ.

It is this difference that exists between the Self and the elevated Self of form that make of us creators of the new, because the elevated Self of form is new. The Self is eternal. Your Self of elevated form is newly birthed, just as I was once newly birthed even though my Self was eternal. One of the major things we will be seeing as we proceed is the difference between form and content and the difference in the way separate forms express

21

content. It will be challenging to become aware that different expressions do not make different. These differences were spoken of within the Course as unique expressions of the selfsame love that exists in all.

As the system of nature supports the life of many different trees, the trees are all still of one life-giving and life-supporting system.

Can this be said of any of the systems you have developed as a learning being? Are your systems life-giving and life-supporting?

The patterns of the new will create only such life-giving and life-supporting systems — as long as the patterns of the new are accepted and lived with your full awareness.

Now I realize that this is just the first step revealed and that many of you will feel already as if you are being asked to learn again and not only that, but as if I have presented you with a concept difficult to learn. What you need remember now is that your separated self already learned this concept of giving and receiving, and that for the elevated Self of form it is simply a shared quality of oneness. It is not in need of learning or even understanding. It *is*. Awareness of what *is,* is a quality of Christ-consciousness. Thus you are already aware of the truth of giving and receiving being one. This awareness exists within you and you cannot any longer claim to be unaware of it through non-acceptance of what *is*.

These are your ideas as well as mine. They are the ideas of your brothers and sisters as much as they are of God. I am teaching you nothing, nothing old and nothing new. I am reminding you of what you know as I have reminded you of your identity.

What this portion of the dialogue attempts to do is to give you a language to support what you already know, and are already aware of, so that you are more comfortable with letting what you know serve you in your creation of the new. All — *all* — that

22

you need in order to create the new is available within you. The power of the universe is given and received constantly in support of the creation of the new. This is what creation is! The entire universe, the All of All, giving and receiving as one. This is *our* power. And *our* power is needed for the creation of the Covenant of the New in this time of Christ.

chapter 4

the New You

This Covenant is the fulfillment of the agreement between you and God. The agreement is for you to *be* the *new*. As you are new, so too is God, for you are one, if not the same. As you are new, so too is the world, for you are one, if not the same. As you are new, so are your brothers and sisters, for they, too, are one, if not the same.

While not the same, you also are not different. The differences you saw during the time of learning — differences that made you feel as if each being stood separate and alone, you are now called to see no more. In unity you are whole and inseparable, one living organism now raised above the level of the organism as you become aware of unity of form.

It is time now for this idea to be accepted, for if it is not, you will remain in the prison you have created.

Prison is an excellent example of a system you created with your faulty perception. As with all systems, it reflects an inward state and shows you what becomes of all of those who see not what it means to be neither different nor the same but to be one.

For the moment, disregard any idea you may have of there being those who deserve the prison system you have developed and any arguments you would cite about the heinous crimes of some. Think instead of prison simply becoming a way of life for those who are incarcerated.

Each of you has had an imprisoned personal self. Each of you who have entered Christ-consciousness has had the cell door and the prison gate thrown open and a new world offered. If you do not accept this opportunity, you remain incarcerated in a system that tells you when you will awaken, how you will spend your day, and when you will retire. You remain at the mercy of those who are incarcerated along with you. You remain at the mercy of those who would have power over you, and you remain subject to the laws of man.

I tell you truthfully that until you are living as who you are and are doing what you love, you are in prison. This prison is as much of your own making as are the actual prison systems that developed when shape and form was given to what you fear and what you believe will protect you.

Just as an actual prisoner, when released from prison, must adjust to a life in which his or her actions are no longer restricted artificially, you must adjust to your new freedom. Your life has been artificially restricted by the prison you have created of it, and the actual prison system merely mirrors this restriction on a grand scale for all to see and look upon with dread. For most, the prison system is a very successful deterrent. The thought of time in prison fills the mind with fear. And yet those who are imprisoned often become so acclimated to prison life, that life on the "outside" is no longer seen as desirable. How can this be?

A life of artificial structure is all any of you have known. An internally structured life will quickly replace the life of the inmate if you will but let it do so. Even those who actually are incarcerated in the prison system you have made are free to follow an internally structured life to a greater extent than many of those who call themselves free.

Your prison was created by the separated thoughts of the separated thought "system." Systems, as you may recall, are the result of your attempts to externalize the patterns contained within. Patterns are both of learning and of design.

25

Let's look at each of these terms separately so that we see the nature of existence in the same way and speak the same language while discussing it.

Let us begin by coming to agreement about the idea of divine design. This divine design could also be called creation, and where we have spoken of creation previously, divine design was also spoken of. Here I am quite confident that you have either seen and learned enough during your time as a learning being that you accept that a divine design created the universe and all that is in it, or that you trust enough in the wisdom of your heart that you know that this is so. Either way, you may still *believe* in a divine design without accepting that a divine design exists and that you are part of it. Remember that our goal here is to deny the old and accept the new. In this case, the old you would deny is the idea of a purposeless existence, a universe with no divine order, a life in which you are at the mercy of fate. The new idea you are asked to accept is that existence is purposeful, that the universe exists in divine order, and that your life is part of that divine design.

Divine patterns are the patterns that made your existence in form possible as well as the patterns that have made your return to your true identity possible. These patterns are both external and internal. External divine patterns include the observable forms that make up your world, everything from the planet on which you exist to the stars in the sky, from the body you seem to inhabit to the animal and plant life that exist around you. From the daintiest and most intricately laced snowflake to the stem of a plant to the workings of the human brain, a divine pattern is evident and should not be beyond your belief. Despite the differences in what you see, think, and feel, there is but one external divine pattern that created the observable world, and only one internal divine pattern that created the internal world.

This pattern is that of learning. The two patterns, the internal and the external, were created together to exist in a complementary fashion. Both of these divine patterns are being newly created and we will talk much more of them and of the creative time we are now entering. Thus far, we are merely working together to create a pattern of acceptance to replace the pattern of learning.

Systems of thought are both divinely inspired and products of the separated self. The idea of giving and receiving as one might be spoken of as a divinely inspired system of thought. In such a way of thinking, one would take the internal thought pattern, enhance it with the external pattern, and by seeing the unity and cooperation of all, understand and live according to the system of thought of giving and receiving being one. Systems of thought are the foundation upon which how you live arises. The truth is a system of thought. It exists in wholeness and has always been available.

Systems of thought that arose from the separated self are those you have accepted as the truth. Some of these systems of thought were part of the divine pattern. Contrast is one such system. As a learning being, you accepted that you learned through contrast, knowing that contrast was provided for your learning. It was upon the foundation of this and other thought systems that your perception developed. Through contrast, you identified and classified the world around you based upon the differences or contrast that you saw.

Other systems of thought were not part of the divine pattern. The ego is one such system. It may seem peculiar to think of the ego as a system, and we have heretofore referred to both the ego and to the ego's thought system, but the ego is quite rightly seen as a system in and of itself. It is thought externalized and given an identity you but falsely believed to be yourself. From this one externalized thought pattern came most of your false ideas, ideas that made it difficult even for the divinely inspired thought systems to provide the learning they were designed to impart.

Such is the case with the system of learning through contrast, since when the ego entered with its false ideas and judgment, contrast did not always provide the lessons it was meant to provide. In addition, believing the ego had become an externalized self took you, the true Self and the true learner, out of the learning loop. Obviously these systems, built as they were upon patterns now being recreated, are part of the old.

Externalized patterns, or systems, were also built from the systems of thought that have been your foundation, the basic building blocks of what you have seen as reality. As such, these systems too are obviously of the old.

Just as obviously, all we are left with is divine design. All we are left with is what was given: A divine universe, a divine existence. That divine universe, our divine existence, is now recreating the patterns that served the time of learning. What was learned in the instant in which you came to know your Self is all that learning was for. Let us not dwell any longer on why this has taken so long or on the suffering that occurred during the time of learning. This would be like dwelling on the inmate's life as an inmate once he has been freed. Let us simply create a new structure around the new pattern of acceptance, a structure that will provide you with the home on Earth you have so long sought and used your faulty systems to but attempt to replicate.

I speak of structure here not as a thing — not as a building in which to dwell or as a set of rules or instructions to follow in order to build the new — but as structure that will provide you with parameters in which to begin to experience your new freedom. It is your questions and concerns that have led me to speak of such, for it is you who have felt such as this is needed. The unlimited freedom offered you is too vast for your comfort. Thus without limiting this freedom at all, let us simply speak of a place and a way to begin to experience it, and of a place and a way to begin to create the new.

This place and this way begins at the prison doors, begins with acceptance of the new and denial of the old. Turn your back on the prison of your former existence and do not look at it again. Do not long for its old structure or the false security you came to feel at times within it. Do not look for a new structure with barred windows and doors to keep you safe. Do not seek someone to tell you anew what to do with who you are now that you are no longer a prisoner. Do not give keys to a new jailer and ask to be taken care of in exchange for your newfound freedom. Instead see the world anew and rejoice in it, just as you would have had you literally spent your life within a prison's walls. Breathe the sweet air of freedom. Be aware constantly of the sky above your head and desire no more ceilings to shield you from it.

Beware of gifts offered in exchange for your newfound freedom. A hungry ex-prisoner may soon come to feel the three meals a day provided in the prison were gifts indeed. So too are the gifts many of you have desired and still feel as if you need.

If you have imprisoned yourself in order to earn a living by doing work that brings you no joy and allows you not to be who you are, then you are called to walk away. If you are tempted by the security of a relationship in which you cannot be fully yourself, you are but tempted by a false security, and are called to turn away. If you are lured away from who you are by a drive to succeed, if you fear doing what you want to do because you might fail, if you follow another's path and seek not your own, then you have imprisoned yourself for the "three meals a day" of the old way.

What has this to do with structure and parameters? Everything. You cannot deny the old and remain in the prison of the old. You have asked, and because you have asked, I am telling you that the permission you seek must come from your own heart and from your commitment to the Covenant of the New. Once again I remind you that there is no authority to whom you can turn. But in place of that "outside" authority, I give you your own authority, an authority you must claim in order for it to be your own. An authority you must claim before your externally structured life can become an internally structured life.

Let this acceptance of your own internal authority be your first "act" of acceptance rather than learning. Turn to this as the new pattern and to the thought system of giving and receiving as one. Let the authority of the new be given and received. Become the author of your own life. Live it as you feel called to live it.

We cannot build the new upon prison walls of old. Whatever imprisons you must now be left behind.

Those of you now protesting having heard what you have so longed to hear, protest no more. You cannot keep your prison and have the new life that you long to have. You may have to examine just what it is that imprisons you. You may find that it is attitude more so than circumstance, or you may feel as if the walls that imprison you are so sturdy and so long barred that they may as well be prison walls. You may even be a prisoner in truth, and wonder how, save a grand escape, you can proceed. But I tell you truthfully, your release is at hand and it will come from your own authority and no place else. It is up to you to accept that your release is possible, to desire it without fear, to call it into being.

Do you not see that you must begin with yourself? That if you are unwilling to claim your freedom it will not claim you?

What is one, or in union with all, draws from the well of divine design. You need not turn to old patterns or systems to accomplish your release. You can only turn to what *is,* to what is left now that the patterns and systems of learning are no longer.

You accept that what has been given is available. You accept and you receive. You realize that the first order of creation of the new is restoration of the original order, or original design. As you

30

have been returned to your Self, now your life must be returned to where it fits within the divine design, to where it is a life of meaning and purpose. This return is the return of wholeness. This return is not selfish on your part, but magnanimous. It returns wholeness to you and wholeness to the divine design. It returns creation to what it is.

Understand — this cannot be fearful. This cannot fail. This will not bring suffering but will end suffering. Your part is to invite it and accept it when it comes. State your willingness, accept the coming of your release, and prepare to leave your prison behind. Invite this simply by inviting what brings you joy. Invite yourself first to this new world, but leave not your brothers and sisters behind. Invite them too. For those who are imprisoned are one with you, and need but your release to find their own.

Dear brothers and sisters in Christ, I hear your protests and the reasons that you feel must prevent you from the acceptance I call you to. Yet as you fully accept that your right to your inheritance, your right to be who you are, and your commitment to the Covenant of the New, are one and the same, these reasons will disappear. All the *different* reasons you would cite become what they are — *one* reason, the *same* reason — and you will see that what is one is neither the same nor different. You will see that there is *one* answer, an answer different for everyone and yet the same for everyone. That answer is acceptance of your Self. That answer is acceptance of the new you.

chapter 5

True Representation

Within the Course your "imitation" of creation was often spoken of. This was about your ability to "remember" much of creation in a non-cognitive, intuitive way. It was also about the minor distortions that occurred between this non-cognitive memory and how you acted upon it, distortions that created major departures from the nature of creation.

These distortions occurred as you assigned meaning or "truth" to things, truly believing in your ability to do so. In this way, you determined what the world around you was meant to represent. It was in much the same way that the ego came to represent you.

What we are doing now is returning the world to its true representation. As was said in *A Treatise on the Personal Self,* there is a huge difference between a true representation and a false representation. While the false representation of the ego self led to the world you see, it did not change the truth but only created illusion. The truth is still available to be seen.

The world without was created as a true representation of the world within, and as you become aware of the truth represented in all that encompasses and surrounds you, the boundaries between the inner and outer world will diminish and eventually cease to be.

Let me provide you with an example that illustrates how one aspect of what was created in the pattern of learning, while not being seen in the way it was intended, still represents what *is* and thus contains all meaning or the truth:

When two bodies join and joy results from this joining, this is form mimicking content — form representing what "is." The form was created in order to show — to teach — that joining is the way. Think of the word *desire* and its association with sex. To desire someone is to desire joining. This desire was created to remind you...to point the way...to your true desire for your true identity as a being joined in oneness. This seeking of completion through oneness, this joining, is a true representation that shows you that completion does not come of standing alone but of joining, as love does not come alone but in relationship.

You have determined sex to be the ultimate fulfillment of love and called it "making love." If it were painful rather than pleasurable, if you did not lose yourself and experience completion, you would not desire it. Sex, experienced for this pleasure and completion, regardless of emotional attachment or non-attachment, still would produce the desired effect of creating desire for oneness if you truly saw and understood the body and its acts as representative of truth. You have thought the things you do represent your drives, but they simply represent what was given to help you remember and return to who you truly are.

Obviously — as you have been told that the ego has represented a false self — it is possible to misrepresent. But the new world you have entered need not be filled with misrepresentations, for you are cause and effect. It is through the representation of the true that the false is exposed as nothing. A lie is nothing but a lie. The false is nothing but the false. It does not become some "thing," for in the becoming it would need to take on the properties of the truth. Think of the ego again as an example here. The ego but seemed to be who you were for a time. Now that you know who you are in truth, the ego does not remain, a separate entity with a life of its own. No. The ego is gone. Because it was a lie its exposure to the truth dissolved it.

Thus must it be now with everything in your world. Everywhere you look the lie of false representation will be exposed and the

33

truth will be represented once again. This seeing of the truth is the first step as it is the step necessary for the restoration of divine design. True seeing facilitates the return to what *is* and we but proceed from this starting point.

While you have learned to take judgment from your seeing, this must be reemphasized now as you are called to see what you might previously have thought of as inconsequential in the light of truth. Everything *given* represents the truth.

Remember now that you are not called to reinterpret but to accept revelation. You will not arrive at the truth through thinking about what everything means. This is the old way that led to so much misinterpretation and misrepresentation. Acceptance of what is given is acceptance of what is given. All was *given* to you to remind you of who you are in the time of learning that is now passing away. All was *given* to you to *represent* what is rather than to *be* what is. Now, as you join with the truth, your representation, in the new time that is before us, will *be* what is, in its representation. Simply put, this means that form will never be all that you are, but will return to being as it was intended and will represent the truth of who you are. This true representation, being of the truth, returns you to the reality of the truth where you exist in oneness.

Love and the loving patterns given in the time of learning are all that exist in all you see. But what now will become of these patterns that are no longer needed as your learning and that of those around you comes to an end? What was created to serve the time of learning, to represent what *is* and aid you in your return to what *is,* will become what *is* once again. What you can see with your body's eyes will not be *all* that *is* but will represent all that *is* truly.

What was *made* of what was created in order to serve the ego will cease to be, just as the ego has ceased to be. To outline and define the differences between what was created and what was made would be to create a tome of information, and this is not needed now. The desire for such is a desire to think through once again the meaning of everything and to have a tool to help you do so. This would assume that you are still a learning being and have need of such help. You are no longer a learning being and need not this assistance.

In this time of Christ, we are not called to recreate the "tools" of learning but to allow all that was created to show the way back to Self and God to be what it is in truth. This is the return of love to love. This is acceptance of your Self.

What then is the call to creation that has been spoken of? This is the acceptance of the *new you* — acceptance that you are going beyond simple recognition and acceptance of the Self as God created the Self — to the living of this Self in form. This is an acceptance that recognizes that while the Self that God created is eternal and the self of form as ancient as the sea and stars, the elevated Self of form is new and will create a new world.

This is the answer to the question of "What is next?" If there is nothing to learn, if coursework is behind you and accomplishment is complete, what then are you to do? You are to create in community, in dialogue, in commitment and togetherness. You are to be the living Covenant of the New.

But while this is what awaits you, I am merely answering the questions that remain and that occur as this dialogue proceeds. What I am attempting to answer now is your confusion concerning what *is*. This is crucial as you learn to accept what *is* and to deny what is *not*. While the question of what is *not* has been answered as fully as is possible, your questions and my answers in regard to what *is*, are somewhat confusing to you because what *is* is not a constant that can be *answered*. That you want answers while I tell you to await revelation speaks to the impatience of the human spirit, the longing that has so long gone unfulfilled that now that you are close you cannot bear to wait

35

another day, another hour. You want release from your prison *now,* and so you should.

Yet what you think imprisons you is also what I am addressing here. As was said earlier, release through death is no longer the answer. Release through life is the answer. Release through resurrection is the answer. You have died to the old. But surely it would seem easier in some ways to have literally died and been released from the prison of the body, the prison of the Earth and your immediate environment, the prison of your mind and the thoughts that so confuse you, the prison of past and future and a now that isn't changing fast enough to suit the new you whom you have become.

This is what we discuss today. We discuss being what you represent in truth. We discuss the elevation of form. And what we have discussed thus far is the acceptance of form as what it is. This is the new reality you have desired: to live as who you are *in form,* to not wait for death's release, but to find release while still living *in form.* Thus we begin with the true content of the form you occupy. We return the form you occupy to its natural state. Only then can we proceed to creation of the new. Because Christ-consciousness is consciousness of what *is* we begin with what *is,* with creation as it was created rather than as you have perceived it to be. From this starting point only can we move forward to the future we create together.

What I am revealing to you here is that what was once a prison may no longer be a prison! If you continue to think of your body as a prison, if you continue to think of your environment, your mind, and time as a prison, how can you exist in perfect harmony with the universe? As you can see, you are now approaching another thought reversal. Fear not that your confusion will last, for with this thought reversal will come your final release.

You will soon wonder, if you haven't already, just how it is going to be possible to live as your new Self while still in form, while

36

still in a form that seems inconsistent with your being, while still in a form that exists within a world that seems inconsistent with your being. You will wonder how, if you are done learning, the patterns of learning will change to help you embrace the acceptance of this new time of no time. You will wonder how to live in time as a being no longer bound by time. And I tell you truly, that once acceptance of what *is* is complete, we will go on to these questions of the new and together we will find the answers.

So let today's dialogue serve as a final call, a most emphatic call, to acceptance. See the importance of this acceptance to everything that is still to come. Hesitate no longer. Let your willingness exceed your trepidation. No longer wait to be told more before you accept what you have already been told. Do not wait for a grander call before you accept the call that has already sounded in your heart. Let this be the day of your final surrender, the day that will usher in a new day.

Discovery

chapter 6

the Body and the Elevation of Form

Within the text of the coursework provided you heard many ideas that either changed or reinforced those you already had about yourself. *A Course of Love* is a teaching text and the goal of its teaching was stated and restated many times so that you would not forget the purpose of the learning you were participating in. Eventually your learning reached an end point as the learning goal of the Course was met, and this you were told as well. I say this to remind you that the time of "teaching" like the time of "learning" had its place as well as its methods.

One of the methods employed by your teacher within the text of your coursework was that of comparison, a method that will be used less and less as the time of learning passes. The thought reversal of which we recently spoke is why I bring this up. During your time of learning, I used a method of comparison — I compared the real to the unreal, the false to the true, fear to love — in order to point out the insanity of your perception and the perfect sanity of the truth. For some of you the repetition of the properties of the false that aided your learning may now work as a detriment to your acceptance as you cling to ideas concerning false representation rather than let them go in order to embrace true representation. In the time of learning, you were so entrenched in your false beliefs that their insanity needed to be stated and stated again. But as we enter this new time of elevated form, these same ideas — ideas that many of you attached to form rather than to your perception of form — must be rejected.

This is what I have already spoken of and speak of again as a re-visioning of what you believe imprisons you.

While the false representation of the body as the self was almost as detrimental to your learning as the false representation of the ego as the self, the body, given your choice to return to who you truly are while still in form, continues, while the ego, of course, does not. Your belief in the non-existence of the ego is now total and has brought a freedom and a liberation in which you rejoice. Your true Self is beginning to reveal itself to you in ways of which you will become increasingly aware. As you identify more intimately with the Self you truly are, the self of form is likely to grow more and more foreign to you and less and less comfortable. Thus what is required now is a new way of envisioning the body and its service to you.

Like all that was created for the time of learning, the body was the perfect learning device. Seeing it as such assisted us in bringing about the end of the time of learning. But now your body — your form — must be seen in a new way. It is with new ideas about the body that we will begin the final thought reversal that will allow you to live in form as who you truly are.

The body, as all else you see among the living, is, in fact, living. It exists as living form. And so we begin with a distinction between what exists as living form, and what exists as inanimate or non-living form. While you might think this is an easily drawn distinction — and it is — it is not perhaps as you have previously seen it, for everything that exists in form is of the same source. Even those things you have made you have not made from nothing. There is not one thing that you have made that does not exist as some variation of what was originally created. Because, and this cannot be repeated enough, creation begins with what *is*. And so even the creations you have *made* are only distinct from what was originally created in your perception of what they are or what you have determined their use to be. There is truth, or what we might call the seeds of the truly real, or the energy of creation, in everything that exists in form.

42

It is your perception of the forms around you as non-living forms that cause them to have rigidity and a particular meaning. But they still are real, even if they are not as they appear to be to the body's eyes.

What is not real are the things that you have made to represent what *is* real since you didn't understand what it was you were making things to represent. These are the systems we have already spoken of: Systems of justice, systems of government, systems of corporations, the systems of economics and science — the systems — in short, of what you think governs you.

In the Bible there were many stories about miracles, both before and after the time in which I lived. If you were to pose to a scientist whether or not these miracles were possible, they would tell you of all the "laws" of science that would be opposed to them occurring. You would be told that if the sun had "stood still" galactic catastrophes would have resulted, that there are reasons Noah's flood could not have occurred as described, or that it would have been impossible to repopulate the earth afterwards even if it had taken place as described.

What these laws of science do not take into account are the laws of God. Although science is beginning to see much as it truly is, scientists still look for natural laws that govern what is in an *if this, then that* world.

This same attitude governs your ideas of the body and of the systems of the world. If you are no longer living in an *if this, then that* world, then the same laws will naturally not apply. *You* developed an *if this, then that* world because it was the easiest way in which to learn. It was the easiest way in which to learn because it seemed to provide proof. Yet if science teaches anything, it teaches that what is proven can be disproved — and often is.

The prayer of the Native Americans who thank the sun for rising each day is a prayer that acknowledges that the sun may not rise.

This is not a doomsday attitude, but an attitude that accepts that scientific or natural law and the law of spirit are not the same.

There are many stories in many cultures that celebrate and bear witness to happenings that reveal that the laws of spirit and the laws of man coexist. Yes, there are natural laws, but these "natural" laws are not the sets of facts you have defined them to be. They are rather a staggering series of relationships, relationships without end, relationships that exist in harmony and cooperation. This is a harmony and cooperation that might one day extend to the sun and a demonstration that the sun need not rise — or perhaps need not set — and the earth would still be safely spinning in its orbit.

Now if this were to happen, scientists would quickly determine the existence of a natural law that allowed this event to happen. It would require the re-working of many previously known "scientific facts," but this would not prevent the discovery of new "scientific facts." I mean no disrespect to scientists and bless them for their desire to find the "truth," as you should bless them for the certainty they have given you in an uncertain world. Even if it has been a false certainty, it served a great purpose in the time of learning. Discovery has been a grand facilitator of the human spirit's quest for the truth and is part of what brought you, finally, to the quest to know your Self.

I am calling all of this to mind in order to begin our discussion concerning the suspension of belief. If you continue into the new with your old beliefs about your body, the old body will be what you carry into the new with you. So let us begin with a suspension of belief in what you think you know about the body, in what science would tell you about the body, in what you have experienced as a body — a suspension of belief that comes in the same spirit as that of the Native American who knows that the sun may rise and may set, but also knows that it may not.

I am speaking of a spirit that is open to the discovery of something new and "unbelievable" and even "scientifically impossible," as well as to the creation of something new. For in this time of revelation, discovery is the new divine pattern that will replace the thought systems we have spoken of. To discover is simply to find out what you did not previously know.

Creation of the new will be predicated on the discovery of what you did not previously know. This will not happen if you cling to "known" truths. Revelation cannot come to those who are so "certain" of what *is* that they cannot allow for the new to be revealed. Your certainty about what *is* is a false certainty, a learned certainty based on the fear that caused you to order the world according to a set of facts and rules.

Be jubilant rather than hesitant about the time of discovery that is before you. Calling what you think you know into question is not a call to return to uncertainty, but a call to allow real certainty to come.

If you think of the "old" as a world in which an attitude of *if this, then that* ruled, and the "new" as a world in which giving and receiving are one, you will begin to see the enormity of the thought reversal that now awaits your acceptance. As I said earlier, we begin by applying this new attitude to the body.

You have been taught that *if* you take care of the body in certain ways, *then* good health will result. You have been taught that *if* your body expends energy, *then* it will need the refueling provided by food or rest. The list could be endless, but these examples will suffice. These modes of behavior concerning the body were given to teach and to represent. What you have done is turn them into implacable rules you call natural laws. When these natural laws have been shown at times to not apply, you consider these instances flukes or miracles.

When a person who has exhibited healthy habits get sick, you think it is unfair. When a person who has exhibited unhealthy habits gets sick, you think, even if you would not say, that they "did it to themselves" or that they could have prevented it by abstaining from the unhealthy habits. You might look now at these two attitudes and see that they are somewhat silly, but still you would cling to them because you would believe the person of healthy habits has a greater *chance* of not getting sick than the person of unhealthy habits. Again we could go into countless examples of this type of thinking, but the examples matter not except to make you see that these attitudes are not ruled by certainty, but by a mere idea of bettering the odds against what fate may offer.

What fate may offer is itself an attitude that puts life at the risk and whim of an external force that has no reality except in your imagination. What is this thing called fate? Like all the systems you believe in, it is a system too, an internal idea given a name, externalized, and blamed for all that you do not understand, all that cannot be made to make sense, all that seems unfair and beyond your control.

When you remember that we have left blaming behind, you will see that belief in fate is just as systematic and in need of being left behind as is belief that illness can be blamed on certain habits. This may not be the type of blaming you see as easily as that of blaming a friend for your hurt feelings, or blaming the past for the present. Ridding your mind of ideas of placing blame takes it one step away from the thinking of the *if this, then that* thought system we are leaving behind. As a non-learning being you are now called to accept that you no longer need this type of learning device and to realize that it will no longer serve you.

Let us return now to the beginning and start with the body as a *given*. It *is* what it *is* in terms of flesh and bone, and it is also the form that is now serving to represent the truth of who you are. How might this change the "laws" of the body, the laws you gave the body in the time of learning, knowing not what the design of the body represented? What might the bodily design now represent?

The first example of the body we presented newly was that of the perfect design of the joining provided through sexual intercourse — a design *given* to lead the way to desire for oneness and completion.

We have talked of but one replacement for the pattern of learning — the pattern of acceptance. What might the body be called to accept? This is an easy answer, as you have already called upon the body to accept the indwelling of Christ. You have replaced the personal self, the self of learning, with the true Self. You have accepted your true identity. How could the body now be the same as it once was?

The body was, in the time of learning, representative of a learning being. But the ego narrowed your ideas of what the body was here to learn to ideas of survival. You learned to survive rather than to live. You increased the life span of the human being, but you increased not its capacity for true living or true learning. And with the extended life span came extended reasons for fear, and a physical form that you came to believe needed greater and greater resources to maintain.

The body is now the embodiment of the true Self, the embodiment of love, the embodiment of divinity. Its existence is *given* as it was always given. But now the very nature of its existence has changed. I say *changed* only to remind you that change occurs in time. Outside of time and form your Self has always existed in the perfect harmony in which it was created.

Now that your Self has joined the elevated Self of form, you exist together both in time and outside of time. Remember, the elevated Self of form will never be *all* that you are. This does not imply that there are portions of your Self missing from this new

47

experience, but that the elevated Self of form is now able to join with the Self in the unity of shared consciousness. You are whole once again and your form will merely represent one aspect of your wholeness in the field of time.

The self of form, as form, could never truly experience the All of Everything that is the natural state of the formless. But the true Self cannot cease to experience its natural state: the state of Christ-consciousness, sharing in unity, the All of Everything. These two states – the state of form and the state of unity – are both in existence right now. In the state of unity, your true Self is fully aware of the elevated Self of form and is fully participating in its experiences and feelings. Yet the elevated Self of form, being a form that still exists in time, must realize the consciousness of the true Self in time.

What this means is that the elevated Self of form may still need time to come to know the changes that only occur "in time" even though they are already accomplished in unity. This is why we have spoken of miracles and of the collapse of time the miracle is capable of providing. We have redefined the miracle as the art of thought, or the continual act of prayer that sustains the unity of Christ-consciousness.

Form and time go together. You have been told that time is a measurement of learning. If you are no longer a learning being, for what is time needed? Time is needed now only for the transformation of the self from a learning being to a being that can accept the shared consciousness of unity and begin to discover what this means.

chapter 7

Time and the Experience of Transformation

Just as when you were a being existing in the shared consciousness of unity you couldn't know what the experience of form would be like without entering into it, you cannot know the experience of unity without entering into it. To enter into the experience of form is something you can picture in your mind, and that you have language to represent, because you are aware of the self of form. To enter into the experience of unity is something more difficult to imagine, and something for which you have little language.

You were told within the Course that what you learn in unity is shared. This language was used because you were still, at that time, a learning being. Now we will adjust our language somewhat to represent the new and restate what was said earlier as "What you *discover* in unity is shared." Learning does not occur in unity, but discovery is an ongoing aspect of creation and of the state of union in which you truly abide.

You were also told within the Course that because you were learning in separation, unity had to be experienced individually before learning could be shared at another level, and that levels are a function of time. We then talked of the integration of levels that collapse time. This integration of levels is the integration of form and unity. When Christ-consciousness is sustained, time will collapse and the sun may not need to rise or set to separate day into night. Resting and waking will be part of the same continuum of being.

The Dialogues

Experiences of form take place in time because experience, too, was designed for learning. Now experience is needed in time to aid your total acceptance of what you have learned. In order to experience the new you must answer the call to let revelation and discovery, rather than learning, be what you gain from experience.

What was created cannot be uncreated. Thus transformation is needed. The miracle makes you fully aware of the embrace and the consciousness of unity and places you outside of time. In this state, no duality exists. Doing and being are one.

Action is the bridge between form and the formless because action is the expression of the self in form. "Right" action comes from the unity in which doing and being are one — from the state in which there is no division between who you are and what you do. "Right" action comes from the state of wholeness. Being whole is being all that you are. Being all that you are is what the elevated Self of form represents.

You have been told that you are time-bound only as a particular self, existing as man or woman in a particular time in history. Now you are called to discover how to exist in form without being defined by this time-bound particularity.

That you are living form does not require you to be defined by particularity. You can accept the body now as what it is in all its manifestations while not seeing it as "bound" by the particularity of time and space. It may still exist in a particular time and place, but this is simply the nature of one aspect of what you are. The nature of form is that it exists as matter, it occupies space and is perceptible to the senses. You have previously seen this one aspect of form as separating it from mind, heart, and spirit — those aspects that are not perceptible to the senses.

All that lives is from the same Source, and there is nothing more alive than mind and heart combined in the spirit of wholeheartedness.

Matter is simply another word for c   need not be maligned. The content of all living th   ergy of the spirit of wholeheartedness. The conten   .hings is, in other words, whole. By seeing only as   .holeness you have not seen content nor matter truly. You   ve not been aware of all that you are. You are now called to discover and to become aware of all that you are. The body, rather than aiding you in learning as it once did, will aid you now in this discovery.

Realize that this is a call to love all of yourself. You who once could love spirit *or* mind, mind *or* body — because of the dualistic nature associated with them — now can love all of your Self, all of God, all of creation.

You can respond to love with love.

We start with the body, returning love to it now. It is what it is, and nothing that it is, is deserving of anything other than love. This call to love all of your Self is a call to unconditional, nonjudgmental love. It is not just a call to nonjudgmentalness, but to nonjudgmental love. This nonjudgmental love is the condition upon which your discovery of all you do not yet know awaits.

Discovery is not the same as remembrance. Remembrance was necessary for your return to your true identity, the Self as it was created. Remembrance was not about what you did not know, but about what you knew but had forgotten. Memory has returned you to your Self. Discovery will allow the new you to come into being by revealing what you do not yet know about how to live as the elevated Self of form.

This discovery can only take place in the reality of love.

51

Being in love is a definition of what you now are as you accept the unconditional, nonjudgmental love of all. This is a transference of love from the particular to the universal. Loving all that you are, including your body, is not love of the particular but universal love. The old way in which you related to your body, be it a love or a hate relationship, was a particular relationship with the vessel that only seemed to contain you. It was a relationship with the separated self. Now, because your relationship is with wholeness, you can transfer love from the particular to the universal by loving all.

We are one body, one Christ.

The observation, envisioning, and desire you have been practicing in order to be ready to accept revelation works hand-in-hand with the new pattern of discovery, but discovery is less time bound.

Observation takes place in time. Even while you have been called to observe what *is,* what you are observing in form are the representations of what *is* in time. Your envisioning too is bound to time and that is why so many of you think of envisioning as envisioning the future. Envisioning is less bound to time than is observation because it is not about what your body's eyes see, and will increasingly join with what you observe until your vision is released from old patterns and guides you more truly.

Desire is an acknowledgement of the uniqueness of each Self, and is a demonstration of means and end being the same. Desire keeps you focused on your own path and leaves you nonjudgmental of the paths of others. Yet desire, like observation and vision, is still related to the self of form. It is a step toward full acceptance and awareness of who you are now and what this means as you become the elevated Self of form.

Revelation is of God. Observation, vision, and desire are steps leading you beyond what the individual, separated self sees, to the revelation of what *is.* These steps that lead to revelation are not ongoing aspects of creation, because they are related to particular forms as they exist in time. Time is not an aspect of eternity or of unity. Time is what has separated the self that exists in form from the Self that exists in union or the state of Christ-consciousness.

By becoming one body, one Christ, you have accepted existence as a non-particular being in a state outside of time — you have accepted existence as a new Self, the Self of elevated form. You just do not yet understand what this means.

Discovery is not bound by time as it *is* an ongoing aspect of creation. As you were told in *A Treatise on the New,* the future is yet to be created. While this seems like a time-bound statement, it is not. It is merely one way of stating that creation is ongoing rather than static. While creation *is* and *is* as it was created, it was created to be eternally expanding and expressing in new ways.

With your new awareness *you* are now linked, through the consciousness of unity, with the entire field of creation, rather than only with the time-bound field of creation of form. As your awareness grows, you will begin to expand and express in new ways. Those ways now include the form of your body without being limited to creation of, and in, form. The body has thus joined creation in a non time-bound way.

Evolution is the time-bound way in which the body has participated in creation. This is why you have been told that you are not called to evolution. Time-bound evolution is the way of the creature, the natural response of the living organism to the stimulus of matter upon matter, and of the creature's perception of its own experience in time. This time-bound evolution is really adaptation. It occurs in reaction to what is perceived as necessary for survival.

Time-bound evolution is still surely going on, and as the planet becomes crowded, as progress has left so many unfulfilled, as environmental concerns mount, even the perceived survival needs are leading you toward new answers of what survival may mean.

You know, in this time of Christ, that the end of the old way is near and that the new is coming. You are moving toward anticipation rather than adaptation, and evolution moves with you. But evolution in time is part of the old that needs to be left behind. It is a provision of the time of learning that allows the learning being to learn at her or his own pace and to pass this learning on in time.

You know that this has not worked to improve the fate of man. You secretly fear that evolution will not keep pace with the changing world and that humanity's reign over the environment will come to an abrupt and painful end. Some even fear an evolutionary setback, and see any threat against civilization as they know it as a return to barbaric times.

These scenarios of fear we leave behind as we abandon ideas of evolution in time and proceed to an awareness of how the elevated Self of form can replace the laws of evolution in time with the laws of transformation outside of time.

In order to facilitate your understanding, I call you now to imagine your body as a dot in the center of a circle and the circle as representing all that you are. The dot of your body is all that is bound by time. What transformation outside of time asks you to do is to see the body as but this one, small, aspect of what you are. In observing both yourself and others, you have learned to view your body in the field of time. This will be helpful now as you begin to imagine the more that you are, the more that exists beyond the body's boundary and beyond the boundary of time and particularity.

This circle in which you have placed your body is not a circle of time and space. It is not a circle that can be drawn around where you exist so as to define, perhaps, a mile of space and say that this is all you. No, the circle that exists around you is the circle of shared consciousness, the circle of unity.

In truth, this circle is everything, the All of All, the universe, God. But just as the Earth can be seen as your home, although you are rarely consciously aware of existing in this "larger" home, you will not always be aware of this circle of the Self as the All of Everything, and it will, in fact, be helpful as we begin, to imagine on a smaller scale.

You might begin by imagining first your actual, physical, home, then your neighborhood, community, city, state, country. You see yourself as most your "self" in your home, your neighborhood, your community. You identify with the citizens of the city, state, and country you occupy. You have an address, perhaps a yard, or farm, perhaps a public spot that has become a favorite park or lake or beach that you consider partially yours. You have a route to and from your work or other places that you go, where you see familiar landmarks, structures, faces. You visit the homes of friends and relatives, your church, perhaps a school or library, certain restaurants or places of civic duty or social engagement. You may expand this small territory you call your own with business travel or vacations, and have more than one locale that feels like home; or you may never travel far from the building in which you dwell.

What I ask you to do is to think of these areas as the territory of your body, and to remember that while this is your territory, it is a shared territory and a territory within the territory of planet Earth.

Thus we begin once again with parameters, with a territory of shared consciousness, rather than with consciousness of the All of Everything. This territory we will call the territory of your conscious awareness. This territory of conscious awareness is shared with the larger consciousness of unity, just as the territory of your body is shared with those who live and work nearby. This territory of conscious awareness exists within the larger consciousness of unity, just as the territory of your body exists within the larger territory of the planet Earth.

We will begin here, with the territory of your conscious awareness, knowing that discovery and revelation will expand this territory, and realizing that no matter how small this cosmic territory may be, it will still at times give way to awareness of the All of Everything.

c h a p t e r 8

the Territory of Conscious Awareness

Continuing to imagine your body as the dot within the circle, I ask you to imagine now being able to take a step outside of the area of this dot, and into the area of the wider circle. In this area of the wider circle, there is no time, no space, no particularity. It is an area of unlimited freedom; but as was already said, we will begin with parameters that make this area as imaginable to you as possible. Because here is where all that you can imagine can become your new reality.

Imagine this first as a place where no learning is needed. Ah, you might say now, this you have heard before. This idea of no longer needing to learn has intrigued you since it was first mentioned, and yet it seems too impossible, too "good" to be true. You are too used to thinking of yourself as a learning being to truly experience the freedom of not being bound by this constraint. In all of your life, you can think of no ability you have not achieved through learning.

Yet most of you have "discovered" something that comes easily to you, something you might have said or been told you have a natural talent or ability to do. These things some of you have practiced or studied to take advantage of your natural ability and in doing so may have found a continued ability to learn faster or achieve more in this area than those who are not seen as having a natural ability of this particular kind. But because you are prone to comparison, many of you have been discouraged by not being able to be the "best" despite your natural talent or ability, and have given up working hard to be the best. Others who have achieved the highest possible acclaim for their talents find this acclaim unfulfilling once it is achieved.

All of these ideas we leave behind as we concentrate instead on the very simple idea of each of you containing a natural ability or talent that existed in some form prior to the time of learning. We concentrate on this idea merely as an *idea* and not in terms of the specific ability it may represent. We concentrate on this idea as the first parameter of the territory of your conscious awareness as you let awareness grow in you that you *have* experienced something that existed prior to the time of learning. And that this *something* was quite wonderful.

You might think of this ability that existed prior to the time of learning as coming from the content of the wider circle of who you are to infiltrate the dot of the body, or, conversely, as the body having taken a step outside of the dot of self to infiltrate the wider circle of the Self. When you have realized that you are "more" than your body, your natural talent or ability has been one of the primary factors leading to this realization. It has been one of the primary factors leading to this realization because a part of you has always known this ability was a "given." That you are gifted — given to — and able to receive. And despite what science might have to say to you about the source of such talents or abilities, you have known that they are not of the body.

To accept this is to accept that you have access to a "given" Self, to something neither earned nor worked hard to attain. To imagine this as an idea is to imagine this "given" Self as the Self that exists beyond the boundary we have described as the dot of the body.

This idea will aid you too in your understanding of discovery, as your natural abilities or talents were *discovered* and in that discovery, you realized that although you had not previously known that this talent or ability existed, it was there awaiting but your discovery. You may also have seen that in the expression of this talent or ability new discoveries awaited you and that you greeted these discoveries with surprise and delight. As was written in *A Treatise on the New*, these surprises of discovery have,

58

and will, cause you to laugh and be joyous. There was never any need, and will never be any need, to figure them out — for surprises cannot be figured out! Surprises are meant to be joyous gifts being constantly revealed. Gifts that need only be received and responded to. Not *learned.*

While discovery of the new will naturally include much that goes beyond what you now think of as your natural talents or abilities, the place or Source of your natural talents or abilities is a place from which to start building your awareness of what is available or given — of what is but awaiting your discovery and conscious awareness. Thus, like the home in which you reside, the idea that you have an already existing awareness of the Source of unity beyond the body will increase your comfort level, and will help establish it as the first parameter in the territory of your conscious awareness.

Now this is not new *information.* Much of this was taught in *A Treatise on the Nature of Unity and Its Recognition.* Between the Course and the Treatises, all of what you needed to learn was put forth. What we are now doing is discussing what was taught from the realm of wholeheartedness. What was learned was only able to be learned because you chose to become the wholehearted. You chose to join mind and heart and it was done. But you do not yet know how to rid yourself of former patterns. Your mind, while it no longer wants to cling to known patterns, is confronted with them constantly. Your heart still seems to battle with the supremacy of mind.

What we are attempting to do with these dialogues is to *open* the mind to the wisdom of the heart. As the mind *opens* and accepts the new, the art of thought will become your new means of thinking. What has been learned will become an ability to think wholeheartedly, or with mind and heart in union, and then that ability will transcend ability, wholehearted will become what you are, and wholeheartedness will be your sole means of expression.

The self and the expression of self that comes from any place other than wholeheartedness is not the true Self or the true expression of the Self but the self-expression that arises from separation. Self-expression that arises from separation is still valuable, as it is a sign of yearning toward the true Self and the true expression of the Self. Thus where you have desired to express yourself in the past is very likely linked to the natural ability or talent you did not have to learn, to that which was given and available just a step beyond where the separated self could reach.

Expand your reach! Step outside of the dot of the separated self and into the circle of unity where all you desire is already accomplished in the fullness and wholeness of the undivided Self.

The divided self is the small self of separation that is constantly yearning for union with that from which it is divided. Enter the place of no division, the place of shared consciousness, the place of wholeness. The natural ability that you recognize as a given and unlearned aspect of your Self is the doorway.

Step through that doorway.

Take the first step outside of the known reality of your conscious awareness, the learned reality of your separate consciousness, and into the realm of shared consciousness.

Do not be surprised if no shaft of light descends upon you, if you feel as if you have taken that step and yet remain unchanged. When you choose to take this step it is taken. What you will become aware of on the other side of that doorway will require a new way of seeing, a new kind of awareness.

chapter 9

Awareness that does not come from Thought

The door that is being opened to you here is the door of awareness of what *is,* a door that swings open and closed on the hinges of your thoughts. Thoughts are a greater boundary than the dot of your body and a greater means of imprisonment than bars and walls. They are why you do not see what *is* and are the reason that you continue to desire to be provided with set answers.

The final thought reversal that was spoken of in the section on acceptance is what is spoken of here. There you were asked to become aware of what imprisons you, only to have it later suggested that what you think imprisons you may not be what imprisons you at all. What you think *is* what imprisons you.

You continue to believe that your desire to know who you are calls you to think about who you are and in that thinking to come up with a definition of who are, a truth of who you are, a certainty about who you are. You have been led to see that this desire has always been with you, and you have thought it is the very desire that, once defined and acted upon, would fulfill you, allow you to be who you truly are, end your confusion, and give you peace to usher in the new.

But you have thought about this desire to know who you are in one way or another all of your life without reaching the place of fulfillment you have sought. Even now, when you have learned all that you are in need of learning, the pattern, even of your wholeheartedness, remains one of thought. This pattern is what the new patterns of acceptance and discovery that we are beginning to lay out here are going to replace.

Thought is a practice and a pattern of the separated and learning self. When it was said within the Course that you are an idea of God, and when ideas were spoken of as if they were synonymous with thought, this was an accurate and truthful way of expressing what was true for you as a learning being.

But your reality has changed, and with that change, new patterns apply. This does not mean that the truth has changed, but that you have changed; and with your change, the truth, while it remains the truth, can now be presented in a way that speaks to who you are now rather than who you were when you began *A Course of Love*.

As we continue, you may feel as if contradictory things are being said, such as being called to consider what imprisons you and then being called to reconsider. The call is still the same, but the means by which you are considering the call has changed. Thus there is no contradiction although there may at times seem to be.

This may seem as well to be inconsistent with the teaching of *A Treatise on the Art of Thought*. If thought is what imprisons you, why would the "art of thought" be taught? You must continually remember your newness and the different aim toward which we now work. The aims we clearly embraced together when you were still a learning being were meant to allow you to come to know your true identity. *A Treatise on the Art of Thought* was but a forerunner to what we now will embrace together. It was a means and an end.

The same is true of the beliefs set forth in *A Treatise on the Nature of Unity and Its Recognition*. What was taught in order to aid your "recognition" will clearly be different from what is revealed once that recognition has been brought about.

Just as the Art of Thought led to abilities beyond the thinking of the ego-mind, the beliefs of the Treatise on Unity were meant to lead beyond the need for beliefs, and *A Treatise on the Personal Self* meant to lead beyond the personal self. Thus the Treatises were not inconsistent with our aims here. Learning always has as its goal leading the learner *beyond* learning. With *A Treatise on the New* we established what lies beyond learning. Now, as we embrace the new together, it must be realized again and yet again, that the new cannot be learned. It must be realized that you cannot come to know the new, or to create the new, through the means of old, including the means of thought.

We thus return to discovery and continue to expand the territory of your conscious awareness. We do this by discussing now the nature of ideas as opposed to the nature of thoughts.

Like the natural abilities you discovered existed within you prior to the time of learning, ideas are also discoveries that you make, discoveries that exist apart from learning. Ideas "come to you." They are given and received. They are surprising and pleasing in nature. You may think that they are the result of learning, of thoughts you have contemplated and struggled with. You may think that all of your previous learning and thinking merely resulted eventually in a new idea being birthed, but this is not the case. Heredity can be cited as a cause for talent, but what is heredity but that which already exists within you? So too is it with an idea. An idea already exists within you, but is awaiting its birth *through* you.

This is how you must now come to see your form; it is that through which what already exists, what is already accomplished, comes or passes through by means of the expression of your form and the interaction of your form with all you are in relationship with.

If we return to the image of the body as the dot in the wider circle and accept that your discovery of your natural talent or ability and your discovery of new ideas are discoveries of something that already existed beyond the dot of the body; and if you accept that these ideas that already exist were able to pass through you in order to gain expression in form; then you are beginning to see, on a small scale, the action that, on a large scale, will become the new way.

the Goal and the Accomplishment of the Elevated Self of Form

What is found outside of the boundary of the personal self in the wider circle of unity is timeless. What comes to you in the form of natural abilities or talents, as ideas, as imagination, as inspiration, instinct, intuition, as vision, or as calling, are ways of knowing that come to you, and through you, outside of the pattern of learning.

Learning is about the transfer of knowledge that was gained in the time of learning, through the process of learning. Notice the inability of teaching or learning to call forth talents, ideas, imagination, inspiration, instinct, intuition, vision, or calling. You may believe that teaching and learning appropriately work with and enable the *use* of abilities such as these, but you also know that these means are limited in what they can do and that they can hinder as well as enhance the creative expression of these givens.

You think that the use you put these givens to, what you *do* with them, how you express them in the world, is your unique and individual accomplishment. Such it is. But when you also think that it is your hard work and diligence, your effort and struggle, that bring the expression of these givens forward, you think in error and limit your expression in much the same ways that the effort of teaching and learning limit them. It is your joyous acceptance of the already accomplished state of these givens that allows expression of what is given to truly come through you and express the Self, because joyous expression expresses the Self of unity rather than the self of separation, the Self of elevated form rather than the personal self.

Now you might be thinking, here, that while these givens come from the realm of unity, your expression of these givens, since that expression exists in the realm of time and space and involves the work and time of your form in your form's separate reality, is not of union but of the individual self. You may feel that to think of this in any other way will leave you with no individual, personal accomplishment, nothing to be proud of, nothing to call your own. You must begin to realize that the bringing forth of the accomplishment that already exists in unity is your new work, the work of the Self of union, the work that can fill you with the true joy of true accomplishment, *because* it is your real work — work with what *is*.

Working with what *is* in unity is not work but relationship. You are called to realize your relationship with what is given from unity. It is in that relationship, the relationship *between* what *is* and the expression of what *is* by the elevated Self of form, that the new is created. What *is* becomes new by becoming sharable in form. What *is* continues to *become* through the continuation of relationship and the creation of new relationships. In this way, sharing in relationship becomes the goal and the accomplishment of the elevated Self of form, the means through which the Self of union is known even in the realm of separation, and what draws others from separation to union.

The goal and relationship of the elevated Self of form is timeless, for it draws from the realm of unity and returns to the realm of unity. This is an expression of the biblical injunction to "Go forth and multiply." It is about increase. To be content with *personal* or *individual* understanding or experience of what is given is to not complete the cycle of giving and receiving as one. What is given must be received. What is received must be given. This is the way of increase and multiplication. This is the way of creation.

In this time of Christ, discovery is about acceptance of your true way of knowing, a way that existed prior to the time of learning and that has always existed. When put into practice and allowed to replace the pattern of learning, this way of discovery will be a constant coming to know of what *is* as well as a constant expansion of what *is,* or a constant expansion of creation — creation, in short, of the new.

chapter 11

the Return to Unity and the End of Thought as You Know It

We haven't, here, been talking of the *art* of thought, but of the *use* of thought. You use thought to solve problems, apply thought to intellectual puzzles, focus your thoughts in order to make up your mind. You make lists of your thoughts so you don't forget what they remind you to do, you order your thoughts to communicate effectively, you take note of your thoughts and you take notes on the thoughts of others.

You might even consider this dialogue the written notes of *my* thoughts. In this one example can you not see the fallacy inherent in all the others? To think of these dialogues in this way, dear brothers and sisters, is insane. To think of the thought or idea of God by which you were created as the same type of thought I have just described would be insane. Are you willing any longer to see me as a lecturer, or even as a great teacher? Am I but a giver of information from whom another is capable of taking notes? You think it is only the content of your thoughts that differentiate you from others. Do you think the same is true of you and me? It is *that* you think that differentiates you from me, not our content, which is one and the same.

You might imagine that the *way* you think is so different from the *way* I think that they are incomparable. But thinking is not an accurate description of what I do, or of what occurs in unity. I *am* and I extend what I am. This dialogue is that extension. God's idea of you extended and became you and me and all the sons and daughters of creation.

In the opening page of this dialogue I said that you give and you receive from the well of spirit. True giving and receiving is of unity. True giving and receiving is not of the separated thought of the separated thought system of the separated self. Your acceptance of the concepts in *A Treatise on the Art of Thought* was but a beginning to the total rejection of thought as you know it that must now occur in order to go on to creation of the new. You create the new from, and in, unity.

Your thoughts are the last bastion of your separated self, the fertile ground, still, of your individuality, your testimony that you believe you are still *on your own,* and that you still desire to be. For only here, in this area of your individuality, do you believe you make your contributions to the world. Your desire to make a contribution — to help to make new the world that you have known — has been enhanced and amplified by what you have learned.

You know you have been called and that a contribution has been asked of you. And so your mighty thoughts have turned their focus on this *problem* and attacked it as they attack all problems to be solved. The idea of making a contribution has begun to receive the attention of your thoughts. The hope of answering your call and fulfilling your promise has lit a bonfire in your heart and begun a stampede of thoughts within your mind. Again, is this not what we spoke of in the beginning of this dialogue? What was spoken of as your desire to prepare?

Let me ask you a question. Do you think desire will still be with you when you have achieved what you have desired? Is it not possible to conceive of a time in which desire will no longer serve you, just as learning now no longer serves you? If you reach a state of full acceptance of who you are, and in that state, fully accept that your contribution is being made, will desire still be with you?

The way to achieve this state is through acceptance that it is already accomplished. And yet, as soon as your thoughts begin to accept this, many of you reverse the direction of your thoughts and turn to ideas of what you still need to do to accomplish your calling, to make your contribution. Such is the way of the mind, the way of the thoughts of the mind.

Now I return you to your idea of how these words have come to you, for if you can fully accept the *way* in which these words have been given and received, you will see that you can fully accept the *way* of unity.

You have been told you give and you receive from the well of spirit. What might this mean? How might this relate to the giving and receiving of these words? To the discussion we have been having about the body and the elevation of the self of form? How might this relate to your desire to make a contribution and answer your calling? How does this relate to your desire to know what to do?

These answers lie within you, at the heart or center of your Self, as do all answers. Your desire to make of me a teacher is the same as your desire to make your thoughts into answers that will provide you with direction. You dare not, as yet, turn to your own heart for answers. Yet your heart is the well of spirit from which true answers are drawn. Your heart is a full well, a wellspring from which you can continually draw with no danger of ever drawing an empty bucket. You need never thirst again when you have accepted this. You need never seek again for answers when this has been accepted. Because you will know and fully accept that the answers lie within.

To *believe* that you are already accomplished and not live from this belief is insane for reasons already enumerated time and time again. What prevents this belief from becoming an ability and prevents it from going from being an ability to simply being who you are, is your thoughts — thoughts that need an explanation for everything, and an explanation that makes sense in terms of the world you have always known.

The giving and receiving of these words will never make sense within the terms of the world you have always known. No explanation will ever be good enough for those who set limits upon the truth. But for those willing to open their minds and hearts to a new way of seeing, for those willing to suspend disbelief, the answer to the giving and receiving of these words will provide the answer to the question your thoughts cannot quite comprehend well enough to even articulate, much less to answer.

These words give evidence of who I am because they give evidence that I know who you are. That these words give evidence that I know who you are and that they give the same evidence to your brothers and sisters that I know who they are, will tell you something of the nature of who you are if you but let this idea dwell within you and take up residence in your heart. We are the sacred heart. We, together, are the well of spirit. We, together, are the shared consciousness of unity. In our union we bear the sameness of the Son of God. In going forth with the vision of unity you become as I was during life. You do not *think* your way through life, but instead draw your knowing forth from the well of spirit, from the shared consciousness from which these words are given and received.

The elevated Self of form does not remain contained within the dot of the body but draws its sustenance from the larger circle, the circle of unity.

What then becomes the contribution, the unique contribution of each elevated Self of form? The contribution becomes a contribution from the well of spirit – from the shared consciousness of unity, that finds its expression – its unique expression, through the elevated Self of form. Why would you retain your desire to make an *individual* contribution, when you

71

can now make a contribution such as this? Is not your unique expression of the whole enough for you? Is it not infinitely greater than the contributions that are possible for the individual, separated self to make? Is not the history of your world filled with individual contributions of incredible scope?

Do you still believe that the contribution made by the man Jesus was an *individual* contribution? I tell you truthfully that the only contributions that endure, the only contributions that are truly lasting, are contributions that arise from the well of spirit.

To seek importance for the personal self would be akin to placing the importance of Jesus on the man Jesus who existed in history. Some do see Jesus only as an important man among many important men. Those who do so miss the point of the life of Jesus just as they miss the point of their own lives. Those who do so seek to make individual contributions as important men and women. They do not seek to give expression to what is in everyone's hearts, to what is shared in unity, to what is the truth of who we all are rather than the truth of who the individual is.

There is no truth inherent in the individual, separated self, but only illusion. Illusion can be described in many different ways that lead to many paths of seeking, but illusion can provide no place in which the seeking ends and the truth is found.

Turn now not to your thoughts, but to the mind and heart joined in unity. *In unity!* Unity is *where* the heart and mind are joined. Unity is the place from which the expression, the right-minded action of the elevated Self of form, arises. Unity is the Source of these words. So is it said. So is it the truth.

chapter 12

the Body and Your Thoughts

In the terms in which you are used to thinking, terms that have put the body at the center of your universe and yourself, there is no mechanism through which thought can enter your mind. You believe thoughts exist *in* your mind and are themselves the product of your brain, which lies within your body. Since it is believed that a cessation of brain activity is equivalent to the end of thought, you accept this as proof that your thoughts originate from within your brain.

You may have pictured the person who first received these words as receiving them either through her thoughts or through her ears, as in the idea of "hearing" words. The receiver of these words, in fact, "hears" these words as thoughts. They are not "her" thoughts, but they also are not separate from her. How can this be?

They are, quite simply, not the separated thoughts of the separated thought system.

This work is called a *dialogue*. A dialogue is most often thought of as a discourse between two or more people and as such is associated with the spoken word. When you enter into dialogue with another person, you listen, you hear, and you respond. This is exactly what occurs here. You have "entered into" this dialogue. While you think these words come to you through the written form of this book, by means of your eyes and the decoding mechanism of your brain, they do not, nor did the words of the Course. You were told within the Course and you are reminded now that these words enter through your heart. As your mind and heart joined in unity and became capable of hearing the same language, you truly began to enter the place of unity, to take the step outside of the dot of the body.

Now you may not "think" that you have been doing this, yet few of you would argue that you have been simply reading these words as you have read the words of other books. While you may be aware that something different is going on here, you might also say that your body has felt no "step" into the realm of unity, and you may rightly wonder now, if you can take such a step and be unaware of it, what its value to you is.

This is why we work now on your awareness and acceptance of your changed state, for without awareness the value of what we do here does remain minimal, and this I cannot allow. The urgent need for your return to unity has been mentioned before, and I remind you of this urgency again.

Let your reception of these words, a reception different from the reading of the words of most and maybe all other books you have read, be a sign to you. Keep this in mind as you consider how the first receiver of these words can "hear" these words as thoughts. Keep in mind that she has thoughts she is not thinking.

We have spoken already of "entering into" dialogue. When you enter into dialogue with another person you "hear" what it is they have to say. You "hear" their thoughts through the form of the spoken word. They do not then become "your" thoughts, but they do "enter" you. Their words *must* enter you in order for them to provide a source for your response — to become a means of communication and exchange. The same is true of the "thoughts" these words symbolize. Thus we continue to expand the territory of your conscious awareness through this realization that the ability of "thoughts" not your own to enter you is already commonplace.

We have already established that the thoughts that arise from unity are not the same as the thoughts that arise from the thought system of the separated self. We might make this a more simple subject to discuss by making a distinction between thinking and thought. This distinction, while it will not be consistent with your dictionary's definition of these words, is still a useful distinction, as "thinking" is seen as what you "do." Even in your dictionary definition, being "thoughtful" is seen as a condition of mindfulness, and mindfulness is much closer to the idea of wholeheartedness, or sharing in unity — the state of which we speak. Realize also that you do not consider it to be the "thinking" of another that is shared with you in dialogue, but the thoughts. This distinction will suffice for our further discussion in this chapter.

Let us now consider "thinking" to be the active and often unwelcome voice "in your head," the voice of background chatter. And let us consider your "thoughts" to be the more meditative version of your "thinking," often even resulting in a conclusion to your thinking, a summary of the finer points, as what might come to you in a reflective moment at the end of the day. Again we will see the idea of thoughts "coming to you" at such times. This is not the "thinking" of a conflicted and struggling mind, but the "thoughts" of a mind at rest.

Thinking is more descriptive of the ego mind; thoughts are more descriptive of the true mind. I am not saying that your ego is still at work because you still think in the same way as before. I am about to make the two main points of this discussion: The first is that thinking, with or without the ego, is a pattern of the separated self and does not serve you. The way in which you think may seem vastly improved since the ego ruled or may seem only minimally improved, but it is the pattern, not the ego, that is still with you. The second point is that although thinking does not serve you, you do have, right now, and have always had, true thoughts that come to you from your Self, the Self joined in unity. These are thoughts you did not "think," just as the first receiver of these words received them as thoughts she did not "think."

What I am striving to help you see, once again, is that union isn't achieved with a flash of light from above, but that it quietly infiltrates the dot of the self in its unguarded moments. I am attempting to help you to become aware and comfortable with the idea that, released of old patterns, the self will join with unity more and more frequently, until finally you will sustain Christ-consciousness and live in the world as the elevated Self of form.

One of the primary ideas that will assist you in leaving patterns of thinking behind is the idea that thought as we are describing it, the thought that is not really thought but the way of coming to know of the Self joined in unity, enters you through the place of mind and heart joined in wholeheartedness at the center of yourself, a place that has nothing to do with the body. That you listen, hear, and respond may at times be of the body, but it may also at times not be of the body. The main idea to hold in your mind and heart is the idea of entry, and the idea that what comes of unity does not need access through your body's eyes or ears or any of what you consider to be your senses. Along with this main idea it is essential for you to realize that this is not so strange and unusual as it may sound, that this access and entryway already exists within you, and that you have already benefited from moments of interaction with, if not awareness of, the state of unity.

Now that you are coming to a more clear idea of what the "thoughts" that come to you from unity may be like, you will undoubtedly realize this: You have had such thoughts already, thoughts that *came to you* with an authority that you are not used to — thoughts that you *know*, beyond a shadow of a doubt, are true or right or accurate. They may be simple thoughts about a situation in which you are involved, or about the situation of another. Or they may be profound insights into your Self or the nature of the world.

You may at such times have been frustrated by an inability to share these thoughts, or to deliver them with the authority of the truth simply because you have *known* that they are true, and because you realized, as soon as the truth came into your mind, how seldom in the past you have been sure of anything. You may have been amazed at this new authority, and you may have desired more than anything to have others realize that you really *know* something, that this wasn't your usual opinion or idea you were offering up for discussion, but something you knew the *truth* about!

Many of you may, as well, have experienced the fading of your certainty about this truth over time. It may have been your inability to convey this truth, another's reaction to this truth, or simple doubt that arose within your thinking, but regardless of this fading of your certainty, you still carry within you the moment of realization — the moment in which the truth was *known* to you without doubt, known to you without uncertainty. And you may begin to realize that what has been said throughout this Course — that all doubt is doubt about yourself — is true. If another challenges you, or if your own thinking challenges you, doubt is quick to arise simply *because* you do not expect yourself to be certain of anything, and certainly do not expect yourself to be certain about the "right" or "true" course of action required in a situation, or of something that has not yet occurred but that you are given the certainty to know will occur. But once you have felt this certainty, you will never be so sure again that you cannot *know* the truth. Adding the phrase "beyond a shadow of a doubt" will be something you no longer need add to your knowing of the truth because you will realize its redundancy.

To know is to know. To know is to be certain. This may seem crazy or impossible, and in your realization that it seems crazy or impossible to you, you may become more aware than ever before that what I have said about your way of thinking being insane is true. You think it is perfectly sane to go through life without knowing anything "beyond a shadow of a doubt," without knowing anything with certainty, when the reverse is what is true. It is *sane* to know the truth. It is *insane* not to know the truth.

Some of you will have credited your personal or individual self with the "figuring out" of this truth. Others of you will have recognized the "voice" of authority with which this truth came to you as something other than your usual thoughts, other than your usual self. Either way, you know that your self was involved, somehow, in this coming to know of the truth, even if this coming to know of the truth wasn't quite of the "you" of the personal self.

The thoughts that come to you from unity can be seen as both your own thoughts and thoughts that arise from union. Union is not other than you, as I am not other than you. Union includes you, just as the All of Everything, the whole of wholeness, the one of oneness, include you. We are, in unity, one body. We are, in Christ-consciousness, one Christ. We are, in wholeheartedness, one heart and one mind.

chapter 13

Sharing and a Refinement of your Means of Expressing What You Know

There is no danger, in this time, that you will *know* the truth and *then* discover that you were wrong. You know the difference between certainty and uncertainty and are far more likely to err, especially in the beginning, in discounting what you know rather than in being adamant in the proclamation of what you know. But this desire to proclaim what you know will grow in you, and while you will not be "wrong" in what you know, you may have difficulty in understanding exactly what it is you have discovered; and you may have difficulty in the expression of what you know, especially as what you know grows beyond the realm of mind and body, form and time.

What you will be coming to know in this new way of discovery will be coming to you from the state of unity, from a state you share with all at the level of Christ-consciousness but that may literally *not* be sharable with those who remain in a separate state *except* through the sharing of who you are and who you know others to be. There are two issues of great import contained within this statement, and we will explore each separately.

The first is that what you will be discovering, what you will be coming to know, will be coming to you from the state of unity, which is a shared state. Although what you will be coming to know is already known to you, it will still come in the form of a surprising discovery, a joyous discovery of the previously known but long forgotten identity of the Self and all that lives along with you. This knowing will, for a while yet, be surprising because it will be reversing the insanity of your life as you have known it thus far. These reversals will be among the first revelations and will seem quite simple and pleasing as they enter your awareness, but they may come to be seen as quite complicated as you begin the practice of living with what you come to know.

What is known to you in an instant through the new means available to you within the state of unity will still seem, at times, to need to be learned anew in daily living. This is knowing that will often come in a flash, and is, in a sense, a humorous metaphor for the idea of a divine "ray" of light descending and granting enlightenment. Take another look at your Bible for many stories such as these, and you will read account after account of people who did not know how to live with what they came to know, with what was received in a "ray of light" from within the state of unity.

What comes of unity is in union and therefore is whole. The knowing that will be coming to you will be given in a state of wholeness. You have previously learned of everything in parts and details and particulars. While you are perfectly capable of coming to know in wholeness, a way that is actually natural to you, it will seem so foreign at times that you will feel "blinded" by the light of knowing. You will realize that you know something you did not know before in form, that it is important, monumental even; but you will be unable to "see" this knowing, to envision it in the world of separation, to translate it into the language of the separated self.

Yet you will know that this knowing must be shared. You may not fully realize at first that this sharing is not needed so much as a means of imparting important knowledge to others, but so that you can come to understand it. What comes of union is a knowing that exists in relationship. Once you have attained a state of being able to sustain Christ-consciousness, this will no longer be a problem because you will constantly abide in awareness of the relationship of unity. But until this state is achieved, this aid to understanding is essential.

This need not overly concern you as it will not affect you as it did those of the past. You are living in the time of Christ, a time when no intermediaries are needed or required. You are not called to become an intermediary trying to bridge the knowing of the separated self and the Self of union. What you are called to do is to share in union with others whose awareness is expanding.

You have been told and told again that you are not alone, and this has been among the biggest hurdles for many of you to overcome because your state of aloneness is all you have known. This perceived state is synonymous with the personal self, with the idea of individuality, with separate thoughts, and with the idea that no one will ever be able to truly know you.

Join with others who are experiencing the expanding awareness of the time of Christ, and you will begin to see the evidence that things are different now. Join with others who are coming to know through the state of unity, and the evidence to the contrary will be overwhelming. You will begin to truly understand that you are not alone and separate, and that even the coming to know of the state of unity is a shared coming to know, a coming to know in relationship.

Just as you were taught that you could not learn on your own, you are now being told by one who knows that you also do not come to the knowing of the state of unity alone. Why then would you think that you could come to full expression of what you have come to know without sharing in relationship? Partial expression, yes. But that partial expression will bear the mark of your *perspective,* and that is why partial truth is never the whole truth, and why the whole truth is the only truth.

Sharing in relationship is what the state of unity is all about. It is what it *is.*

81

We come now to the second part of what we are exploring together here, the idea that what you come to know may literally *not* be sharable with those who remain in a separate state *except* through the sharing of who you are and who you know others to be. All this means is that while you may feel unable to share or express all that comes to you from unity, and while you may feel unable to share or express the authority and truth you know it represents, you will, by living according to what you know to be the truth, form the very relationships and union that will allow the truth to be shared. The relationship or union precedes the sharing of what can only be given and received in relationship.

This is why you were told specifically not to evangelize or attempt to convince. These are actions of the separated self attempting to fulfill intermediary functions. Relationship, or union, is what negates the need for such intermediary functions. By being who you are, and seeing others as who they truly are, you create the relationship in which sharing can occur. Without relationship there is no willingness and no union. Without relationship, you behave as a separated self attempting to communicate union from the state of separation. This does not work.

Join with your brother and sister in Christ and sharing becomes effortless and joyful and effective. Cause and effect become one. Means and end the same.

chapter 14

New Frontiers Beyond the Body and Mind, Form and Time

Discovery is more, of course, than the acceptance of your accomplishment and these beginning steps into the real state of unity. Discovery is also consistent with the way most of you have thought of it throughout your lifetime. It is consistent with the action and the adventure of discovery within the world around you.

Here it will be helpful to keep in mind the idea of *as within, so without.* We are not leaving the Self to explore, because the Self is the Source and Cause of exploration as well as the Source and Cause of discovery. And yet the Self is far more than you have experienced as yourself in the past.

The Self is not separate from anything, not from anything in the physical world or anything in the state of unity. This is why the key to unlocking the secrets of all you might want to know before beginning the creation of the new are the ideas we have just explored, ideas of how what is not of the body can still be known to you. This is why this exploration and discovery needs to be invited and experienced *before* you become partners in the creation of the new.

Let me remind you again of your invulnerability and the cautions given within the Course concerning testing this invulnerability. In a certain sense, these cautions are now lessened. While you still are not to view your invulnerability as a testing ground against fate, you will, to a certain extent, need to remember your invulnerability in order to be a real explorer, and to fully participate in the discovery that lies beyond the body and mind, form and time. You will need to put into practice the suspension of belief that was spoken of earlier. You will need, in short, to set aside the known in order to discover the unknown.

I would suggest beginning this exploration with simple questions posed during the course of your normal life. Questions such as, "What might this situation look like if I *forgot* everything I have previously known about similar situations, and looked at this in a new way?" Questions such as, "Do I really need to worry about this situation, or can I *effect* this situation simply by not worrying about it and allowing it to be and unfold as it will?" Questions such as, "While I realize that the facts would tell me this or that is true, I wonder what would happen if I disregarded the facts and was open to this being something else?"

These questions could be asked in situations as commonplace as balancing the checkbook, or as momentous as a doctor's diagnosis of a disease. These questions could be asked when decision making seems to be called for, and when plans seem to need to be made.

One of the major benefits of questions such as these is that they can circumvent the usual thinking you would apply to these situations. They can circumvent the labeling of many situations as problems or crises. They can leave the way open for revelation.

It has been said often that revelation is of God, but remember now that God is not "other " and that the God who seemed so distant from you when you abided in separation can now be heard and seen and felt in your experiences of unity.

Your openness will not only leave the way open for revelation but for cooperation. Cooperation comes from the All of All

84

being in harmony and relationship. When this harmony and relationship isn't realized or accepted is when you believe you have need of planning rather than receiving, when you believe you have cause for stress and effort rather than for just being open to what comes.

Your awareness of the harmony and cooperation that naturally extend from the state of unity in which all exist along with you was advanced by the idea of acceptance you took to heart earlier and paves the way for discovery as a constant coming to know and coming to be.

Coming to know is the precursor of coming to be; the precursor to manifestation; the precursor to creation of the new. It paves the way much as each step of learning that was needed in the time of learning paved the way for the next and then the next. But while I say "much as," this is only to provide you with a way to understand this, for learning is incremental and discovery is not. Learning took place in parts in an effort to lead to wholeness. Discovery comes to you in wholeness. So these steps are not about parts or levels but about the expansion of your awareness of what is.

To expand is to open out, to spread out, to increase, to *become*. It is, for us, about bringing out what is within. As you become aware "within" your Self, you enable the expansion of awareness into the world. As within, so without. An explorer seeking a new continent to "discover" first became aware "within" of the possibility of the discovery of something more. The awareness "within" became awareness "without."

Becoming is all about a movement into form or manifestation. You already *are* manifest in form, and so the idea of *becoming* that has been with humankind throughout time must signal a recognition that what you are is not complete, has not yet become whole, has not been fully birthed. Your forms are complete in the physical sense of sustaining life. Your form was birthed and you have celebrated many birth "days" since your actual birth, progressing from youth to adolescence to maturity, as well as many days of birthing new aspects of the self, all without *becoming* more fully who you are.

Again, these ideas can be likened to the ideas put forth in *A Treatise on the Nature of Unity and Its Recognition* when it was said that "a treasure that you do not as yet recognize is going to be recognized. Once recognized it will begin to be regarded as an ability. And finally, through experience, it will become your identity." That *treasure* is the new way of thought put forth in *A Treatise on the Art of Thought,* the thought that is the miracle, or miracle-readiness, the thought that comes of unity and that extends and expresses itself through your form, elevating the self of form.

It is awareness, acceptance, and discovery of what is beyond form that allows the beginning of the transformation of what is beyond form into expression in form. Awareness, acceptance, and discovery are what allow form to *become* the *more* it has so long been seeking to become.

What is discovered is discovered in the state of unity (by means of your awareness of your *access* to the state of unity, as well as by *what you discover there),* and only *becomes* through the expression you give it. Here *becomes* could be stated further as what is known and sharable in relationship, what is actualized through the expression of thoughts, feelings, art, beauty, kind interactions, or miracles. What is real in the state of unity is what is real, yet you have known this reality not even though it is the more subtle memory of this state that is behind your striving to become. Now you are beginning to see the vastness of what is meant by creation of the new. What is meant by creation of the new is creation of a new reality.

This reality begins with awareness of what is beyond body and mind, form and time. It proceeds to this awareness being accepted, adopted as an ability, and then to becoming your new identity. It proceeds to the transformation we have spoken of, to the act of becoming the elevated Self of form. You are entering the time of becoming, the time of becoming the new *you* which must precede creation of the new *world*. For as it has been said: As within, so without.

Being whole is being present. Being whole is being all you are. Being whole is being present as all you are. When this occurs you are All in All, One in being with your Father.

Wholeness of being is what lies beyond body and mind, form and time. *Becoming* the elevated Self of form is becoming whole, and will be the *way* in which Source and Cause *transform* body and mind, form and time.

Becoming

chapter 15

Becoming and the Principles of Creation

Before creation of the new can begin, you must come to know the way of creation as it *is*. It has not always been the same, and it will not be the same in the future as it is now. But there are certain principles that govern creation. These principles are like unto the patterns that were created for your time of learning, and that will be applied anew to the creation of new patterns for the new time that is upon us.

The first principle of creation is that of movement. Rigor mortis, or the stiffness of death, is nothing but a lack of movement, a lack of movement of the blood through the veins and the consequent stiffening of the muscles. The Dead Sea is called a *dead sea* because of lack of movement. These are excellent examples to illustrate the principle of movement as life itself, the idea of lack of movement as lack of life.

Life and the movement of *being* into form is what occurred when God "spoke" and the Word came into being. Movement is energy, the life force of creation and of being, both in unity and in time. By being you are *in* movement. By being you are an expression of being.

The second principle of creation, then, is that being *is*. It is what *is* and it is the expression of what *is*.

Life is movement through the force of expression. The third principle of creation is expression.

Movement, being, and expression, are not separate principles, but a single unifying principle of wholeness. One did not occur

91

before the other, as they are not separate. There was movement *into* being and an expression *of* being. But what was there to move before there was being? This is the way the mind looks at principles, one coming after the other and building upon each other. This is not the way of creation, which is why these principles of creation must be seen as the undivided wholeness of the principle of unity before creation of the new can begin.

Let me use the creation story of what was once my tradition as an example. Before God "said" anything, a mighty wind swept over the wasteland and the waters. The wind, which is as great a signifier of movement as rigor mortis is of lack of movement, is the first element mentioned in this particular creation story. This first mention of movement is literally present in all creation stories because there is no story without movement. There is no story to tell without movement. Nothing is happening. So movement might be likened to something happening — to the beginning, the beginning of the story and the beginning of creation.

Then God, a being, spoke. Here we have both the introduction of a being and the continuation of movement. Speaking denotes not only a speaker, the being, but the movement of sound. Then we are told the content of the words: It was said, "Let there be light." More movement. Only when movement, being, and *expression* came together was there light. Light might be seen, in this example, as the first act of creation.

I repeat this story not as fact, or to still any doubts about these principles of creation, but to give you an example that is easily understood, an example of the way in which these principles work together. What I have left out of this story — the formless wasteland, the earth and the water that the wind first swept across and upon which the light first descended — is an interesting omission, made by many. What were the earth and water if they were not form?

They were barren form. Form unable to create or bear fruit. Form was simply *barren* form before movement swept across it and animated it with the attention and awareness of spirit — with sound, light, and expression. Could these barren forms not be compared to the forms of the not yet elevated? What if the existence of form was seen to predate the animation of that form with life and spirit? Would this not be consistent with what we attempt to do here? With our continuing work of creation? Would this not even be consistent with spirit existing in every living form from the beginning of *time* until the end of *time?*

Time is what begins and ends. Time is what began when life took on existence in form and space. It is temporal rather than eternal. Along side it, in the state of unity, rests all that is eternal, all that is real. What is real is but another way of saying what is true. What is true is eternal life, not temporal life. There are no degrees of life. One form is not more alive than another. All that lives contains the breath or wind of spirit, which is eternal and complete.

Expression, movement, and being are about what is eternal passing through what is temporal. Thus I return you to the lesson on "pass through" which was contained within the Course. The Course sought to teach you to develop a relationship with all that passes through you. Now is the time when the fruit of those efforts will be reaped. For what passes through you now is a relationship without end. What passes through you now is the eternal come to replace the temporal.

To try to capture the eternal would be like trying to catch the wind. But just as the wind can power many machines endlessly when it is allowed pass through, so too can spirit endlessly empower form when it is allowed pass through.

You might say that the wind comes and the wind goes. It blows in mighty gales and whispers in gentle breezes. Any sailor knows the wind is fickle. But any sailor also knows the wind never dies.

93

You have all been sailors here, animated by the wind of spirit and at one time sailing — flying along with the wind at your back — and at another time sitting still or seemingly bobbing along with no apparent direction. You have attempted to build better sails to catch the wind, or motors to replace it, never realizing its constant and continual presence only needs to be allowed to pass through you to be in relationship with you, never realizing that this is, in truth, what animates you, that this is that without which you cease to be. Continual and unblocked and aware pass through is what we now consider.

You have been prepared for this by the realization that your thinking mind will no longer be necessary as your access to unity, or Christ-consciousness, is maintained and sustained. Let us begin with the idea of maintenance and proceed to the idea of sustenance.

Maintenance is thought of most often as keeping what you have, and as keeping what you have in good repair. It is not often thought of as a lasting measure, which is the primary difference between the idea of maintenance, and the idea of sustenance.

Maintenance assumes that you already have something of value, and that you wish to take care of it so that it will continue to be of service to you. Maintenance implies a certain attitude, an attitude of care, vigilance, anticipation, and a knowing that without this care, vigilance, and anticipation, the value of what you seek to maintain will be lost. Thus we look at maintenance as the work, or relationship, with the desired service. In this example, maintenance is what you give in order to receive the maximum connection to unity that is possible in this time. You realize that some breaks in service will still occur, that maintenance will not make the connection perfect, but that it will keep it of service to you.

And so we begin with the idea of maintenance of your relationship with unity. You have experienced unity now and you wish it to continue to serve you. Consequently you must strive to maintain the conditions that will allow it to do so. This is, as with all maintenance, a temporary measure, but one you desire to have discussed, just as we discussed parameters to your state of conscious awareness.

To move from maintenance to sustenance is our goal. To sustain is to keep in existence. To recognize unity as sustenance is to recognize it as that which sustains life. Sustaining unity or Christ-consciousness is being done with the need to maintain conditions that allow it to be present. Maintenance will lead to sustenance.

Let this idea enter you now. You have left behind the conditions of learning. Why? Because they are no longer needed. The time of learning has ended. When this time of becoming has ended, the conditions that allow your acceptance and discovery of all that is available within unity, or Christ-consciousness, will no longer be needed. This will be as big a step as was the step that left behind the conditions of learning, a step from which you at times feel as if you are still reeling.

This step was like the final step after your ascent of the highest mountain. These dialogues might be seen as taking place there, with the guide and the team of climbers who accompanied you on your ascent. And at this highest point of the highest peak of the highest mountain, you pause and become accustomed to the thinner air, the view from above, to what you now can see. You catch your breath and let the wind of spirit fill your lungs once again.

Here is where you work in relationship to maintain what you have learned, for you know that when you return to the level ground from which you climbed, you will be different as a result of having made your ascent. The hard work is done. What you

95

gain here you gain from what is beyond effort and beyond learning and from the maintenance of the state in which you reject the conditions of learning. You maintain here, in short, all of the conditions necessary to reach your goal.

What you will have gained on your return will be the goal itself — the sustenance — for what you will have gained will never leave you but will sustain you forever more.

chapter 16

From Image to Presence

Barren forms might be seen as forms that existed before the onset of the state of becoming. You are now in the final stage of the state of becoming. You now know who you are, and so now you can begin the work, or the relationship of this final stage: The stage of becoming who you are. This is the stage in which movement, being, and expression come together into the re-creation of wholeness that will be expressed in the elevated Self of form.

The creation story is occurring, right now, in each of you who have reached this final stage of becoming. This is both the beginning stage and the final stage, for once begun, the story of creation moves inevitably to join with the accomplishment and wholeness that already exist in unity. Creation occurs in each of us, seemingly one at a time. Creation is our coming into our true identity, and is the extension or expression of that identity into the creation of wholeness in form.

To be barren is to be empty. Empty is the opposite of full, the opposite of wholeness. It is the perceived condition of lack. It is the belief that what animated form with life did not remain. The belief that in the passing through, a relationship did not form. But as can be easily seen, the earth is no longer a formless wasteland. Form was animated with spirit and entered a state of becoming. You were animated with spirit and you too entered a state of becoming. You can be an expression of being and yet not express the wholeness of being. This is a description of the state of becoming. It is a perceived state. It is a state in which the unified principles of creation are seen to be taking place as separate steps. This is so because of the condition of time. Once these principles are unified, time will have ended just as time was once begun.

The unified principles of creation, once unified within each of us, bring light to each of us; they bring the ability to see, the ability to know, the ability to be, the ability to create. Through the art of thought, these abilities become who we are.

You have been told that God and Creation are synonymous, and you are reminded of that here as you and God become synonymous through Creation. Means and end are one. Cause and effect the same. Creation is means and end as God is means and end. Creation is cause and effect as God is cause and effect. When you move from the state of becoming to the state of being whole, you will have moved through the act of creation and you will have become a creator. You will be ready for creation of the new.

You were told within the Course that being *is* as love *is.* Here you are told that being is a principle of creation and you are not told that love is a principle of creation. Love is not a principle any more than it is an attribute. This is because love remains in eternal wholeness. Love cannot be learned, and so has stood apart from the time of learning. Being could be *learned* here, because it was not yet whole. Being is synonymous with identity. When your being and your identity, your Self and your awareness of Self, are whole and complete, being, like love, is no longer capable of being learned, for it no longer has attributes.

Love *is* the spirit of the wind that animates all form. Love *is* spirit, *is* God, *is* creation. Love is a description of the All of All because it is whole and rests in eternal completion and wholeness. Love *is* the state of unity, the only relationship through which the Self and God become known to you. Love, God, Creation, are all that remained in union, in eternal completion, when form came into being.

Movement, being, and expression are what *is* because they are the givens. Love, like God, like Creation, is the giver of the givens. Life was given through the extension and the expression of God, of Love, of Creation — through the extension of wholeness — into the seemingly separate identities of form. The way of that extension was the way of the unified principles of creation, the way of movement, being, and expression.

The difference between the *way* that *is* and *what is* lies in choice. While you think that you can choose to stand apart from God, apart from Love, apart from Creation, you cannot. But you *can*, while existing in time and form, choose to stand apart from movement, being, and expression. You can choose to *exist* without allowing spirit to move you, without allowing yourself to be who you are, without allowing for self-expression. You might think that you can *be* simply because you exist and that as long as you exist in form you are *being* because you are being something. You are alive. You have form. You think and feel. You have even been told that you would cease to *be* without the existence of spirit, and so, you think, you must at least *be*. You are, after all, called a human *being*.

While you are becoming you are still being acted upon by creation. You are still being acted upon by creation because you are not yet whole. When you are whole, creation's principles will be what you do and what you are rather than what is happening to you. Creation's purpose, creation's cause and effect is wholeness and the continuing expression of wholeness. While it was said in *A Treatise on the New*, that "Now is the time to move out of the time of becoming who you are to the time of being who you are," it was not said that this time of becoming was completed.

And yet giving and receiving are one in truth. All of the principles of creation are in accord with this truth, and these truths occur in unison or in union. Becoming *is* movement. Movement is given and becomes movement in form. Being is given and becomes

99

being in form. Expression is given and becomes expression in form. Since you were conceived in form, you were in movement. Since you were conceived in form, you were being. Since you were conceived in form, you were expressing. It would be impossible for these principles of creation not to be constantly occurring in everything that lives because all that lives, lives because of creation's continuing creation.

Becoming is the movement from image to presence. It is upon you as we speak. It is not a learned state or process and it should not be seen as a cause for disappointment. Perhaps you thought you were beyond this point of becoming. And yet, as you have begun your practice of awareness, acceptance, and discovery, you have felt as if you still have a long way to go. You have often thought that even though you may be done with learning, you don't feel quite complete, or possibly even feel as if learning has not quite been accomplished in you. This is precisely why we now discuss this state of becoming, this movement from image to presence.

There is creation going on in this becoming, the very creation promised you. This is the creation of the new you that you were told will precede the creation of the new world. This is what is meant by *as within, so without*. Only a new you can create a new world. The new you is the elevated Self of form who you are in the process of becoming. This time of becoming is the time in between your awareness of and access to Christ-consciousness, or unity, and your sustainability of Christ-consciousness, or unity in form. In your time of directly experiencing the movement, being, and expression of unity, you are being who you are. At other times, you are becoming who you are.

In your time of directly experiencing the movement, being, and expression of unity, you are whole and complete, you feel no lack, no uncertainty, no doubt. You are confident in what you know. You realize fully that you are no longer a learning being and that you have no need for teachers or for guidance other than for that which comes from your own heart.

At times when you are not directly experiencing the movement, being, and expression of unity, you realize the state of becoming. To realize the state of becoming is to realize that an in between exists between the time of learning and the time of being the elevated Self of form; that times still exist in which you are not wholly present as who you are.

When you are not wholly present as who you are, you are experiencing, still, the image or after-image of who you are. This image is like a lingering shadow. It encompasses all of your former ideas about yourself, all of the patterns of the time of learning, all of the moments in which you feel an inability to join in union, and in which you recognize still the image of your former self.

This is only an image. This is not your personal self, your ego self, or your separated self, come to reclaim you. This is why we have also described this as an after-image. This is but a photograph that remains, a copy of what you once might have thought of as your "original" self. It is but an impression, as in clay, or a reflection, as in a mirror. It is as removed from who you are as is the picture of an ancestor or a landscape that hangs on your wall separate from what it is an image of.

There may be striking beauty in this image, as there is in art of all kinds. This may be an idealized image of your former self, the image of your *best* self, who you may imagine now, through the grace of God, you finally are. But this may also at times be an image of a type, a construction of the subconscious, which still sees in forms and symbols. This kind of image may leave you thinking that you are "acting" as if you have changed, while even within your new actions you see archetypes of the previously known and previously experienced.

The stimulus for these after-images is gone. They are but sensations that remain, like memories of childhood. This time of becoming is a time of coming to acceptance of them as what they are — images. This time of becoming is a time of coming to acceptance that they are not real. They are no more real than the mirage of your future, another aspect of the image you have held of yourself. They are no more real than was your image of heaven, or any image you have had of heaven on earth, paradise found.

The time of becoming is a time of letting these images be without reacting to them. It is a time of coming to no longer "hold" these images in your mind and heart. It is a time of letting them first cease to affect you, and then of letting them go entirely, for without letting them go you are not fully present. Without letting them go, your presence is not wholly realized, you are not fully here, not whole, not complete. You are *at times* who you are, but you also are, at times, but an image of who you have perceived yourself to be.

This image, being but an image, is incapable of true joining in relationship. You must be fully present in order to join in relationship. All of your images are false images, and when you retain them you do not allow for the time of learning to be replaced with the only replacement that will sustain Christ-consciousness, the replacement of learning with sharing in unity and relationship.

chapter 17

the Secret of Succession

To succeed is to follow after, and to follow into inheritance. It is a following after that occurs in time and space rather than in truth. It is never about one. It is not about replacement. It comes in a never ending series rather than in singular form. It is not true succession if there is a break in the chain or in the line of succession for true succession does not stop and start, but is continual.

The series build to a climax, to what, during the time of evolution, might have been called evolutionary leaps.

The secret of succession is simple. It is but a matter of wholehearted desire. Do you wholeheartedly desire to follow me to your true inheritance? To come after me and be as I was? To be the inheritor of the gifts that are ours? Do you desire this? Are you willing to claim it? Are you willing to claim it in form and time?

Can you understand that what you claim in form and time was always yours?

Little can be had without desire. Desire, unlike want, asks for a response rather than a provision. Desire is a longing for, a stretching out for. Imagine yourself at the summit of this mountain we have climbed, standing with arms raised, hands wide open, gazing jubilantly into the heavens rather than toward the earth below. This is the stance of both desire and fulfillment. Of longing and attainment. Of having asked and having received.

Of having striven mightily and succeeded. It is what comes after the embrace of homecoming, and what comes before the passing of desire and the reverence that replaces it. It acknowledges a certain "taking over" of the spirit of desire. Having "arrived," the desire to "get there" has not been satiated but only has grown into something different. With having arrived comes the "presence" of Self so long awaited, the joy of accomplishment, the taste of victory.

But the desire, the desire is stronger than ever before. The influx of attainment has begun. The height of achievement has been reached.

Your glory is realized. But the desire, the desire is stronger than ever before.

You are not alone in your glory or achievement and you marvel that this takes nothing from your feeling of accomplishment. You want to share it with the whole world. From the top of the mountain, arms outstretched, this desire too has caused your arms to rise as if of their own accord. You feel the power of giving and receiving as one, for this is what this gesture symbolizes, a great and steady flow of giving and receiving as one, an unbroken chain of giving and receiving as one. You offer up your glory and call it down from heaven, both at the same time.

But the desire, the desire is stronger than ever before.

You know instinctively that this desire is not a desire to hold on to what you have. That this moment of achievement and glory is a gift of this moment, a gift of presence. Your gesture, so like unto that of a champion who has crossed a finish line and won a race, is not meant to remain as it is in this moment. It is not a trophy for your wall. It is not an achievement you would hope to best. It simply is what it is: A moment of presence full of both desire and fulfillment.

Hope, as was said within the Course, is a condition of the initiate. You have now passed hope by as you have moved beyond the state of initiation. You are no longer hopeful for what will come. Hope is desire accompanied by expectation. To expect is to await, and you are no longer waiting. You have arrived. You have passed through the stage of initiation. You have reached the top of the mountain.

You stand now at the threshold. The stimulus has been provided, the journey taken. You are present. Now is the time for your response.

That response is wholehearted desire, which is the power that *A Course of Love* came to return to you. You were told within the Course that wholehearted desire for union would return union to you and return you to your Self. This is the moment of realization of that accomplishment. But your desire has not left you. Your desire is stronger than ever before.

What is different now is that your wholeheartedness, as well as your desire, has moved beyond the pattern of thought.

Let me return you to the questions that were asked of you earlier, for they are even more pertinent now. Do you think desire will still be with you when you have achieved what you have desired? Is it not possible to conceive of a time in which desire will no longer serve you, just as learning now no longer serves you? If you reach a state of full acceptance of who you are, and in that state, fully accept that your contribution is being made, will desire still be with you?

Your heart is a full well. It is because you have now turned to your heart, instead of to your thinking, that you feel both fulfillment and desire. But my earlier questions seemed to indicate that once fulfillment was reached, desire would no longer be with you. But your desire is still with you. It is stronger than ever before.

The only reason why this might be so is that it is meant to be so. Something is still desired.

Desire asks for a response. Earlier it was said that desire asks for a response while want asks for provision. What is the difference we speak of here?

Provision is about preparation for future needs. This is an appropriate response to want, but it is an inappropriate response to desire. It is an assumption of needs unfulfilled. You now stand in fulfillment. This is the secret of succession.

Desire asks for a response. From where is this response sought? You now must understand the fullness of the well of your heart, the interrelationship of desire and fulfillment. The interrelationship of desire and fulfillment is what occurs at the threshold. Beyond the threshold is the state in which desire has passed and been replaced by reverence. To revere is to feel awe, which, it has been stated, is due nothing and no one but God. To move beyond desire to reverence is to move into the state of communion with God, full oneness with God, wholeness.

You have realized now that you remain in a state of becoming, and any disappointment you may have initially felt with this realization has been replaced by acceptance. Acceptance has come because you recognize the signs of becoming that we have been discussing. You recognize them because they are what you are feeling. Yet you may wonder how you can be told that you have arrived at your journey's end and still have farther to go.

You have nowhere to go. The journey *is* over. You stand at the threshold, the gateway to the site you have traveled so far to reach. You are here, and desire fills you, even while you know the glory of having arrived.

Having arrived here, it is as if a new question is asked of you. Just as in the myths that are as ageless as they are timeless, you are asked for something. You are asked for a response.

Only in myth is this response to a specific question, but even the specific questions of myth, when seen truly, were questions of the heart, calling only for response from the heart.

Desire calls here, louder and stronger than ever before, because of your proximity to what you have desired. Every hero's journey returns him home. To where he started from. In story form, this takes place with movement. Years are spent traveling many paths and many miles. All the heartaches are experienced along the way. All the experiences and learning occur on the journey.

This is why you have been told the time of parables, or stories, has ended. This is why you have been told: "As within, so without." This is why you have been taken to the top of the mountain without leaving home. You have taken the inward course, the inward journey, the only journey that is real in the only way that is real.

We will spend forty days and forty nights here together, at the top of the mountain, fasting from want, becoming aware of desire, responding to desire. This is the final stage of becoming. Herein lies the secret of succession.

The Forty Days
and Forty Nights

The Forty Days and Forty Nights

Day 1: Accept me

Acceptance of me is acceptance of your Self. Acceptance of me is acceptance of your inheritance. This is nothing new to those of you of the Christian faith. To others it will seem an acceptance beyond your ability, an acceptance that there is no real cause to request. Why must Jesus be accepted? Why cannot the truth be accepted? Why cannot everyone hold their distinct beliefs as long as they are beliefs in the truth?

Beliefs are not what are being spoken of here. *Acceptance is*. Acceptance is not belief, it is not prayer. I care not in what form of the truth you believe, nor to what god you believe you send your prayers; although if you do not believe in your Self above a form of truth, and if you continue to send your prayers to a god who is other than you, you will not cross the threshold.

We are here on the top of the mountain together, beginning our work together. I am no longer your teacher, but there is a reason that you are here with *me*. You have been listening to *my* words, and these words are what have brought you here, not to a place but to an ascended state. Without your acceptance of who I am, you will not fully accept who you are. Without your willingness to achieve this acceptance, you will not receive the secret of succession presented here. You can read of it still, but it will not convey to you what it will convey to those who have accepted me. You will return to level ground with eyes unopened and listen to parables once again and learn once again from the stories of others.

Why should this be so important? Why not leave well enough alone? If acceptance of Jesus is a stumbling block for many, why

111

should it be required? A college education has requirements. If math is a stumbling block for some, a foreign language for another, are these requirements waived? Let us just accept that requirements are prerequisites for many states you value. To marry one man you must choose to leave others behind. This is required. This does not mean the married woman will not relate to many men in many ways, have many male friends, teachers, guides. It means that one is chosen as a mate to the exclusion of others not chosen as a mate.

In these examples we are talking of simple requirements, requirements of daily life rather than of eternal life. The requirement asked of you here is not to exclude others in whom you believe and have found a connection to eternal life, only to accept me as who I am.

Now that you have moved beyond the thought system of the ego self, you look back on it and realize why you could not know your Self while the ego was your guide. You were required to make a choice between the thought system of the ego and the thought system of unity. This choice was made and you have arrived here. You have left behind the state of the initiate, the time of waiting. You have chosen. You are merely asked now to look at what you have chosen and to understand what you inherit through the secret of succession.

If you are to succeed me, you must accept me, much as you must accept your ascension to this mountain peak and this dialogue that is occurring here. If you believe this mountain peak is merely metaphorical, you will not realize that you have ascended or that you have left behind the conditions of the initiate. If you believe these are words of wisdom and that you can remain ambivalent about their source, you will not know me nor accept me, and you will not know or accept your Self.

Why are we so linked that your ability to know your Self is contingent upon your ability to know me? Because I am. This is akin to saying *Love is*. I am what *is*. I am the way, the truth, and the life.

Not accepting me would be like training to be an astronaut and, at the moment of take off, refusing the requirement of the spacecraft as the way to reach outer space. This would be akin to non-acceptance of the way that has been given to bring your desire to fruition. The spacecraft could be seen as a response to your desire. So too can I.

This would be like saying, "If I am an astronaut, I can reach outer space without a space craft. I have been trained, I understand the truth about outer space, I believe in my abilities; but I do not accept the spacecraft as necessary."

Many people now are discovering the power of healing. Some think this power comes from one source and some from another. You may think that, as long as the power is called forth, it matters not the name by which it is called. You may think that it all comes from the same source, regardless of what the practitioner of healing calls it, be the practitioner a faith healer or a medical doctor. You may make one exclusive choice to attend to your needs of healing, or you may make many choices. You may think these choices matter not, but only the power of the healer. Some of you may see this example as an example of why you should not need to accept me. You may claim that you understand that this power is of God, whether it be the power of granting life to grow within the womb, or the power of giving new life to a limb withered or broken. You may wonder why it should matter whether this power be called Buddha or Allah, Muhammad or God.

It matters not. The power of God is not what is being spoken of here. It is *our* power that is being spoken of here. The power of the god man. The power of God brought into form. The power of who we are rather than the power of who God is.

God cares not what you call Him. God knows who He is. It is you who has not known who you are, and it is through me that this knowing can be returned. This is simply the way it is. It is not about being right or being wrong, about one being more and others less. This is simply the way to sameness of being, to the reunion of all, from the holiest of the holy to the lowliest of the lowly.

Had any of the holy women and men who walked the way of the world since my time learned, accepted, and lived the teachings that have brought you to this point which I now would like to lead you beyond, the world would be a different place. Have I not called you to a new time in which the conditions of learning exist no more? In which the suffering and death that have obscured that love is the answer are banished, rejected, and a new world of love accepted in their place?

You are all beloved daughters and sons of love itself, no matter what you call that love. You all are equally beloved. That you give your devotion to one religious tradition or another matters not. That you accept that I am he who can lead you beyond your life of misery to new life matters absolutely. I am not your teacher and you are not called to follow me blindly. But you are called to follow, or succeed me. Only in this way can new life be brought to old.

Your desire to know me has grown as you have read these words and grown closer to your Self. This is because we are One. To know me is to know your Self.

Let us return a moment to the creation story and my acknowledgment that this creation story is occurring in each and

114

every one of us. Let me move forward and speak a moment of Adam and Eve and the fall from paradise. Let us extend our idea of the *creation story* to include the creation of man and woman. Adam and Eve represent your birth into form. I represent your birth into what is beyond form. Adam and Eve represent what occurred within you at the beginning of the story of your creation. I represent what occurred within you recently, the story of your rebirth through this Course.

The story of Adam and Eve, and the story of Jesus, are within you. *As within, so without.* In each of you is Adam and Eve represented in form. In each of you am I represented in form.

The New Testament was the beginning of the new. My life represented fulfillment of scripture, of all holy writing, of all learned wisdom. In fulfillment are endings found and beginnings created.

This fulfillment of scripture has now occurred within you. When it occurred within me, it occurred within all. It became part of the continuing story of creation, of creation acted out within the created.

The story came after the fact. Thus the fulfillment was always part of the story of creation. It was always part of you as it was always part of me.

There is no story to project what comes next — no accomplished story. There is only scripture unfulfilled, the promise of inheritance or the threat of doom. Myth too stops short of fulfillment, of return to paradise.

The return to paradise, to your true Self and your true home, is written within you. It only needs to be lived to become real. You must accept me because I lived it and made it real for you. You must accept me because I am the part of you that can guide you beyond what I accomplished to the accomplishment of creation, and beyond creation to the story not yet written, the future not yet created. To the realization of paradise and of your true Self and true home, in a form that will take you beyond time to eternity.

This has been spoken of as the second coming of Christ because my story goes unfulfilled without your fulfillment. It is only in your fulfillment of the continuing story of creation that my story reaches completion. It is a story whose completion cannot occur in singular form, but as with any true inheritance only in a series, only in a joining together of all of the parts of the creation story into the wholeness of the story's end. As a story is seen to move from one element to another in an unbroken chain of events, so too is the story of creation. As history proceeds with gaps only waiting to be fulfilled in current time, so too is it with the story of creation.

You are living history. You are living what will tomorrow be history. You are living creation. You are living what will tomorrow be the story of creation. A chain of events is merely another way of saying cause and effect. The chain of events of creation include, thus far, the movement of being into form and the movement of being beyond form. What will be realized through the secret of succession is the elevation of form.

You can only fast from wanting by realizing what it is you desire. My forty days and forty nights on the mountain succeeded my baptism and my acknowledgment as the Son of God, and preceded my time of living as my Self in the world. So too does it with you. You long for and desire me because our story is the same. You are living my story as I lived yours. They are one story.

Lay aside your want of other answers, other stories, and accept the story we share. The Bible and all holy texts can be seen clearly now as one creation story. One story of one beginning. One story with many promises made. Promises of inheritance and fulfillment, promises that give hints to, but never quite reveal, the secret of succession.

I am the secret of succession, the way and the life, the beginning of the end of the story that is to be fulfilled, brought to completion and wholeness in you and in me, so that together we bring about the second coming of Christ and the elevation of the self of form.

The Forty Days and Forty Nights

Day 2: Accept Yourself

Acceptance of your Self is acceptance of me. Acceptance of your Self is acceptance of your inheritance. Now is the time to come into full acceptance of the human self as well as the Self of unity. It is time for the final merging of the two into one Self, the elevated Self of form.

You have let go the ego, re-viewed your life, unlearned previous patterns, and now see the difference between the image you hold of yourself and your present Self. But still, in unguarded moments, in moments in which you would desire peace, memories of your life continue to play within your mind, often still bringing you sadness and regrets.

All of these moments you review have brought you here. But I realize that you have not as yet developed the capacity to accept this fully. For most of you, much of what you have considered your mistakes and poor choices have been reconciled. You can see the pattern of your life as clearly now as if a masterful biography had been written of it. It is this clarity that has brought a new "haunting" to some of you. Your life is being seen more as a whole now. The parts are fitting together. You can see how you have moved from seeming purposelessness to purpose.

You are like an inventor who wasted many years, much money, and endured many hardships over many projects that did not come to fruition, and now has succeeded in inventing just what was always envisioned. This is the moment of fulfillment and desire coming together, the time in which you realize "it was all worth it."

This is the time of revelation of meaning. You who have so long striven to give meaning to the purposeless, here see meaning revealed.

And yet you cannot still some of your regrets. The feeling is not as strong as it once was, and you are very unlikely to still experience guilt or shame; but the hurts you have done others may weigh heavily on you now. It is as if, at this mountain peak, you have discovered a lightness of being, and yet within it is this stone of regret. You continue to have a nagging feeling that this stone of regret will always keep you anchored to the self you once were, that no matter how high you ascend, it will continue to drag you back.

This is the feeling that will prevent you from receiving the secret of succession. It is like the force of gravity, a feeling that you will not be able to remain at this height long enough to benefit from what will be shared here.

Part of this feeling arises from erroneous ideas that remain regarding your unworthiness. Part of this feeling arises from the erroneous idea that you can fail, even here. These are the temptations that confront those who have dared to ascend the mountain. It is not the height you have attained that causes your fear of falling. It is the depth to which you feel you once descended that calls forth your fear here.

These are mainly, in truth, judgments, judgments that arise from your conscience, from that part of you that has compared your actions to the laws of man and God and found yourself guilty.

Let me ask you now, are these feelings that are attached to your beliefs that you have harmed others not feelings of sorrow? Are you not sorry for these actions? Have you not expressed your wish that you had acted differently? Can you see a way to change the past or to "make up for" what occurred in the past?

119

Now is the time for acceptance, even of these actions that you would rather not accept. They happened. They were what they were. I ask you not to forget that they occurred, but to accept that they occurred. If your home had been destroyed by a tornado or a flood rather than adultery and divorce, would you not see the benefit of accepting what had occurred and moving on? You might counter this by saying that if you had been the adulterer, the cause of the divorce, this was different than a tornado or a flood. Yes, this was different, but this difference does not place these actions beyond the idea of acceptance.

Conversely, were you the innocent "victim" of an adulterous mate, a mate whose actions led to divorce and the destruction of your home, can you not accept that this is something that happened? We leave aside, for the moment, any considerations of other outcomes of such actions, whether they are negative or positive in your judgment. We look for a simple acceptance of the "facts" of your life.

I could give thousands of examples here, but we are not looking for degrees of wrong-actions, or wrong-doing. You all have moments you wish you could re-enact, decisions you wish you could change. These "actions" are unchangeable. This is why simple acceptance is needed. We speak not of forgiveness or even atonement here, for these have been thoroughly discussed earlier. You have all been through the time of tenderness, the time that preceded your giving and receiving of forgiveness, your request for and granting of atonement, your re-viewing and unlearning of the perceived lessons of your life.

But just as you are called here to accept me despite possible misgivings such as religious beliefs, you are called to accept yourself. This unconditional acceptance is necessary. I will give you one final example in order to make our discussion as clear as possible.

This is an example from my own life, an example the idea of which still plagues many of you. This example is that of the crucifixion.

For many of you the crucifixion is among the reasons you hesitate to fully accept me. It is hard for you to believe that my suffering was symbolic of the end of yours when so much suffering has continued. I will add here the example of my resurrection. It is hard for you to believe that my resurrection heralded eternal life when death has been a constant companion of all those who have lived since my time. It is difficult for you to believe that by following me you will not walk in my footsteps. Perhaps you will be granted eternal life, but not until you have suffered as I suffered. This idea would hardly be a joyful idea with which to begin our work together.

As was said within the Course, my life is the example life. The way in which I have talked of it recently may have led some of you to consider it as a symbolic life rather than an actual life. All of our lives here are symbolic rather than actual. Just as the creation story is symbolic rather than actual. This does not mean that my life did not happen, that it did not occur in time and space, just as yours is occurring now in time and space. What this means is that what occurs in time and space is symbolic, that it is representative of something more.

So let us consider my life again, just briefly, and let us consider the something more it may represent.

My life consisted of many of the same major elements as yours: Birth through childhood, maturity, and with that maturity action in the world, suffering, death, and resurrection.

You have accounts of my actions that begin with the appearance of my form in the world, but that mainly occur during my time of maturity. These accounts do not stress the time of childhood as it is a time commonly held to be one of innocence. The accounts of my maturity generally begin with the recognition of who I am. This is symbolic of the idea put forth here that until you are aware of who you are, your life has not literally or symbolically begun.

It was in awareness of who I Am that my life took on meaning. It could be argued that this awareness existed at my birth, and this too would be accurate, since all births are meant to be eagerly looked forward to as beginnings of I Am. Since most births are seen in this way, and most mature lives are not, we concentrate here on mature lives.

My mature life began with the recognition of who I Am, as does yours. This time was followed by my "example life," a life that began with the forty days and forty nights spent upon the mountain, and continued with my joining with my brothers and sisters, with the bringing of light to darkness, power to the powerless, health to the sick, life to the dead. My life touched all those willing to be touched, changed all those willing to be changed. But great unwillingness remained. Willingness was not yet upon humankind. The choice was made collectively to remain in illusion. The choice for continued suffering was made. And so I responded to that choice. An example of response was needed. The example was that of a symbolic gesture. It, too, was a choice. A choice to take all that suffering upon myself and kill it. To say, here is what we will do with suffering. We will take it away once and for all. We will crucify it upon the cross of time and space, bury it, so that it need be no more, and demonstrate that new life follows the choice to end suffering.

"I" did not suffer, for I knew who I was and chose no suffering. This is what is meant by the idea that has been repeated as that I died for your sins. My death was meant to demonstrate that the end of suffering had come, and with it, eternal life.

Here, then, is where *you* need to make the choice that those in my time could not make, the choice to end suffering. This is the choice I made "for all." This is a choice you make for all as well.

Willingness is now upon humankind. What my life demonstrated but needs to be demonstrated anew. But this will not happen if you cling to suffering. If you do not accept your Self, all of yourself, you cling to suffering.

This is why you first needed to accept me. To accept me is to accept the end of suffering. To accept the end of suffering is to accept your true Self.

The Forty Days and Forty Nights

Day 3: Accept Abundance

Accept your anger for it is the next step in the continuum upon which we travel. When a person is dying, just as when a person is undergoing this final surrender, there are stages through which one moves. The first is denial, the second is anger. We have already spoken of denial, albeit in a new way. Now we will speak of anger, in both an old and a new way. Let me suggest to you what it is truly all about. It is about the way you have learned and your lack of understanding of what this did to you.

What was it that was "taught" *to* in the time of learning? It was the mind. Your mind has been trained for learning and you are most willing to have new insight, new information, and even new discoveries, enter through your mind — because this is known to you and is that with which you are familiar. In the area of the mind were you most willing to accept teachers, leaders, guides, authorities, for only *through* them did you learn. You are beginning to see now that this learning was not a choice but only the way you knew life to be. While the freedom of childhood learning might be seen as the way learning was meant to be, the time of this pure learning has grown shorter and shorter while the time of enforced learning has grown more entrenched.

In the area of the body came another form of learning about which you saw yourself as having little choice. When the body had something to teach you, what choice did you have but to listen? So the mind and body were both conditioned to have learning thrust upon them. You long ago quit resisting most of this learning and accepted it as "the way things are." This kind of acceptance is what we are reversing with a new acceptance.

124

With your heart you grew less accepting of these "outside" attempts at influence. You, who as both individuals and as a species, have been conditioned by thousands of years of learning through the mind, learning in often painful ways, said "no" to learning through the heart. Many of you will admit to growing a bit angry with the beginning of the Course and its challenge to your ideas regarding love. Most of you approached learning through the heart with even more openness than you did new ideas about love, not realizing that they were one and the same.

So our first point of discussion in the realm of anger is that no matter where anger seems to arise, anger is a product of the condition of learning. It always was, but now this is being revealed to you not just through my words, but by your experiencing of anger in new ways. You may not have felt a great deal of this anger yet, but it is there, and here we will discuss its function.

There is one area that is greeted with even more anger and more resistance in regard to both old learning and new than is love. This is the area that you call money and that I call abundance. Feel your body's reaction to this statement. Some of you will feel excitement at the idea of this issue being finally discussed; but be aware of your feelings as we proceed, for I tell you truly, here is where your greatest anger, and your greatest lack of belief and acceptance, lie.

You may believe a spiritual context for your life can change your life, make you feel more peaceful, give you comfort of a non-physical nature. These ideas, whether you realize it or not, are all associated with mind. It is through your mind that these new ideas will change your actions and your life, your mind that, through increased stillness, will give you more peace, your mind that will accept comfort of a certain type, even extending to a new comfortableness of being. You believe having a spiritual context for your life can change your inner life, but are more skeptical in regard to its ability to affect your outer life; and nowhere are you more skeptical than in regard to money or abundance. The area of money, or abundance, is where learning fooled you and failed you the most.

You may believe that having a spiritual context for your life will assist you in feeling more loved and possibly even assist you in finding some *one* to love. You may believe that this spirituality can help mend a feeling of broken-heartedness, can cause you to extend forgiveness to those who hurt you, to make amends to those you hurt, or to simply quit feeling guilty or bitter, shamed or rejected because of them. But you do not believe this spiritual context is capable of bringing you the lack of want you associate most strongly with money.

Just posing the idea that having a spiritual context for your life will assist you in living abundantly will cause you to think, *I doubt it.* Or, *I'll believe it when I see it.* You might think spirituality can assist you in living a more simple life, a life of limits of which you are more accepting. But given time to consider such an idea, you are likely to become more and more agitated, to go back and forth between the general and specific, thinking of both your own lack in life and that of those whose lack is more pronounced than your own. Fairness seems non-existent in terms of who "has" and who "has not," and the world seems made up of haves and have nots and to function in the insane way that it does largely due to this discrepancy.

In such a case, would it make sense that we not address this issue, this blatant cause of so much insanity? This cause of such anger?

Let us return for a minute to the base idea behind the issue of money or abundance: the way you have learned. The mind would tell you that nothing is given, and that all must be either learned or earned, most times both. You have learned in order to earn, learned in order to advance yourself in the world in one way or another. Since money or abundance is not a given for all, but only for a few, you think of it much like the givens of natural gifts or talents, the givens of fresh and inspired ideas. You do not see that these are in truth linked as givens, for you do not see that all are gifted.

It is only because some are gifted more abundantly than others that they can use the givens of talent and inspired ideas to bring them wealth. This is the idea of bartering, which we have spoken of before, or bargaining, which we will speak more of here. It is the base idea that is behind all ideas of lack, an idea you so thoroughly learned during the time of learning that letting it go, even now, still torments you with worry and anger. It is the idea of an *if this, then that* world. An idea of a world in which the beliefs set forth within this Course are neither seen nor lived by.

This is the basic fallacy that the time of learning supported. The idea of *if this, then that.* The idea of abundance earned. The idea of nothing being truly free. Not you, and not your gifts. Everything coming with a price. Abundance comes, even to those gifted, only through the exploitation of gifts. Abundance remains, even to those born with it, only through the exploitation of others. Only through some having less do some have more. To think in such terms, and then to see such thoughts as even capable of having spiritual value, is something you think of as insane. There seems no remedy, and so you would rather not even attempt an understanding of how things might be different. As far as you have come, these ideas are still with most of you to one degree or another. Even though you know these are false ideas, and in that knowing may even say to yourself as you read them that you no longer think in such a way, they are there in the learned pattern and you know this too.

They are what prevent you from believing that the ideas set forth in this Course, when practiced, are capable of making a difference, especially in terms of monetary abundance. This is one of those situations in which you know and have no idea what

127

to do with what you know. Being unable to replace, in application, the false with the true, the pattern of the false remains.

Yet how can you accept yourself when you have feelings such as these? How can you accept the idea of inheritance with ideas such as these? How do you accept me when you see me as symbolizing a life of "godly" poverty, and of calling my followers to abandon their worldly goods?

Thus must this source of your anger and discontent, this source of your non-acceptance, be revealed in a new light.

Let's go back to the idea of money when it is seen as a given. It is seen as a given in one case only: In the case of inheritance, in the case of those born to money. Thus this is a good place to start, since inheritance is that of which we speak. Let's be clear that we are not speaking of money or abundance as being given when it is hard work to attain. Not even when it seems to come from some event of luck or fate. We are talking specifically here of the money given through inheritance, the money some lucky ones are born with.

These are those who are resented most within your world. And yet envied. This resentment and envy fills you with anger. If you feel any anger now, pay attention to its effect on you. You can feel, perhaps, the strain and tension in your stomach, back and neck.

The degree of your discomfort with this issue is something you only imagine to be greater than that of your brothers and sisters. A few of you will not feel this, and if you are among those few, do not skip past this dialogue, but join in so that you understand, as do those for whom this dialogue is meant, the power of this aspect of your brothers and sisters lives, and the power and function of anger.

The power of money to affect you is a power that is denied, rarely acknowledged, seldom spoken of. Think you not that the shame that comes from heartaches or mistaken actions is any greater than the shame those feel who feel no abundance, who suffer a lack of money. There is still a commonly held belief that abundance is a favor of God, and as such those who do not experience abundance have thus done something wrong. We will return to this, but first let's continue with the denial of money's affect.

The shame and pain of heartaches and mistakes is more often and more easily spoken of than the shame of monetary failure. Certainly much complaining and general fretting are done, but only to the degree in which you feel you are in the same circumstances of those to whom you complain. To speak of money matters with someone who might have more than you, you would consider a shaming act. You would fear that they might think you want something from them and you would suffer embarrassment. To speak of money with anyone who has less might open the door for a request for what you do not feel you have to give. To reach a position in which you feel you need to ask for money from others, even from a bank, is seen as a dire situation indeed. This asking will likely be an ordeal of some consequence. Even those who are seen by others as constant "takers," unafraid to ask for a "hand out" or free lunch, experience these same emotions, the build-up of anger, resentment, and shame.

In the realm of money lie your biggest failures, your greatest fears, the risks you have taken or not taken, your hopes for success. What you wish for is contingent upon having the means to pursue it, and few of you truly think that money would not solve most of your problems. Even those of you on this spiritual path think money is among the greatest limits to what you can accomplish, to how you can live the life you would choose to live. You may have left behind aspirations of wealth, and replaced them with ideas of having more time, more fulfilling work, simpler pleasures, and yet you still see your new state as one that does not touch upon this aspect of "reality." The better life you might attain will be a by-product rather than the effect of Cause.

Here is the *real* of the old *reality* most solid and unrelenting. Not having enough is the "reality" of your life because it was the reality of the learning life. Even if you are one of those others consider lucky, one of those who always has "just enough," little do others know that your fear is as great as theirs. While you admit you have "enough," you are sure it will not be enough for what the future holds. And if you ever need evidence for this position, it is quick to come. As soon as you get just a little bit ahead, a need arises. The roof leaks, the car breaks down, and an endless series of needs arise. This "evidence" is exactly what you have sought.

This is the way fears operate. They operate in the pattern of the ego, a pattern that was learned, a pattern that was emphasized and reemphasized through external events so that it would not be forgotten, so that it would reinforce wants until this attitude of wanting seemed impossible to unlearn. It is a pattern of survival, but not of *your* survival. It is the pattern of the ego's survival, and even though the ego is no longer with you, the pattern remains. Because what you learned and the way in which you learned it remains.

Remember, you have learned that nothing is given, for what use would you have of learning if such were the case. In our dialogue, we have begun to use examples of what you did *not* learn in order to demonstrate that what you learned is not true. What you learned is insane. But to realize the truth you must now fully reject the untruths that you learned. You must fully reject the ideas that taught you that you do not have enough, that you will only have what you can earn or learn, that only through effort will you gain, and that with your gain will come another's loss. Here is where you must accept the teachings of this Course.

Do not feel dejected that you have not learned these things. They *were* learned to the degree that you could learn them within the teachings of *A Course of Love*. But beyond learning is where we now stand. We now stand at the place of the rejection of learning — the rejection of *all* you learned.

Let me set your mind at ease, for you are not called to sacrifice, as you have been told time and time again. I do not ask you to give up what you desire, but to expect and accept a response to what you desire. Remember that we are headed even beyond desire, and know that desire must first be met before you can be taken beyond it.

The condition of want, like all conditions of learning, ended with the end of learning. The condition of want was a learning device — not one of divine design, but one of the thought system of the ego. It was a trick to keep you constantly striving for more, a trick to guarantee the survival of the ego-self, a trick that provided the small rewards of time-bound evolution, the small rewards that would keep you assured of progress through effort, and just as assured of ruin through lack of effort.

You think abundance is the most difficult thing to demonstrate when it is actually the easiest. You think you could learn what is for you the most difficult type of learning, be it philosophy, math, or foreign languages, before you could learn how to make money, or have abundance. You think you could more easily find love than money, even those of you who have felt loveless for too long to contemplate. And those of you who scoff at these remarks because you feel you have learned the secret of money, the secret of success: Answer truly if you really believe this, or if you are merely covering over your fear of not having enough with an incessant drive to prove it is not so.

Just as so many of you are thankful for your good health while at the same time dreading the disease that may at any point take it from you, those of you who have money see it in the same way.

131

You may go along just fine for weeks or months or years, unworried about your health until the slightest pain makes you think of cancer. In this same way, there are not any of you, those who have money or those who have none, who feel that your financial "health" is any more secure than the "health" of your body.

How can you live like this? How can you have any peace when you live like this? What succor will your inheritance provide if thoughts like these accompany your inheritance? Were this a monetary inheritance, would you not squirrel it away for a rainy day, or spend it only with trepidation and an eye upon the bank account? Even those of you who would feel prepared to let it bring you joy would err in thinking that it could. How many times has what you thought would provide you with reason for joy failed to do so once acquired?

And so you might think, here, of what *has* brought you joy. A home, a garden, a musical instrument, the equipment that enabled a hobby or talent to be developed, a well-loved book, dinner with a friend, a new car, a new pet, the ability to provide a child with a good education.

You might think here too that money made from what you love to do has a different quality than money earned from toil. You might think that money earned from what you love to do is the answer, just as you might think that money spent on the more lasting pleasures such as the things described above is the secret.

For you are quite certain that there is a secret you know not. There is, and it is a secret I will try to share with you here, if you can let your disbelief and anger at this suggestion fall away. I know you expect a flowery answer, and surely not one that will be a "one, two, three steps to abundance" answer; but I will try to address you in an in between tone, one that will not cause you to feel spoken down to or incite your hostility. One that will not only be truthful, but as practical as you need it to be.

132

You have been told that the time of the Holy Spirit, the time of a need for an intermediary between yourself and God, is gone. You have been invited to know God directly, and to develop a relationship with God. It is only in knowing God that the relationship of abundance will be made clear to you and break forever the chains of want.

Learning is no longer the *way* for good reason. It exemplifies the difference between information and wisdom, between finding an answer and finding a way or path. Many have read the words of the Bible, the words of Lao-tzu, the words of Buddha. To teach is to convey the known. To speak of a *way* is to invite dialogue and a journey. This is what all master "teachers" taught, often throwing the questions posed back upon the poser in order to say: Use me not as an intermediary. It is only in relationship with the God within that the way will become clear.

To read the inspired wisdom of teachers such as these in order to "learn" has prevented the very relationship that these teachers sought to impart.

What you have "learned," and since the time of learning had revealed to you, is a new *way,* the way of direct relationship with God, the way of knowing through discovery. Remember always that knowing through discovery is knowing what was not known before, and keep this in mind as we consider the knowing of abundance.

When you have felt the reality of union, you have felt the place in which no want exists. You felt this through the responsiveness of the relationship that is unity. You perhaps desired an answer that "came to you" through no process you had known before. We spoke of this as thoughts you did not think. We spoke of these thoughts you did not think coming with authority and certainty, a certainty you previously lacked. When I said earlier in this chapter that you are most comfortable learning through the mind because of your familiarity with the pattern of learning through the mind, you can perhaps see why these first revelations of union would come to you in a way associated with the mind.

You have accepted now, because of whatever experiences of unity you have had, that the knowing of unity is available to you. You may not have given great consideration to the access through which that availability arose, but since for most of you it has arisen as thoughts you did not think, if you were to make an association in regards to entry, you would likely say the entry point was the mind. This is, in a sense, true, as wholeheartedness is comprised of the mind and heart joined in unity. It would be more true to think of this joining as creating a portal of access, a new source of entry. But these points do not advance our discussion now and can be returned to later. The point here is your concept or idea about what you have gained from unity thus far being that which *can* be gained through the mind. As you advance, and as you become more open to other means of accessing the wisdom you once sought through learning, or through the mind, other means will open to you. You may see, audibly hear, and interact with what comes to you from union.

The idea I am trying to open to you here is the idea of a responsive relationship with unity that does not exist only within the mind of the wholehearted.

It is the visible world, the outer world, through which your wants find provision. It is the world of unity, the true reality, through which your desires are responded to. This does not mean that unity does not interact with form. It *is* interacting with the world of form *through you*.

Do you not see? You are the entry point, the only channel through which all that is available in unity can flow.

Abundance is the natural state of unity and thus your natural state, just as certainty rather than uncertainty is your natural state, just as joy rather than sorrow is your natural state. What you are

134

being asked to do here, is to open the self of form to the place of unity, thus allowing this divine flow of union into the elevated Self of form.

Being open to the divine flow of union is the exact opposite of the condition of anger. Anger could be likened to an argument, a debate, in which you are on one side and determined to be the one who is right, the one whose side will win. What you hope to win, in this insane argument about abundance, is an acknowledgment, even from God, that you do not have what you need, that you are lacking, and that because of this, you have no choice but to continue to struggle and strive, to earn and to learn, to, in short, carry on in the world as you always have.

Even those of you who would claim to know this anger not, who would claim to wait in trusting silence for God's provision, are still waiting for provision. Even those of you who have asked God for abundance, and opened yourselves to receive it, even those of you who have seen some improvement or evidence you could cite as a response to your requests, see not the truth of the situation.

You still believe the truth of the situation to be the reality of physical form and of what you have or have not within the confines of that form. This would be like still seeing the mind as the only source of learning, and learning as the only source of knowledge. What you have begun to see is that the mind is not the source of certainty, no matter how much knowledge it attains. What you have perhaps begun to see in similar terms, is that money is also not the source of certainty, no matter how much it enables you to attain. Certainty comes from somewhere else. This somewhere else we have defined as your true reality, the reality of union. Living in this reality, the reality of certainty, is the only key to abundance.

These words are just what you may have expected to hear, and you may feel a return of feelings of anger here. But we have said that there is a function for your anger. The function of anger is to lead you to the step beyond it, the step of action and ideas, the step often called that of bargaining.

Many of you will have already entered this step, this step of considering how what you might *do* might affect the response of God. You take this step without realizing that you are still acting in accord with ideas of it being an *if this, then that* world. You try to guess what God might want you to do, be it being still and not worrying about money, or taking actions, right-actions now, as opposed to your idea of the wrong-actions of the past, in order to bring money or abundance flowing to you. All that this period of bargaining represents is yet another stage in your movement toward acceptance. It is still based on the belief that *you* are responsible for the abundance or lack of abundance in your life. That it is *you* who, by changing your beliefs or your actions, can change your reality.

This is often a hopeful period and it, too, is not without value. You may have many good and even inspired ideas within this time. You may feel as if you are on the right track, that through the planning out of strategy and action, through putting all that you have learned into practice, you are sure to begin to see the benefits that have been promised. But many of your ideas and actions at this stage will be tinged with the anger that came before it. Here is where you may rail at the unfairness, at the unseen benefits of what you have acquired from this learning, of promises seemingly made and not kept. Where, you may ask, is the lack of struggle that has been promised? Why do you still have to try so hard? Work so long? Endure so much? Why isn't the end in sight?

The final stage in this process, this movement toward acceptance, is depression, a lowering of spirits and energy, a lack of desire, a lack of activity, a sinking feeling of going under, of going into the depths of sadness and despair.

Each stage may contain hints of the other, but in regard to money, or abundance, each stage is experienced and felt. This experience has only one combined value, one combined purpose, the purpose of the final letting go, the final surrender that is necessary for the final acceptance to come into being.

Just as you were told you cannot think great ideas into being, or great talent into fruition, just as you were told that the givens are not to be dealt with by the conscious, or thinking mind, so too is it with abundance. Abundance can only be accepted and received, just as great ideas and great talent can only be accepted and received.

You might argue now that what you *do* with great ideas and great talent is of consequence, and this is true. A great idea or great talent that is not brought into form, that is not expressed, that is not shared, is no greater than a seed not planted. But the gift of the great idea, the great talent, must first be seen and recognized, acknowledged and accepted, before it can be brought into form, expressed, and shared. What good would it do you to say *If I had talent,* I would accept and receive it, express and share it. *If I had a great idea,* I would accept and receive it, express it and share it. And yet you continue to think that *If you had money or abundance,* you would accept and receive it, express it and share it.

This *IF* is all that stands between you and abundance.

You do not believe this, and the functions of denial, anger, bargaining, and depression are to lead you to this belief and, finally, to this acceptance. Acceptance first that you do *not* believe. And then acceptance itself.

Do you see the difference even here in belief and acceptance? Can you begin to see acceptance as an active function, much as learning was an active function? Acceptance *is* an active function. It is something given you to do. You think it is difficult, but it is only difficult until it becomes easy.

137

While you think of acceptance as just another word, another concept, another trick of the mind, you will not see it as the end of learning and as such as an active state, a state in which you begin to work with what is beyond learning, a state in which you are in relationship with what is beyond learning. It is in truth a state in which you enter into an alternate reality, the reality of union — *because* you accept that reality.

Like all that was taught within this Course, this is a matter of all or nothing. You cannot accept part of one reality and part of another. You cannot accept, for instance, the compassionate and loving benevolence of the universe, of God, of the All of All, and still accept the reality of lack. You cannot accept that in the reality of unity all things come to you without effort or striving *except* money. You cannot accept that you no longer have to learn and accept the condition of learning that is want.

Active acceptance is what allows the great transformation from life as you have known it, to death of that old life, to rebirth of new life. By clinging to some of the old, you prevent its death and you prevent the rebirth of the new. You prevent the very life-giving resurrection you await. You prevent the elevation of the self of form.

This does not have to be. You have wanted something to *do* to change your circumstances in this earthly reality. This is what you have to do. This is the action required. The active acceptance of abundance is the way to abundance. Active acceptance is a way of being in relationship with all that flows from unity. This you cannot learn but you can practice. Thus your practice begins.

The Forty Days and Forty Nights

Day 4: the New Temptations

While we will broaden the focus of today's dialogue beyond that of money or abundance, we will still be addressing this area of your concern, as well as all other concerns that may be surfacing as you begin to move through the steps toward acceptance. Your anger will be serving you here as it brings attention to these areas most incorrectly influenced by the time of learning. Remember here all the "arguments" that I needed to present in the early part of the Course just to convince you that you are not alone and separate. Although my arguments were not fed by anger, your response will almost surely have been tinged with it at times. Although *my* arguments were not fed by anger, the arguments that arise now for you *will be* and as such are actually appropriate to this stage of our dialogue. We can argue here before we go on. We face together here the temptation of these arguments, these temptations of the human experience.

Yet we do not argue simply by engaging in debate. To engage in debate is but a strategy for proving one side right and one side wrong. We must begin with the realization that we are on the same side. The arguments we will be having will be meant to show you this: That on one side are the temptations of the human experience, which is just another way of saying all that you have learned; on the other side will be the truth, the new temptations that will incite you to leave behind the temptations of the human experience.

How can you feel as if you have a choice when the temptations of the human experience are the only choices that have been

139

known to you? Thus you must be given the opportunity here to see what other choices might be before you.

Real choice is the first new temptation.

As we discussed in yesterday's dialogue, learning has not been a choice. Both as divine design and as a pattern of the thought system of the ego, learning has been with you and within you. Although the divine design of the time of learning is being recreated, the ceaseless pattern of learning remains.

The divine design of learning was a given and a natural part of you, much like breathing. You have no choice about breathing, yet neither do you, under normal circumstances, have to think about breathing. You might begin to imagine the givens of unity as those things that require no thinking.

Learning was not meant to be linked with thinking. Again I'll draw your attention to the learning of childhood. Learning begins long before the onset of the time of language that constitutes your ideas about what it means to think. In evolutionary terms this was true as well. Despite the creation story that symbolizes man's journey, early man was not a being who learned in the same way that you do. Early man had no language. His mind was not full of thoughts. Early man and early childhood can thus be linked as examples of a kind of learning that, despite evolution, has not left any of you. You all begin life without the ability to think in the terms you now associate almost exclusively with thinking, the terms of having thoughts, or words, in your mind.

Even after the onset of language, children continue to learn without thinking. Does this not sound odd, foreign to you? And yet this is the way learning was designed to be. Learning was given as a natural means of access to all that was available to you, but not through effort any more than breathing was designed to be effortful. Learning was designed, like the intake of breath, to be taken in and given out. Inhaled and exhaled. Inhaled and expressed.

The ability to learn is given to all in like measure.

The conformity of learning, as the product of an externalized system, has you all attempt to learn the same things. In coming to identify the world in the same way — the way that has been taught — you think that you have succeeded in learning. This is the cause of the insanity of the world and of your anger with the way things "are" within the world. This is an anger that stems from lack of choice. When you are "taught" the "way things are," where is the room for choice? Where is the room for discovery? And to find out that you were "taught" incorrectly! Why should you not be angry?

You are here now not to re-learn or be taught what life is all about, not to re-learn or be taught the "way things are," but to discover what life is, and to discover the "way" to remake things as they are.

This is the new choice, the first new temptation.

The second new temptation is access.

You have been told that in unity a "place" exists that is your natural state, a state free from want, a state free from suffering, a state free from learning, a state free from death. To be told that such a place exists is no more comforting than consoling words if you do not feel you have access to this place. It is like being told that all of the treasure you might desire is locked away behind a gate to which you have no key.

Access, then, is the key to the treasure.

We have spoken at some length about access that seems to come through the mind. We have spoken of thoughts that arise that you didn't think. We have spoken of talents that were not learned. We have spoken of ideas that were not gained through effort. We have spoken of these things to begin to familiarize you with the given world as opposed to the world of your perception, what we might call a world-view attained through learning.

If you will contemplate for a moment what you know about the example left by my life, you will almost surely realize fairly quickly that my life challenged the world-view of the time and that it is still challenging the world-view of your time. Why might this be?

Let me assure you of what you already know, that everything about my life was purposeful. That challenge was meant then and continues to mean now, a call to a new choice. It asks that you challenge your world-view in a most thorough manner.

The problem with this throughout the centuries has been a tendency to challenge one world-view only to replace it with another of no greater truth or value. My challenge has been reacted to as a challenge to be externalized, a call to create a new system. But nowhere in my example life is such a system found despite all attempts to make it so.

The example often used for the creation of a system is that of my attraction of followers, my claiming of disciples. The term disciple can be linked here with the idea of succession. What I asked of my disciples is not more than I ask of you. I asked them to follow in my *way*. I asked them to be — not as they once were — but to be as I am. I asked them to live — not in the world of their former perception, not in the world-view that had been taught to them – but to live in a new world and, by so doing, to demonstrate a new way.

In the time of learning, it was natural that my example life was seen as something to learn from. In order to "teach" what my life represented to those who did not know me, methods of teaching were devised. From these methods of teaching, rules developed. The teaching was externalized and institutionalized. People began to see following me as belonging to an externalized institution, trying to learn what it would teach, and trying to live by the rules it would have them obey. Much progress was made within these institutions, but much misleading was also done.

This feeling of being misled is another cause of your anger — one of the primary causes, in truth. Not only has all that you have learned led to an inaccurate world-view in the here and now, but to an inaccurate world-view of the past, of the hereafter, of me, and of God. Not only has your mind been misled, but your heart and soul as well.

What could bring solace to an anger so profound? How can you be certain you are not being misled once again?

The answer to both come in the stated purpose of *A Course of Love:* Establishing your identity. You needed to first know yourself as a being existing in union before you could know anything else with the certainty you seek, for union is the treasure that has been locked away from you.

What many forgot, after the passing of the first of my disciples, was that they had access to this treasure. They still knew that it existed, but since they knew not how to access it, they called it the Kingdom of Heaven and longed for access to it after death.

Your anger here extends to yourself as well, for all of you know how many of my words have been forgotten, how many of the truths I expressed were still available to you, even within your religious institutions. You feel, perhaps, that you did not try hard enough, or pay enough attention to separating the true from the false. But blaming yourself does no more good than blaming others, for without the dismantling of the ego-self, without the dismantling of the self as separate and alone, you could not learn the truth no matter how much attention you paid, no matter how mightily you tried. On your own you cannot learn the truth. On your own, only illusion can be learned for your starting place is illusion.

Union is both the treasure and the key to the treasure. Union is both access and the place to which you desire access. As all that exists in truth, union is means and end.

To know the basic truth of who you are — that you are a being who exists in unity rather than in separation — is the first step to the access that you seek. Without knowing this, without knowing the truth of your existence, how could you be done with learning? This was what learning was for: to bring you awareness of the truth of who you are. It is "who you are," not learning, that will show the way to the access that you seek. As all that exists in truth, the truth of who you are is means and end as well.

Within you is the access that you seek, just as within you is the Kingdom of Heaven.

The access that you seek is not a tool that can be purchased through your right-actions or even your longing and desire. For this access is not a tool but a function of who you are. This access is, like breathing, something that is natural to you until you begin to think about it. Realize how unnatural your breathing becomes when it becomes the focus of your thought. Thinking about breathing imposes an unnatural constraint upon a natural function.

Thinking, in this time beyond learning, could be rightly seen as a constraint you but try to impose on all that is natural. Your thinking, since it is a product of learning, does nothing but attempt to learn or teach. These are the natural responses of its training. Thus, a major key to your discovery of all that exists within you in the state of unity, is an end to thinking as you know it.

144

In practical terms, you might consider this as a disengagement from the details. Thinking is about details. I am imparting to you the key to abundance and all the treasure that will come with the end of the time of learning. You, on the other hand, are thinking, yearning, grasping for the details. You would like to know how, what, when, and where. While you concentrate on such as these, you impose a function unnatural to this time of Christ-consciousness upon this time.

It is as if you ask to see clearly and then hold your hands over your eyes. You "cover over" the portal of access to unity with a film of illusion. You hide the gate in mist. Remember your breathing and how your concentration upon it affects it. Even learned skills react to this type of concentration. A pianist who suddenly thinks of the notes she is playing, falters. An athlete who suddenly thinks of the requirements of the athletic task he is about to perform, fails to perform with excellence. Why? Because a film of the unnatural is placed over the natural.

Access simply exists within your natural state, much like breathing is simply a fact of the natural life of the body.

Many have applied a certain kind of focus to breathing as a form of meditation. In doing so, they let the natural serve the natural. Some might "go into" the breathing and become one with it. Others might become the observer and in so doing remove themselves from the body entirely.

There is a similar type of focus that will serve you now. It is not a tool, as is meditation, for you are no longer in need of tools. But you have taken yourself away from the ordinary world. You are on top of the mountain. What is this all about? Why have we gathered together here? It is said that during my forty days and forty nights I meditated or prayed. It is said that I fasted. You have been told that you are here to fast from want. You know that you are here to experience both the old temptations and the new. You realize that this is the purpose of our time together even though you have not put this purpose into words and put these words into your mind. What is the focus of which I speak, the focus that is not meditation, the focus that is not a tool?

This is a focus on access itself.

You might think of the mountain top as symbolic of a place close to God. If God was once seen as a figure in heaven, and heaven as a place beyond the clouds, then the mountain top was symbolic of proximity. It was symbolic of a place from which God was almost touchable; as if one could raise ones arms and touch God; stretch just a little more and reach heaven.

You thus may think of this time on the mountain as a time of getting in touch with your own access to God, your own access to heaven. You might think that if you stretch your idea of reality just a little bit farther, stretch your mind just a little beyond where it is comfortable going, that there you will find this access, this portal to all that lies beyond time and space, to all that exists in the place of unity.

We talked earlier of this as a time of fulfillment and desire. We acknowledged that your desire is stronger than ever before. Now is the time to focus on this desire and fulfillment, to stretch this desire to its limits, all the while realizing that its fulfillment lies already accomplished within, in the access that lies within.

This is a longing that carries with it the desire to go beyond thinking, the desire to go beyond words, the desire to go beyond where your imagination is capable of taking you. It is a desire for true discovery, a desire to access the previously unknown.

You must realize that here is where fear must be totally replaced by love. If you fear to go where the portal of access will take you, you will not go. Thus your desire needs to be greater than your fear. Love needs to reign. Love of self and love of your brothers and sisters, love of the natural world, of the world of form that *is,*

146

love of the idea of the new world that can be, all of these must come together and be victors over the reign of fear.

What choice have you made my sister and my brother, if you have not made a choice of love? If you have not made the choice to reject fear? If you have not made the choice for the new? If you are still willing to say that you can go only so far in your acceptance of the truth of who you really are, then our purpose in being together here on this mountain top will go unfulfilled.

What tempts you here? To turn and look toward the towns and cities below? Or to turn and look up to the portal of access to unity?

Do you turn and look back at form and matter? Or do you turn and look up where no form exists? Do you believe you can choose the formless and still return to the towns and cities, the green grass and the blue sea below? Why are we here but to show you these two choices? From where else could you so clearly see the choice between form and the formless?

But what, you might ask, of the elevated Self of form? Why is this suddenly a choice between one or the other? It is the first choice of the new temptations, the first real choice of Christ-consciousness, of the time beyond learning.

Smile with me now, as you think of yourself in this elevated place. You are still the self of form despite the truth that you are literally with me in a place of high elevation.

Is this what you choose to remain?

Do you choose to remain a self of form elevated by circumstance? A self of form on a high mountain? Or do you wish to carry this elevation back with you when you return? Do you wish to return the self of form who once visited an altered state, this state of high elevation? Do you wish to go back and tell tales of your experiences here and be made special because of this experience you can recount? Or do you wish to go back transformed into the elevated Self of form?

Do you want to know this place of access and carry it within you, or do you only wish the opportunity to revisit it when the need arises? Are you here to fast and pray only to have to return when you have once again become a glutton of want, when you once again feel the lack that you would pray for? Surely this you can do, for I deny no one the journey to the mountain top, not once or many times. But this is not what I call you to.

You have been brought here for revelation. You have been brought here to be tempted by the unknown of your inheritance, an unknown that, while it remains unknown, is still what you have longed for all your life. This unknown has been described to you in terms both specific and obscure. It has been described as all you have desired and more. It has been described as the end to the life of misery you have known and the beginning of new life. And I tell you truly, here is where this new life either begins or is once again delayed. Here is where you say, I want it all, desire it all, accept it all — for you cannot have of this in parts. Once full access has been revealed, what is yours is everything. But you will be different.

This is real choice. What is a choice that leads not to difference of any kind? These are the only choices you have made in a lifetime of endless choices. There is only one requirement for this choice: Wholehearted desire. *A Course of Love* taught you wholehearted desire so that you could be taken to this place and tempted to leave behind the temptations of the human experience.

I do not have to spell out this choice for you, for you know exactly what it means. It means you will be as I am. It means you will live from love rather than from fear. It means that you will demonstrate what living from love is. It means that you will resurrect to eternal life here and now. It means no turning back, no return to fear or anger, no return to separation, no return to judgment. It means no longer trying to leave these things behind for they will be gone. It will mean no longer striving. It will mean no specialness. It will mean the individual is gone, and the Self of union all that continues to exist. It will mean peace, certainty, safety, and joy with no price.

The old challenges, the old reasons for existing will be gone. All that will be left to do will be the creation of a new world in the only way that it can come about — through unity.

Your desire and your access are one and the same. If you desire this transformation wholeheartedly, if you make this choice with wholehearted desire, it will be done, and we will continue our dialogue so that you know more of the difference you have chosen. Once this difference is wholly known to you, we will begin true discussion of creation of the new, for you will be done with becoming.

These are the only temptations of the new that I can make you aware of until you have made your choice and have full realization of your access to unity. You will be able, of course, to continue on without making this wholehearted choice, but you will read only to learn and learning will not transform you. If you do not truly and wholeheartedly desire this choice, if you do not truly and wholeheartedly meet the condition of being fearless, you will know this, and you will pass through the time of coming to acceptance again and again until you are ready. You cannot fail but can only delay. For some the time of delay has passed. For those who linger in the time of acceptance, there is reason for this as well.

This may seem odd timing as you have just been asked to accept your anger. Just think. Anger was discussed rather casually alongside accepting me, your Self, and abundance. But none of these things are meant to be dwelt upon. The acceptance of abundance no more so than the acceptance of anger. You are called to accept and not look back, not to dwell in any of the states through which you arrive at acceptance, nor to focus on acceptance of one thing over another. You are not to label good or bad. Just to accept. Accept all. You do not have to hesitate here because you *think* you are still angry, or *think* you are still depressed. When you hesitate you have not accepted but dwell with the cause of your hesitation. When you accept you move on.

To be called to make a new choice before full acceptance of what *is* would be confusing. You who are thinking that you have not moved through the stages to full acceptance answer now as to what is stopping you. Do you choose to dwell or to accept? All, *all* you cannot bring forward with you is fear, for fear is the cause of the state of learning. You may have thought separation was the cause, but separation into form, had it occurred within the realization of continuing relationship, would not have been cause for fear in and of itself. Had you still known relationship, fear could not have separated you from truth and you would not have dwelt in illusion. The relationship of union is what you are here coming to know once again, which is why the time of fear, and along with it the time of learning, can cease to be.

I have not so directly linked fear and the time of learning before, but now you need to see their connection, for if you do not, you will not realize that fear is all that needs to be left behind. You will still *think* you have more to learn because you are angry, depressed, in a state of denial contrary to the denial asked of you, or because you still feel like bargaining with God. These things are only reactions to faulty perceptions, only the steps *toward* acceptance until they are accepted.

As we move into full access and awareness of unity, love is all that is required. Acceptance has been the means chosen, by us, to move you through the layers of illusion that have disguised your fear, to move you beyond false learning to the truth that only needs to be accepted. If you can move forward without fear, you can move forward. If you can move forward without fear, you will move forward only with love. If you move forward only with love, you will have realized there is nothing unacceptable about who you are except fear.

You but think that you can wholeheartedly desire to move forward with love and without fear and that there is still anything that can hold you back. This is what the time of acceptance was meant to show you! Nothing can hold you back except fear! You do not have to be perfect — perfect is but a label, and all that labels of any type cause is delay. You only have to be accepting. Accepting of all that you are. Fear is not a part of what you are, which is why it cannot remain with you as the way opens for you to fully know the Self of unity. You are about to achieve your first glimpse of wholeness, of oneness with God. To know the truth of your inheritance.

Recall the story of the prodigal son. All that the prodigal son was asked to do was to accept his own homecoming. Do you think he would have considered himself perfect as he approached his father's presence? Surely he would not have. You are asked but to accept your own homecoming and to leave behind the time of wandering, seeking, learning. You are asked to leave behind fear for the embrace of the love and the safety of your true home.

This choice has come earlier you might have expected it to come. It does not come at the end but at the beginning of our time together for a reason. This is simply because this choice *is* the beginning. This is the choice that allows us to continue our dialogue as one; to talk heart-to-heart; to have the kind of discourse that can only be had without fear; to truly experience relationship. It is from this beginning that you will come to be as I am.

We are here for the final stage of your becoming, but not because you have reached some ideal of enlightenment or what you might think of as perfection. If this were asked of you, how many of you would have felt free to join me? Yet in your acceptance is

151

your perfection realized without judgment. In your becoming is your enlightenment realized without judgment. These things become not achievements, but the acknowledgments of the accomplishment that has always existed within you and all of your brothers and sisters.

Here is the beginning point from which we continue to burn away the remnants of attachment to the old, the attachments that cause some of you to continue to feel sadness, anger, depression, or nostalgia for the way things were. These things will not leave you before you leave them. But you will leave them.

Join me in this choice, and we will leave behind the old and continue our movement toward creation of the new.

There are many discussions still to be had. We are only at the beginning of our time together.

Our forward movement must be achieved. But one is needed to begin this movement. Followers will naturally succeed the first although this will occur with no fanfare and no "one" to follow. The first will create a series. Thus will the secret of succession be returned to you and put behind us forever the temptations of the human experience.

The Forty Days and Forty Nights

Day 5: Access to Unity

A point of access will no longer be needed once full entry is attained, just as a key is no longer needed once a door has been unlocked and passed through. Even though it will not be permanently needed, this point of access will remain crucial as long as you *maintain,* rather than *sustain* the state of unity. This point of access will thus now be discussed, both as an initial entry point and as a continued entry point so that it is available to you until it is no longer needed.

For each of you this access point will in truth be the same, but perhaps quite different in the action which you use in order to enter it. For those of you who have felt the point of entry to be the mind in experiences already registered, there is no need to combat this feeling. For those of you who have felt the state of unity through experiences of the heart, there is again, no need to struggle against this.

For many of you, "thoughts you did not think" are among your first experiences of unity. Thus, just as when you might look up when trying to remember something, or tap a finger at your temple, there is, in a certain sense, a "place" to which you turn for these experiences. This does not mean that these experiences come from your mind or from a place just beyond your physical concept of the mind. *You* are not your body and the idea of what originates "within" coming from a point beyond the body is not now too unbelievable to contemplate.

As we said yesterday, our form of meditation, a meditation that is not a tool but a function of your natural Self, is a focus on access.

Thus we begin with what feels natural to you. We give access a focal point in the realm of form.

This focal point must be of your own choosing. Your point of access may be your head, or a place just above or to the right or left of your head. It may be your heart, or some mid-point just beyond the body. It may, for some, feel like a connection that arises from the earth and as if it is just below the form of the physical body. Some could feel it in their hands, and others as if it comes directly from their mouths as speech is enabled that bypasses the realm of thought completely. Do not fight these feelings or any others that I may not have named. Just consider them givens and choose what feels most natural to you as a focal point for your focus on access.

What we have focused on for some time now is love. Love never changes. It is the same for each of us. Yet not one of us expresses love in the exact same way as another. This is important to remember now as you begin to work with your access to unity.

Unity and Love — as we have within this work shown them to be — are the same.

Access too is the same. It exists. It is there for you. It is given. It cannot be denied unless you deny it. It is only because you have not known this that we speak of it in this way here.

Just as it is helpful in some instances to associate love with your heart even though we have identified heart as the center of the Self rather than the pump that functions as part of your body, it will be helpful to have identified this chosen access point for unity even while remembering it is not of the body alone.

While the purpose of this work was to have you identify love and thus your Self, correctly, there is still fine-tuning to your understanding to be done, and this will be done as you come to

154

know what unity is, and so more fully come to know your Self and love.

There would seem to be one major difference between unity and love and that difference would seem to be love's ability to be given away.

Access to unity will seem, at first, a quite individual accomplishment, something one may have and another may not. While this remains the case, you may desire to give others what you have and feel unable to do so. Yet, like love, unity is known through its effects. All the benefits of union can be given away to any willing to receive.

While you do not consider yourself as having or needing an access point to love, and while you may treat love still as an individual attribute intimately associated with the self you are, you know love is not an attribute and that all love comes from the same Source. You know you have been able to give love only when you have felt you have love to give. You thus have long known the truth of giving and receiving as one within your own heart. You might think of access in the same way — as enabling you to realize that you have the benefits of union to give.

Like love, unity has one source and many expressions. It will be in your unique expression of union that your Self will come to wholeness and you will be fully who you are and able to express love fully.

Realize that although you are now a part of a community with the same goal, the realization, or "making real" of your accomplishment and its expression, will not look the same way twice. What you each desire from union most will be what finds the greatest expression through you.

A "healer" for instance, might, feel her access point as being the hands and express what is gained through unity by a laying on of hands. Similarly, you might say healing is one of the ways the healer expresses love. In truth healing and love are the same.

Who you are now, what your desires are, and where your talents have been recognized, are as given as the goal you desire to realize. I remind you that the sameness of union is not about becoming clones or one specific type of idealized holy person. Union is being fully who you are and expressing fully who you are. This is the miracle, the goal, the accomplishment that is achieved through the reign of love, the maintenance and finally the sustainability of union.

Realize that while you want to know the specifics of how this thing called "access to unity" will work, you are also impatient with specifics. You want immediate results, not more practice. You want relief and an end to effort, not another lesson to learn that you will be told is not a lesson; not another cause for seeming effort in order to arrive at the effortless. But realize also that this effort that you rail against is still of your own choosing. The realization of a way to make things as they are is never effortful in and of itself.

As you may seem to pause here in your movement in order to understand the way in which that movement is achieved, you will almost surely once again have doubts. Doubts are never more pronounced than when specifics are being dealt with. Yet you continue to desire specifics. This is because you are still entrenched in the pattern of learning, as your earnest effort to leave effort behind implies. Remember that union cannot be learned, for if it could be, the time of learning would be perpetuated rather than ended.

Remember that you are tired of learning. You are tired here, after your climb. You simply want to rest and have whatever transformation is to come to you to come. If you could indeed give in to this desire fully, it would speed the transformation along quite nicely. So please, listen to your weariness and to your heart's desire to rest. Listen to the call to peace and let yourself recline in the embrace of love, feeling the warm earth beneath you and the heat of the sun above you. Let languor enfold you and apply no effort to what you read here. Just accept what is given. What is being given are the helpful hints you have desired from an older brother who has experienced what you, as yet, have not.

In this frame of mind, we can return more specifically to our focus on access. Wherever your chosen point of access lies, imagine now the needle that was discussed as passing through the onion in the Course Chapter on Intersection, and imagine the point of intersection connecting with your chosen access point. Imagine this now, not as a needle, but as the wisdom you seek. Imagine this wisdom not being stopped by the layers of thinking and feeling that we used the onion to illustrate, but as entering and passing through. What comes of unity enters you and passes through you to the world. This is the relationship you have with unity while in form — a relationship of intersection and pass through.

No longer will what enters you be stopped by layers of defenses. No longer will it meet the road-block of your thinking, your effort, your attempts to figure out how to do it and what it all means. There is no cause for such effort. Effort is only a layer of defense, a stop gap between what you would receive and what you would give in which the ego once made its bid to claim ownership.

Effort, as translated by the ego, was about turning everything that was given into what you could only work hard to attain, and thereby claim as your individual accomplishment. Obviously, union is not about this. While the ego is gone, the pattern of effort remains. While it remains, you will not realize full access to what you are given. We are speaking here of letting your form serve union and union serve your form. This service is effortless for it is the way of creation. This is why the "effort" of learning must cease.

Let's return to the image of the healer that was mentioned earlier. While many will heal, all attempts to teach or learn "how to" heal must be thwarted, for if not, the pattern of learning will remain. This is why there have always seemed to be "secrets" held among the great healers and spiritual guides. They have understood that what they have gained access to cannot be taught. This has not meant that they were not eager to share, only that the means of sharing was not one of teaching or learning.

Each expression of union must remain as what it is — untaught and unlearned. Each gain from unity will only, in this way, be seen as the new givens come to replace learning.

Remember this as you focus on your access to unity. Focus does not mean thinking. Focus does not mean learning. Remember the example of how your breathing becomes unnatural when you think about it, and contrast this with the increase in awareness of breath that comes from the focus of meditation. A focus point is a point of convergence. A focal point is a point of intersection that gives rise to a clear image.

The intersection spoken of here is that of pass through. Although we have spoken of this focal point as an entryway, this does not imply that something that is not of you is entering you, and it does not imply entry without exit. When you think of breathing, you may think of inhaling as taking in air, and of air as something that is not "of" you. But the air you breathe is "of" you.

You may think of the air you exhale as being more "of" you, but there is no more or less to the relationship of entry and exit. You are in continual relationship with the air you breathe and in continual relationship with unity. It is a constant exchange. When you are fully aware of this is when full access is attained. So we will continue our work now in releasing you from those things that would still block your full awareness.

The Forty Days and Forty Nights

Day 6: the Time In Between

We now will discuss *being* the true self while *becoming* the true self — the time in between your awareness and access to Christ-consciousness, or unity, and your sustainability of Christ-consciousness, or unity. As was said earlier: To realize the state of becoming is to realize that a state exists between the time of learning and the time of being the elevated Self of form. This is what our time on this holy mountain is largely comprised of. We are in an in between state of time. We stand at the intersection of the finite and the infinite in order to complete the creative act of becoming.

While you know this is the focus of our time together, few, if any of you, feel as if you have truly taken leave of the every-day world of your "normal" existence and feel fully present on the holy mountain. This is not a second-best situation. Although it is being handled in this way partially because to ask you to walk away from your "normal" life for forty days and forty nights would cause too much anxiety and exclude too many, this is not the only, or even the major reason for this chosen method.

Before we can continue to expand on your awareness of the difference you have chosen, we must address this time so that any confusion it seems to be causing will not delay your progress.

Since we have often discussed the similarity between the creation of art and the work we are doing here, we will return to this example. We have spoken of becoming as the time of movement, being, and expression coming together. We have further spoken of your point of access to unity as one of convergence, intersection, and pass through. Can you see the similarities between these actions despite the difference in language used?

Movement	Being	Expression
Convergence	Intersection	Pass through

How might these things be linked to the example of creating art? I chose this particular example to address this in between time. Let us consider the creation of a piece of music. The creation of a piece of music, like the creation of a painting or a poem, takes place in stages.

At one time the creation of a piece of music is only an idea in the mind and heart of the creator. The creation of a song or a symphony may begin as simply as with a few notes "running through the mind" or a particular turn of phrase that inspires the creator to see these words as lyrics. At some point after this gestation within the mind and heart, the artist puts pen to paper, or picks up a guitar, or sings into a tape recorder. Much starting and stopping may be done, or the piece may find its expression easily, in a way that the artist might describe as flowing.

Depending on the disposition of the artist, the piece of music might be shared with others at each step of the process, or only late in its development. But at some point, the sharing will take place, and the reactions of those with whom the music is shared will impact the artist and the piece. Positive reactions might validate the artist's instinct and encourage even more boldness. Negative reactions might cause the artist to doubt her instincts, to make changes, or to be more determined than ever to see the piece through to the point where it will be appreciated. Finishing touches will be put on the piece. Some collaboration might take place to get it just right. By the time the artist has completed the piece of music she began, it may have little resemblance to the piece originally intended, or it might be quite true to the original idea.

Every creative piece of art that comes to completion includes a choice. At some point along the way a commitment is made between the artist and the piece of art; a commitment to see it through. This commitment may come because the artist knows it is "good enough" to deserve the time and attention, or the commitment may come as a recognition that a relationship of love has developed, and "good enough" or not, completion is necessary. It may even be a commitment simply to practice, with the artist feeling no certainty about the value of the piece, but determining to see the project through, knowing that it will make the next piece or the next a better piece of music.

In all stages of its creation, the piece of music exists in relationship to its creator. Be it only an idea, a partially completed rhythm, lyrics without notes, or a completed work that will qualify more as practice than as art, the piece exists. In each stage of creation it is what it is.

Yet only when it is a complete, and full, and true expression of the artist's idea will it achieve oneness of expression.

You are a work of art headed for this oneness of full and true expression. No stage you pass through to reach this oneness is without value. Each stage contains the perfection of that stage. Each stage contains the whole and the whole contains each stage.

You have been told you are in the final stage of becoming. You have committed to completion of the becoming that will create oneness between creator and created. You have developed the creative relationship that is union. You are *in* and *within* the movement of the creative process where there is no distinction between creator and created. You are being who you are right now and eliciting the expression that will take you to the final stage of being who you will be in oneness.

You are not separate now from who you will be when you reach completion! You are *in* and *within* the relationship of creation *in which* created and creator become one.

Now, in returning to one of the main themes of this chapter — the simple truth that you are having to go about this creative process while remaining embroiled in daily life — I want to acknowledge the difficulty some of you will seem to be experiencing even while pointing out to you that life is life.

Let's begin with the seeming difficulty. It may take on many forms, but its main source is almost surely a desire to focus on the relationship developing between us, and a corresponding desire not to have to focus on the details of daily life. You may be thinking that the ease so often spoken of in our conversations would be there *if only* you could be truly "taken away" from it all and experience nothing but our relationship, focus on nothing but your point of access, have a chance to really begin to invite abundance without having to look at the bills that arrive by daily mail or worry about the many other aspects of your simple survival.

Yet realize that if you were told to leave these worries behind and to get away from it all, you would likely rebel and find many reasons not to make it so. And so, abundance will have to come first, lack of cause for worry will have to come first, an ability to focus on other than daily life will have to come first. These are what these continuing dialogues will facilitate.

They will facilitate this by facilitating the acceptance of life as it is. This is why this dialogue is occurring on the holy mountain *without* taking you away from life as you know it. We are, after all, speaking of the elevation of the self of form. This elevation must occur *in* life, in *your* life *as it is,* rather than in some idealized situation *away* from what you consider normal life.

163

This does not mean that this elevation can be postponed, put-off, or can wait for some convenient time. Quite the contrary. We are having our dialogue on the holy mountain while you remain within your life for the very purpose of not allowing this to happen.

It also does not mean that many of you will not have changed or will be changing the very fabric of your daily life. Changes you feel called to make are not discouraged here. But removal from life is not possible or desirable.

Learning takes the student away from "normal" life and creates a place for teaching and only calls this place elevated. Awareness, acceptance, and discovery cannot occur in a place set apart from "normal" life. Believe me when I tell you that the elevation you are currently experiencing is the only elevation you would want. *As within, so without* is the operative phrase here. It is not the other way around. You cannot find a place outside of yourself that will allow for the elevation of which we speak. There are no hallowed halls of learning that will accomplish this. There is no mountain top in any location on Earth that can accomplish this. It is only the relationship we are developing in this elevated place *within* that will bring to your full realization and manifestation *without* the accomplishment that already exists.

I know it doesn't always seem so. Give your attention for a moment to the temptations associated with the mountain top of my own experience. They were temptations of the world, of the normal, daily life of my time. They were attempts to distract me from my purpose, to change my focus, to engage me in debate, to lure me from the place of elevation I knew I had attained. The temptations of the human experience are the same now as they were then. They are the same on the mountain top as they are on level ground. A "place" that seems externally removed from them cannot remove them. Only a created place within can do so.

This place within is what we are creating here. It is a truly elevated place. It is as real as a mountain top, in fact much more real. Were your scientists to know what to look for, they would find it. It is being created to exist both within the body and beyond the body. It is, in truth, the portal of access we have spoken of, a connection with the state of union as real as if a tether were stretched from here to there.

Quit trying to remove yourself from life! If this were required it would be done! Think not that I cannot arrange the ideal environment for our dialogue. This is it!

Consider a new job or some other endeavor in which you apprenticed. In such a situation a person is taught and shown the skills and activities needed for the accomplishment of the tasks he or she is to perform. But often it is only when the teacher steps aside and the apprentice is able to gain experience that the apprentice is in a position to be able to begin to perform with any certainty. Even learning is accelerated by hands-on activities, by *doing* what one has previously only learned.

You have done your learning and your teacher has stepped aside as a teacher and become a companion. Would you desire to prolong your time as an apprentice by being removed from the performance of your tasks? Perhaps you would. But as has been stated from the beginning, there is an urgency to your task.

Seeing our relationship as that of colleagues as well as companions, as fellow workers or work-mates with a task to accomplish as well as conversationalists, is not an erroneous way to think of our relationship. We are both friends and co-workers; colleagues as well as companions.

Our dialogue is not without purpose. You know this or you would not be here. You know this or you would not feel the devotion to me and to what we do here that you do. And what's more, you feel the eagerness of your brothers and sisters. If you

165

felt our goal was unlikely to be accomplished, or that it would elevate only a few and leave all others behind, you would not feel this devotion. You *know* our task is holy and incomparable. You know there is nothing more important for you to be involved in. All other areas where you might previously have placed your devotion pale in comparison to our task.

As your belief grows in our ability to accomplish together our given work, you are almost surely feeling this devotion extend to others, particularly those who, along with us, work toward its accomplishment. In doing so you are not creating new special relationships but the true devotion that will replace special relationships forever.

But this very knowing of the sanctity and incomparability of our task is what seems to create the difficulty so many of you are currently experiencing in one way or another. Your desire is where it belongs — here — in the passionate acceptance of our work together. And so the lack of desire you are experiencing for other areas of the life that you still seem so deeply involved in is disturbing to you. Yet why should this be disturbing? Why should you continue to desire the life you have had?

Let's address this seeming paradox. You have been told to do only what you can feel peaceful doing, to do only what allows you to be yourself, and yet here are you told not to try to remove yourself from life.

Do you need to feel desire for what you do in order to do it peacefully? Do you need to be other than yourself in order to navigate your daily life? What you are being shown here is that you do not. What you are going to realize from this time of seeming difficulty is an end to difficulty, the growth of your ability to do whatever you do peacefully, and the ability to be who you are in whatever situation you find yourself in. There is no time to wait while you learn, or think you learn, the qualities that will allow this. This is the way of movement, being, and expression coming together; the way of convergence, intersection, and pass through. This is it! Right here in your life as it is right now.

There is no call to be discouraged. This is not delay, but what you might think of as trial by fire. Be encouraged rather than discouraged that you are able to embrace this dialogue and remain in your life. Realize that this is just what we work toward! This difficulty will pass through you as you allow for and accept where you are right now and who you are right now.

Does this work of acceptance seem never ending? It is until it is replaced by reverence, just as learning was unending until it was replaced by acceptance. The conditions of this time of acceptance are not the conditions of the time of learning, and so you will soon see that the difficulty of the time of learning truly is behind you.

Let us speak now of the conditions of the time of acceptance, for these will cheer you.

The Forty Days and Forty Nights

Day 7: Conditions of the Time of Acceptance

What does the idea of only now coming to acceptance imply but that you were previously un-accepting? And what does being un-accepting imply but the very denial of yourself that you have come to see as your former state?

Denial of yourself was the precondition that set the stage for the time of learning. The time of learning would not have been needed had you not denied your Self. When you saw yourself as separate and alone, you could not help but suffer fear, loneliness, and all the ills that came from the base emotion of fear. Fear is degenerating. Nothing about fear is life giving. You thus were given life only to have it become degenerated by fear.

Acceptance of your Self is the precondition for the *time* of acceptance. You are no longer denying your Self. You are no longer denying unity. You have replaced fear with love. Love is life-giving and life-*supporting*. There is nothing now degenerating about life.

Life is now supported. Support is a condition of the time of acceptance.

You must realize here that the pattern of learning is now all that is left that can be degenerating to you. While you always were supported, the *idea* of learning that you accepted during the *time* of learning was not one of support but one of effort. You must accept, now, that the pattern of learning is an extension of fear and be willing and vigilant in replacing it with a pattern of acceptance. I say this because so many of you still do not feel supported in your daily life. You may feel supported in your spiritual life, in your progress toward full awareness and the elevation of the self of form, but as in the discussion of abundance, you may still feel unsupported in form. Realize now, that this makes no sense when our goal is the elevation of form. If for no other reason, begin to accept this support of form because it makes sense. It is logical. And realize further that love is not opposed to logic but returns true reason to the mind and heart.

Love replaces fear and is life-generating rather than life-degenerating. Your bodies will thus regenerate rather than degenerate. Love is not a condition, as it is not an attribute, but the *effect* of living from love rather than from fear will cause a major transformation within form in this time of acceptance. Regeneration is a condition of the time of acceptance.

Another condition of the time of acceptance that will be of great service to you now is that of the different relationship that you will have with time. This is a time of convergence, intersection, and pass through of the finite and the infinite, of time and no time. Time has not yet ceased to be, but as you are in a state of transformation, so too is it. Again I remind you, *as within, so without.* As you let go of time's hold on you, it will let go of you. Time will seem to expand but will actually be contracting into nothingness. Time is replaced by presence, by your ability to exist in the here and now in acceptance and without fear.

Again let me remind you that you are in an in between time. These conditions I have spoken of, and those I have yet to speak of, are also in an in between state. They exist along with the new you. They exist in acceptance and union. They do not exist in learning and separation. They exist in love. They do not exist in fear. Like with Christ-consciousness, you are moving from a place of maintenance of these conditions to one of sustainability of these conditions. They do not come about from changes in your external circumstances but from changes in your internal perspective.

The conditions that affect life are conditions that affect the body. Yet it was only your mind's acceptance of the condition of fear that led the body to exhibit the conditions of fear in the time of learning. It is the mind's acceptance of love that will lead the body to exhibit the effects of love in the time of acceptance.

A further condition of the time of acceptance is that of expansion. The singular self you once believed yourself to be was not capable of true expansion and true sharing. The singular self withdrew into its own little world and created its own universe. The elevated Self of form will expand into the world and create a new universe. This condition of expansion is operative now and beginning to find manifestation through the sharing we are doing here.

Conditions of the time of acceptance are conditions of creation and include those we have already spoken of as movement, being, and expression; and convergence, intersection and pass through.

There are many lesser conditions that are nonetheless extremely transformative, such as the replacement of special relationship with the devotion of Holy Relationship that we have already spoken of. Another replacement is that of control with grace. This occurs as you give up the control you have but thought you exerted over your life and its circumstances, and live in a state of grace, meeting grace with grace by accepting what is given for your regeneration.

It is easy to see from here how the dominoes fall and each condition of learning is replaced, always by a far gentler and more compassionate alternative. There is no need for me to list every new condition here. As you become increasingly aware of your relationship with union, each of these new conditions and your relationship with each of these new conditions will become clear to you.

Obviously your relationship or access to union is of supreme importance, since all else will come of this. Access is not an *if this, then that* situation even if it may seem so. Is the process of breathing an *if this, then that* situation, just because breathing sustains life? Your access to union sustains real life, the life of the Self, and will come to sustain the elevated Self of form in a way as natural to you as breathing.

Access to unity is a phrase that will only be used in this in between time. You have always existed in unity and once this is fully realized you will no more need access to unity than you need access to breathing. Unity will be your natural state.

When your natural state is fully returned to you and sustained within Christ-consciousness, the conditions of the time of acceptance, like the conditions of the time of learning, will pass. There are no conditions in the state of union as there are no attributes to love. The natural created Self is all that is. Reverence prevails.

There will be a new stage following the time of acceptance in which the elevated Self of form will be created and come into full manifestation.

What we are concerned about now, however, is the present. It is here, in this present and given time on the mountain, that you must realize that the conditions of the time of acceptance, like the conditions of the time of learning, arise from within. Life has always existed within the conditions of the time of acceptance. The conditions of the time of learning were but imposed conditions that also arose from within.

The conditions of the time of acceptance that we have spoken of are not new conditions. They are conditions natural to your Self, to a mind and heart joined in union. It was the disjoining of mind and heart, of the real Self from the ego-self, that created the need for learning and the imposition, from *within,* of the conditions of the time of learning.

The condition of the time of acceptance that will most clearly reveal to you your status in regard to maintaining or sustaining your access to union will be that of the replacement of doubt with certainty. Certainty is a condition of the present. Realize you may say you are certain of the future or the past but that you cannot make it so. Thus your ability to maintain and then sustain your access to union and thus your certainty, goes hand-in-hand with your ability to live in the present. This ability is also contingent upon your recognition of what certainty really is.

There is an acceptance of the present that some of you are finding difficult and a false sense of certainty that some of you may be experiencing. These will be the subject of our next dialogue.

The Forty Days and Forty Nights

Day 8: Accept the Present

Some of you have felt, once again, a bit of disappointment or resignation as a result of our dialogue concerning not removing yourself from life. Your whole purpose in pursuing the course of this dialogue may have been, at least subconsciously, the idea of removing yourself from normal life. Even the conditions of the time of acceptance may not have cheered you fully. Now, with the ideas of the conditions of the time of acceptance fresh in your minds and hearts, let's return to that earlier discussion.

If you can't remove yourself from life, what choice have you but to join with it? Love it. Love yourself. Love yourself enough to accept yourself. Love will transform normal, ordinary, life into extraordinary life. Loving exactly who you are and where you are in every moment is what will cause the transformation that will end your *desire* to remove yourself from life. All those frustrations you currently feel have a purpose: To move you through them and beyond them — to acceptance.

But here is the point that needs clearing up. This is *not* about acceptance of what you do not like. Do you really think you are being called to accept "normal life?" Called to accept those conditions that have made you feel unhappy? No! You are being called to an acceptance of new conditions!

Realize that your desire for your life to be different, your desire for your unhappiness to be gone, is very unlikely, in truth, to stem from the details of your life. Even so, you are not called to accept what you do not like, but to accept that you don't like whatever it is you don't like. Then, and only then — when you have accepted how you *feel* — can you respond truly. Only when you have accepted how you feel do you quit labeling good or bad; only then can you deal with anything from a place of peace.

Does accepting that you don't like something cause a judgment to occur? Do you judge peas if you do not like them? And yet, do you not accept that you are at the mercy of situations of all kinds? A job you do not like? You may not like it, and you may say often that you do not like it, but you may just as often say that you accept it. You may, in fact, need a job that you do not like, but in acceptance of the simple truth that you do not like your job, you have accepted your Self and where you are now, rather than the external circumstance. We are not, when talking of acceptance, talking of externals, but of internals. We are not talking of the old adage or prayer that calls you to "accept what you cannot change" but of acceptance — absolute, unconditional acceptance — of your Self.

Yet to state that you do not like your job is to pre-judge your job, to assume that the conditions you did not like yesterday will be the same today.

Now you may have been thinking — again, at least subconsciously — that your "real" Self has no feelings of dislike, and in this confusion been trying and even struggling to accept what you do not like in order to be more true to an ideal self. This ideal self is not the self you are right now. You cannot accept only an ideal self. This is nonsense. Can you not see this?

All power to affect change comes from acceptance — not acceptance of the way *things* are, but acceptance of who *you* are *in the present*. Not through acceptance of the way you want to be but of the way you are now. There will be many things within your life that will take some time to change, but many others that can change instantly through this radical acceptance. You will find, once you have begun to practice acceptance of the present, that there will be far fewer things you do not like and that you will be shown, in the relationship you have in the present, the response to those you still do.

Gossip would be an easy example. Gossip goes on in many environments. You are highly unlikely to like gossip, but you may have felt that to say you do not like it is to judge it, or that to accept what *is,* is to accept that people gossip. These false ideas about acceptance may then have blocked your own true feelings and true response. A simple acceptance that *you* do not like the gossip taking place in a present moment situation, will enable you not to participate, judge, or appear to accept that which you do not truly find acceptable.

Not all situations will seem as easy as this example. Acceptance does not require any specific action but it will lead to action that is consistent with who you are when you are fully comfortable in your acceptance of who you are. Understand that this eventual outcome will never occur without the initial acceptance.

This acceptance is the only thing that will truly prevent judgment, for it does not require you to be your brother's keeper but only your own. It requires you to know yourself without judging yourself.

Will knowing your dislikes cause you to be intolerant? This is an important question. You have been intolerant of yourself and it was easy to extend this intolerance to others. Once acceptance of the Self begins to be practiced, you will realize that the self of intolerance was the self of fear. Acceptance of yourself, in love, leads to acceptance of others. Knowing this aspect of how you feel – what we are here calling your dislikes – is but a first step in this beginning stage of acceptance and only of importance *because* of your intolerance of your own feelings.

Remember that you have been told that your real Self will be intolerant only of illusion and that this intolerance will take the form of seeing only the truth rather than attempting to combat illusion. Thus when you see others gossiping, you are called to see only the truth of who they are — to see beyond the illusion, what would seem to be the "fact" of their gossip — to the fear that feeds it, and beyond the fear to the love that will dispel it. You are not called to walk away in disgust, showing your righteous contempt for the actions of others, but to accept who you are within the relationship of that present moment.

Even this type of seeing will have remnants of righteousness attached to it if you do not accept the feelings generated by it. You may know that you dislike gossip only because you have been both a participant and a victim of it. It may still call up feelings of shame or irritation. It may even still intrigue you if you are interested enough in the subject of the gossip. To walk away from gossip, accepting that you do not like it without accepting the feelings associated with it, will make of it a mental construct, a rule you have set up for your new self to follow. If this becomes the case, you will find yourself adhering to a standard rather than acting from who you are. You will, in fact, have returned to judgment because you will have made a predetermination, just as in saying you do not like your job, you predetermine a continuing dislike. Soon, you might see a group of people who often gossip and *assume* that they are gossiping rather than observing the situation for what it is and responding in the present.

If you replace the act of gossiping with a mental construct or rule that says you do not tolerate it, then you will become intolerant. And because you will then act from a predetermined standard rather than feeling the feelings associated with gossip in the present moment, you will soon find that a bit of gossip will crop up in your own speech, couched as something else, something even worse than gossip. You will sigh, and reference something someone said or did that but shows that they are not yet as "advanced" as you, only revealing, through your reference, that it is you who are not as "advanced" as you think you are.

This is the importance now of accepting yourself in the *present* and of understanding certainty. Certainty cannot be predetermined, just as you cannot predetermine either your likes or dislikes. Being aware of how you feel *in the present moment* is the only way to certainty. Thus to say that you are certain that you do not like gossip, or certain that you do not like your job, or even certain that you do not like peas, is an inaccurate use of the term of *certainty*. It may have been consistent with the term or word *certainty* as it was used in the past, but you will not want to confuse the *term* and the *condition*. You may think that taking away the type of certainty associated with the term of certainty will cause you to be even less certain than you were before. You will be less certain in your judgments and opinions, but this is highly appropriate and much needed practice for true certainty.

We have talked little of feelings here, and there has been a reason for this discussion coming so late in our time together. To accept the feelings of the self of illusion would have been to accept the feelings generated by the fear of the ego thought system or the bitterness of your heart. It would have been to accept the feelings of a personal self who had not yet unlearned the lessons of the past or taken these steps toward elevation. Now it is crucial that you come to acceptance of yourself — in the present, as you are — for only by doing so will you come to *full* acceptance of who you are and be able to allow the Self of unity to merge with the self of form, thus elevating the self of form. You will also, only in this way, come to true expression of the elevated Self of form. Access and expression are both conditions of the present.

Another error can occur if you deny your feelings in favor of the perceived higher path to enlightenment. In denying your own feelings you will tend also to deny the feelings of others. You will

177

think that you know the real from the unreal, truth from illusion, and so will disregard the feelings of others as if they do not matter. This will only happen if you allow yourself to deny and thus become distanced from your own feelings.

Does this seem confusing? To be called to see only the truth, to see beyond illusion, and then to be told to accept the feelings of others? It should not. While true compassion sees only the truth, this does not mean it holds the feelings of anyone — not those living in truth, or those living in illusion — in disregard. This disregard is a temptation of those who live in peace, a temptation unlike the more pleasant temptations that were spoken of earlier. This temptation stems from one thing only — from not living in the present. Distancing, or non-acceptance of your own feelings, *is* not living in the present and will create an attitude that will not be compassionate. This is why we talk specifically here of dislikes. While you are prone to acceptance of that which you "like," to those feelings you think of as "good" feelings, you are still prone to non-acceptance of that which you do not like in yourself and others and even to, at times, the false sense of certainty about your non-acceptance that we have spoken of.

When you develop a false sense of certainty, you see not the true Self and the holiness of the true Self being expressed in the feelings of a present moment situation, but see a future where the true Self will be more evolved, evolved enough not to feel the anger or hurt, the bitterness or guilt that you do not like. You hold others to the "standards" you hold for yourself, thus the only "standard" that is consistent with the time of acceptance is that *of* acceptance.

Now you must realize that you no longer have cause to fear your feelings. They will no longer be the source of the misdirection of the past *if* you accept your feelings in present time and begin to be aware of your natural ability to respond truly *because* you have accepted your feelings in present time. This is a recognition that by being in the present you know your feelings are of the truth.

178

This is certainty. This is all that will prevent you from "reacting" to feelings out of your previous pattern.

If anger arises in you now, it does not mean that you will react in whatever way anger once called you to react and it does not mean that something is wrong with you or that you are not spiritual enough! It simply means that you are involved in a situation or relationship that has called forth that feeling. It is in the expression of that feeling that who you are is revealed, not in the feeling itself. The feeling is provided by the body, a helpmate now in your service as a route to true expression.

Remember always that we work now to unite the Self of union with the self of form. The self of form cannot be denied now. This is a continuation of the reversal of some of the ideas of yourself that began in *A Treatise on the New*.

Let me repeat a passage from that Treatise here, a passage about the power to observe what is:

It is not about observing a potential for what could be if your brother or sister would just follow in the way that has been shown to you. It is about observing what is. The power to observe what is, is what will keep you unified with your brothers and sisters rather than separating you from them. There is no power without this unity. You cannot see "others" as other than who they are and know your power.

Non-acceptance in any form is separating.

The very idea of potential, you may recall, is a product of the ego thought system that would keep your true Self hidden. You are used to hiding the self of the past about whom you are not well pleased, and you are used to hiding the self of potential, the future self you think you can only dream of being. The ego-self was the self you felt safe presenting to the world, the self you believed the world would find acceptable. If you are still

179

presenting this self, you are still in a state of non-acceptance and whatever peace you are feeling will not last. Whatever access to unity you have experienced will not last because you will not be choosing the time of acceptance.

I have called this time both the time of unity and the time of acceptance because you cannot only focus on unity when you are still in need of this full acceptance or you will not reach the place of sustainability. Every situation and every feeling that you do not like will pull you from union toward separation. All feelings of non-acceptance lead to a feeling of needing to learn "how to" reach acceptance of that which you do not like, or "how to" create a situation that you will like. It is the by-passing of this "how to" function — a function of the time of learning — that we are heading toward.

Realize how freeing it will be to not go through the gyrations of attempting to figure out "how to" reach acceptance of what you do not like! How freeing it will be to realize you have no need to do this! How freeing it will be to accept *all* of your feelings and not to puzzle over which are true and which are false! To realize that you no longer have false feelings. That your feelings are not misleading you but supporting you! That they are but calling you to expression of your true Self! To true representation of who you are — who you are now!

Remove all thinking that says that you can err in following your feelings. This is the thinking of the old thought system, not the new. This is thinking comprised of the time-delay of the time of learning — of a time when you used your feelings, opinions, and judgments interchangeably and either "thought" about them in order to know how to react or suffered the consequences of reacting without "thought." Judgment has been left behind and with it the need for opinions and for "thinking" about "how to" react. Reaction has been replaced by response. Calculated mental constructs have been replaced with true expression. It does not seem so only if you have not allowed yourself to enjoy the freedom of the new, the freedom of being your true Self.

I call you now to embrace this freedom.

The Forty Days and Forty Nights

Day 9: Freedom

Freedom from want, freedom from lack, freedom from repression, are what we will now enjoy together on our mountain top retreat. We have not removed ourselves from life in any way, and yet we have reached a place of retreat, a place of safety and of rest, a place away from "normal" life and the lack of freedom you have experienced there. I am your refuge from the past, your gate of entry to the present. You have fled the foreign land, where freedom was merely an illusion, and arrived at the promised land, the land of our inheritance.

Allow yourself, now, to experience your arrival, your return to your true home, your return to your Self. Laugh. Cry. Shout or wail. Dance and sing. Spin a new web. The web of freedom.

In other words, express your Self!

You who do not feel confident in your feelings, who do not feel confident in your ability to respond, who do not as yet feel the freedom of the new, allow yourself now, to do so. Allow freedom to reign, for it is your allowance, your choice, your permission, that will make it so. The only one who can stop you now is yourself. The only permission you ever needed was your own.

We will practice here to build your confidence, a confidence sorely lacking. What confidence is it of which we speak? The confidence to be yourself. This confidence is what must precede true certainty in this time of elevation of the self of form. The certainty that arises from unity is different from this confidence in the self of form and they must be realized together for the elevation of the self of form to take place. What good will be the certainty of unity if the self of form has no confidence in its ability to express it? *Expression* of the certainty of unity is what the elevated Self of form is all about. Certainty of mind and heart has been realized by many. The *expression* of that certainty in form has not.

Freedom is nothing other than freedom of expression. No one can block the freedom of what your mind would think or heart would feel. But take away the ability to *express* what the mind would think or heart would feel, and freedom is no more. It is not an outward source that you must fear or protect your freedom against. It is none other than yourself who has not allowed you the freedom of expression.

Realize now the truth of what you have just heard. While you know you have not allowed yourself freedom of expression you believe you have allowed yourself freedom of thought. You believe you have allowed yourself freedom of feeling. And yet if the truth be admitted, you know that even this is not quite true. You know that you censor your own thoughts and feelings, accepting some and not others. You know you have repressed your emotions. You know you have lived in a state in which you believed yourself to be lacking. You know you have never known freedom from want.

Today, I would like you to know freedom.

Let's begin this day with a consideration of the idea that you may have an inaccurate idea of an ideal self.

Where might your notion of what an ideal self is have come from? It may have come from your ideas of right and wrong, good and bad. It may have its source in your religious beliefs. It may have come from someone you have idolized, someone you believe to be the spiritual titan you still but hope to be. Your image of an ideal self may have sprung from your reading, from descriptions of those the world has come to see as enlightened ones. It may be linked to your ideas of being able to express wisdom or compassion. The image of the ideal self you hold in your mind, no matter what form it takes, is still an image, and must now be done without if you are going to realize freedom.

All of your images are false images. Isn't it possible that none are more false than this image of an ideal self? Not having false idols is an ancient commandment. An ideal image *is* an idol. It is symbolic rather than real. It has form only within your mind and has no substance. To work toward, or to have as a goal, the achievement of an ideal image is to have created a false god.

Realize now that your ideal image, no matter how it was formed, is a product of the time of learning. It became an image in your mind, and maybe even within your heart, through the process of learning. It arose from the learning of right from wrong, good from bad. It arose from the learning of moral and religious beliefs. It arose from comparison. It arose from seeking. It arose from your perception of lack.

This ideal image is intimately related with the time of learning. It is the epitome of learning. It is what you have seen learning as being *for*. While other learning goals may have receded, this one seems a learning goal worthy of your *effort*. It seems to be a true goal amidst many illusory goals. Just as you may have believed that if you worked hard enough you would achieve a position of status within your profession or material wealth, you have believed that if you work hard enough you can maybe, someday, if you are blessed or lucky, achieve this ideal image.

But this ideal image is as much a product of illusion as have been all of your worldly goals.

As with most goals of the time of learning, it was an ego-centered goal, a carrot of fulfillment the ego but dangled before you in the place it called the future. As with all messages of the ego, it but says that who you are is not good enough.

The idea of your potential was a useful learning tool and one that served the purposes of the Holy Spirit as well as those of the ego. The idea of your potential and your ability to be "more" than what your limited view of yourself would have you be, was a necessary tool to call you to the learning that would return you to your true identity. But the time for such tools is over.

How will you ever realize, or make real, the Self you *are* when you strive to be something else? Just as "finding" brought "seeking" to an end, accomplishment brings striving to an end.

An idealized image, like a rule, is a mental construct. All mental constructs are pre-determinations.

All ideas such as those of advancement or enlightenment are mental constructs. They are pre-determinations.

While language cannot be completely stripped of usages such as these, and while some use of similar terms, like our use of the term *elevated,* are still necessary, it is only in your understanding that our use of these terms is not a cause for predetermination that we can proceed. For if you believe that we are proceeding to some predetermined ideal state, we will not succeed in the work we are doing here together. If you believe this, you will not accept yourself as you are. If you do not accept yourself as you are, you will not move from image to presence. If you do not move from image to presence you will never realize your freedom. If you do not realize your freedom, you will not realize your power.

To *represent* an image is to *become* an image. To become an image, even an idealized image, is to still become a false idol or even what is referred to in more common usage as a spiritual leader or

185

guru. True spiritual leaders or gurus have no need nor desire to be seen as such and are often made into images such as these only within the minds of those who would seek to follow their teachings. This desire of followers to accept an image is less prevalent now but still a common danger.

What an image does is separate. The holder of an image, precisely because he or she holds an image as a goal, holds him or herself separate. They realize not that they are the same as the one they idolize, but realize only that they are different. In "wanting" to be the same and not realizing sameness, they fail to celebrate their own difference and do not bring the gift of their sameness, or of their difference, to the world, but hold it in waiting for such a time as the ideal is reached.

You are the "same" or "as" accomplished as every enlightened one who has ever existed. Without realizing this your unique expression of your accomplishment will not be realized.

Your freedom is contingent upon your ability to give up your images, particularly the image you hold of an ideal self. It is contingent upon your ability to accept that you *are* your ideal self. Yes, even right now, with all your seeming imperfections.

What are these imperfections but your "differences?" Have we not spoken of these differences as givens, as gifts? These are not just the givens of talents or inspired ideas, but all the givens that combined create the wholeness and the holiness of who you are. A creator who desired only sameness would not have created a world of such diversity. You are a creator who created this diversity. It was and is a choice meant to release the beauty of expression in all its forms. You have a *given* form that is perfect for your expression of the beauty and truth of who you are. You cannot express the beauty and truth of who another is. You cannot express the beauty and truth of a future self. You can only express the beauty and truth of who you are now, in the present. And you do. You just have not realized that you do. You have

186

not desired to do so but desired to do something else! Desired to wait, desired to learn, desired to imitate.

What might happen if you change what you desire? You might just realize your freedom.

Nothing, not even the ego, has been able to keep you from expressing the beauty and truth of who you are. You came into the world of form incapable of not expressing the beauty and truth of who you are. That you *are* is an expression of beauty and truth. You express the beauty and truth of who you are by being alive. It has only been your inability to accept this that has caused your grief and pretensions. In a certain sense, your ability to express the beauty and truth of who you are has been taught out of you by learning practices that sought for sameness, and saw not your differences as the gifts they are.

All of these learning practices were the product of false images of the way things — and *you* — should be! Can you not see the extreme urgency of not perpetuating such a practice?

All you need do is look at a young child to see the joy, beauty, and truth of expression. You, too, were once a young child. You are still the same self you were then. You are a self in whom the freedom of expression has been diminished. Diminished, but not extinguished.

Now we must return to you the freedom and the *will* to fan the flames of your desire to be, and to express, who you are in truth.

You can see that a key step in doing this is the debunking of the myth of an ideal self. An ideal self, like a god seen as "other than" puts all that you would long for in a place outside of, or beyond, the self you are now.

You might ask now what is wrong with desiring to have the freedom to strive to be more and to do more. You might ask what life would be *for* without this type of freedom to strive, to achieve, to accomplish, to work toward and realize goals. This is the second myth that must be shattered if you are to know true freedom. It begins with the simple realization that you do still *desire,* or *think* you desire, learning challenges of this type and with the realization that this is all these are — learning challenges. You seek learning challenges now only because of the consistency with which you did so in the past. In the past you moved quickly from one learning challenge to another. You have just completed a monumental learning challenge and so your natural pattern would be to keep going now, to use the momentum of this learning success to achieve another.

This pattern will be easily replaced as your acceptance of yourself as you are, the *real* challenge of this time, begins to grow and to build your confidence. Unity and your access to unity will be your certainty. Trust in your own abilities — the abilities of the self of form joined with the Self of union — will be your confidence. Only these *combined* abilities will release your power.

The Forty Days and Forty Nights

Day 10: Power

Power is the ability to *be* cause and effect. It is the ability to harness the cause and effect power of love. It is a quality of form as well as a quality of union. Form *is* the ultimate expression of the power of creation. The power of creation, harnessed *by* form in the service *of* form is the next step in the expansion of the power of creation. It is the power of the elevated Self of form.

See you now why the certainty of union must be combined with the confidence of the self of form? Certainty is knowing that this power exists. Confidence is the expression of your reliance upon it. To rely on your own power is to rely on the connection that exists between the self of form and the Self of union and to, through this reliance, tie the two together so that there is no seam, no boundary, no remaining separation.

We have talked before of conviction and your willingness to, like the apostles, let your conviction spring from your willingness to experience its cause and its effect. I am asking you now to be willing to move from conviction to reliance. I am not asking you to do this today anymore than I am asking you to move from maintenance to sustainability today, I am merely making you aware of this difference, just as I made you aware of the difference between the states of maintenance and sustainability. As with the states of maintenance and sustainability, I am giving you cause for movement, the effect of which will be the movement from conviction to reliance.

Conviction is tied to belief, and to a former lack of belief that has been overcome. Reliance is not tied to belief nor to the overcoming of disbelief and thus releases you from the need for belief. Certainty is complete lack of doubt and any perceived need for doubt.

Realize that in the time of learning, you felt a need for your doubt just as you felt a need for your beliefs and for the reassurances that were important to your self-confidence. These needs are tied to your feelings and thus we will return to a discussion of feelings in connection with the ideas of confidence, reliance, and certainty.

Confidence in your *feelings* will lead to confidence in your Self. While you think it is your access to unity that will be the more difficult to achieve and sustain, this will not be the case for most of you, for the simple reason that the certainty that comes from union will seem to come, at least initially, from a place other than the self. Because certainty seems to come from a place "other than" or beyond the self of form, you will instinctively have greater trust in it. You will believe it comes from a place "other than" or beyond the self of form *because* it comes in the form of certainty.

The feelings that lead you to either a state of confidence or to a state of lack of confidence could be spoken of most succinctly by considering your concept of intuition. You all understand intuition and each of you have had intuitive moments. You may have felt, for no good reason, as if you shouldn't do something you were about to do. You may have trusted the intuition and then learned that had you done what you planned to do, an accident or some other event you would not have welcomed might have occurred. You may have never had any proof that following your intuition was the correct thing to do but still felt as if it was. Or you may have doubted your intuition and had something occur that made you think back and wish that you had not doubted it.

This intuition came as a feeling, but not necessarily as a feeling of certainty. You may have reacted to the intuition with confidence or with lack of confidence.

There are other instances of intuition that come, not as these seeming warnings, but as what you might call intuitive flashes of insight — intuition that causes you to make connections between point A and point B, be point A and point B distinct points in a scientific puzzle or murky points about relationships between lovers.

This type of intuition seems to come more as thought than as feeling, but even so, it is your feelings about such thoughts that will often determine how you act upon them. Do you trust in your intuition or do you doubt it?

What you have trusted in the most is rational thought, and intuition is different than rational thought, as are feelings of all kinds. You think of feelings either as that which comes to you through your five senses or as emotions, and you have not trusted in these feelings as much as you have trusted in rational thought. This lack of trust works both for you and against you now. It works for you in that you do not have to resist and reject an existing trust as you do with the thoughts of the mind you call rational. It works against you because all feelings are capable of providing what you have called intuitive knowledge or insight and your distrust of this knowledge and insight will need to be overcome.

Feelings come from the innate knowing of the self of form — in short, from the body. The body is the given form and while it was the perfect vehicle for learning in the time of learning, it is now being transformed into the perfect vehicle for the realization of the elevated Self of form. During this transformation, we work with what *is* as well as with the new and the forgotten.

191

In developing the confidence of the self of form, we work with what has been in a new way. As you know from the time of learning, it is often more difficult to become adept in doing something in a way different than you have done it before than to do something completely new. This is why the certainty that comes from access to unity may be less difficult for you to become aware of and accept than the confidence in the self of form that must accompany it. Old patterns or habits must be done away with before achievement of a new way is possible.

This also relates to our discussion of image versus presence and to the image of your personal self that was discussed at the beginning of our dialogue. While you still hold an image of your personal self, you still hold inaccurate ideas about the feelings of the personal self. This is because your image of the personal self is based on the past and the feelings of the past. Your image of the personal self is a mental construct, and not a simple mental construct but a whole set of thoughts, beliefs, and mental pictures.

Because you believe that your feelings have mislead you in the past, you now still doubt your feelings. Because you have doubted yourself in the past, you now still look for reassurances and proof that you are right before you feel confidence and the ability to act. To know before you act is wise. But to think that doubting your feelings or seeking outside assurances of what you know will lead to either confidence or certainty is foolish.

Pause a moment here and consider our need for a distinction between the certainty you feel from unity and the confidence you need to feel in the self of form. Reflect further on your idea of certainty coming from a place "other than" the self. Realize in these reflections that you are still reliant on means other than the self, including your image of the state of unity and including your image of me. Although you have been called to union you still hold an image of the state of unity as separate from your self.

192

Although I have removed myself from the role of teacher and entered this dialogue with you as an equal, you still hold an image of me as "other than" yourself. You will never fully rely upon your Self while you hold these images.

When I call you to replace conviction with reliance, I call you to replace belief in an outside source with reliance upon your Self.

Part of the difficulty you find in accepting reliance on your Self is what you have "learned" within this Course. As you "learned" to remove the ego and deny the personal self, you transferred your reliance to me and to the state of unity. This was purposeful. Now you are asked to return to wholeness, a state in which you are not separate from me or from the state of union.

You have "learned" the distinction between Christ-consciousness and the man Jesus. You have "learned" the distinction between your Self and the man or woman you are. Now you are called to forget what you have "learned" and to let all distinctions slip away. You are called to forget what you have learned and to realize what you know.

Thus I will speak to you from this point onward as the voice of Christ-consciousness, the voice of your own true consciousness, the consciousness that we truly share. I came to you in the form of the consciousness of the man I once was because you were, prior to this point, unready to give up image for presence, the individual for the universal, reliance on an outside source for reliance on yourself, Jesus for Christ-consciousness. You needed the reference point of a "person," of a being who had lived and breathed and met challenges similar to your own. You have been unable to see the two as the same for you have not realized this sameness in yourself. This sameness of the person you are and Christ-consciousness, of union and presence, of the individual and the universal, is what the elevated Self of form must encompass.

I do not ask you to give up your relationship with me as the man Jesus, but to accept that the man Jesus was simply a representation, in form, of Christ-consciousness. I do ask you to give up your identification of the voice of this dialogue as that belonging to the man Jesus who lived two thousand years ago. To continue to identify this voice with that man is to be unable to recognize this voice as the voice of your own true consciousness — the voice of Christ-consciousness. Yet to realize that this is the same voice that animated the man Jesus two thousand years ago will aide you in realizing that this is the voice that will now animate the elevated Self of form, or in other words, you.

I have spoken with you throughout this time as the man Jesus so that you realize that man and Christ-consciousness can be joined. That you, as man or woman, existing in this particular time and space, can join with Christ-consciousness. You can be both/and, rather than either/or. As I speak to you now as the voice of Christ-consciousness — as your own true Self — you will not have lost Jesus as your companion and helpmate but will only know more fully the content of the man Jesus. As you join with Christ-consciousness in this dialogue, you will realize you have not lost your Self but will only know more fully the content of your Self.

Remember that you have been told since the beginning of *A Course of Love* that the answers that you seek lie within, and that their source is your own true identity. You have been told since the beginning of the Course that this is the time of the second coming of Christ. What we have just discussed is what both of these statements mean. This is the culmination point of these two great objectives coming together in you and your brothers and sisters.

I will still be with you to point the way, but if you can cease to think of this as the wisdom of an outside source, if you can hear it and feel it and think of it as a true dialogue, a true sharing in relationship in which an exchange is taking place, you will further your progress greatly.

Let us talk a moment of this exchange, for it is a key to your understanding of your Self and your power. This dialogue, as one-sided as it may seem when presented in this way, *is* an exchange and will only become more so as we proceed. I am not imparting wisdom that you are unaware of but reminding you of what you have forgotten. I am not having a monologue, but we are having a dialogue in which you are a full participant. As much of what you read in these dialogues comes from your own heart and those of your brothers and sisters in Christ as it does from me. It comes, in truth, from our union, from the consciousness we share. This shared consciousness is the source of wisdom *because* it is shared — shared in unity and relationship.

Before we move on to the all-important discussion of unity and relationship, let me spend my final time with you as the man Jesus talking more of feelings.

It is highly unlikely that in your image of an ideal self you left much room for feelings of the type you currently experience. This is why we have recently spoken of anger and of those things which you dislike — why we have spoken, in short, of the feelings you would think would have no place within the ideal self or the elevated Self of form.

I asked you once before to review your ideas about the afterlife, a life in which most of you believe peacefulness reigns and the spirit is free of the body. Yet if you were to think now of a person whom you know who has died, you would not be likely to think of them much differently than they were in life even while you are able to imagine them being peaceful and free of the constraints of the body. This is as good an idea as I can give you of how to imagine the elevated Self of form, as not much different than you are now, but peaceful and free of the constraints of the body.

Let's continue with this idea a while longer as you consider a particular person you fondly remember from life and how you have thought of him or her since death. Do you not occasionally think that this person would be happy or sad to see you in the state you are in when you think of them? Do you not at times shake your head and think that a dead loved one was lucky not to have lived to see the current state of affairs of the world because you know they would not have liked it? And do you not, in all honesty, think that even in whatever form or lack of form they now occupy, they do not like it, even now, even beyond the grave?

And do you not, when thinking of idolized spiritual leaders, see them as *world* leaders as well, leaders not only capable but bound to taking a stance against the many situations there are to dislike in the world? Do they not feel for the suffering? Do they not dislike poverty? Are they not called upon at times to take unpopular stands against popular leaders? Do not even your ideas of saints and angels include concepts of their feeling compassion and mercy, and of their acting upon those feelings by championing the cause of good over that of evil or of the powerless over the powerful? Isn't history replete with idols who have done just this?

I am not calling you to be as these people are or were or to act as these people have, but I am calling you to acknowledge that feelings are involved at every level of every being you can imagine. Consciousness is about what you are aware of, not about what you think. And you are very much aware of your feelings.

If you are being called to acknowledge these feelings, what are you being called to do with them? You are being called to respond to them with acceptance and love. As a man, I took a stand for the powerless and called them to power. I am still doing so. Not because any of you are powerless but because you do not know your power. If there is one thing associated with my life more so than any other, it was this. I was an advocate for all to know their power. Do you think that my advocacy was a social statement for the times in which I lived? Or do you not see that it is the same now as then?

All the issues those you would call spiritual leaders are called to champion or censor have their roots in timeless and universal spiritual truths. It is the timeless and universal that you are called, in unity, to respond to and with. But this response will not be generated without the feelings that precede them! When speaking of gossip we used a simple example of a relatively harmless situation. When speaking of the many issues facing your world in this time, we are speaking of situations that would seem to be extreme and to call for extreme measures. The only extreme measure called for now is the same extreme measure that I called for during my life. It is the call to embrace your power.

My dear brothers and sisters in Christ, turn your thoughts not to ideals of social activism, to causes, or to championing any one side over another. Turn not to your thoughts but to your feelings and go where they lead. And everywhere they lead you, remember one thing only. Remember to embrace your power. The power of love is the cause and effect that will change the world by returning you, and all your brothers and sisters, to who you are in truth. This cannot be done from without but must be done from within. It is the transformation that is caused within that will affect the world without.

The power you must come to rely upon is the power of your own Self to create and express the cause and effect that is the power of love.

Although I need no awareness of the issues facing your time in order to speak to you of such things, I am aware of them. So is every other living thing because all that lives exists in relationship. What I have often referred to as the urgency of this time has been partially because of these issues and partially because of your readiness. It is no accident that these two aspects of urgency

197

are converging. When your reliance on all that exists apart from your Self — your reliance on science and technology and medicine and military might — has been shown to be unfounded, a new source of reliable power is finally sought with the tenacity with which these other sources of seeming power have been sought. This is what has occurred. This is the time at which we stand.

All of the solutions to the issues facing the world and those who live upon it have been pursued separately from one another and from God — until recently. Now unity is being sought and unity is being found.

But these issues, when removed from feelings, still remain issues. They remain social causes, environmental causes, political causes. The cause of all these issues is fear. The cause and effect of love is all that will replace these causes of fear with the means and end that will transform them along with you. You are means and end. It is within your power to be saviors of the world. It is from within that your power will save the world.

As you can see, it is difficult for me, even now, even in this final address to you as the man Jesus, to speak of feelings without addressing the grand scheme of things. I want to comfort and reassure you in this final message. I want to tell you to be embraced by love and to let all the feelings of love flowing through you now find their expression. I desire, more than anything, your happiness, your peace, and your acceptance of the power that will cause these things to come to be. Yet I know you and what you want to hear. I know you have long waited for your feelings to be addressed in a more personal way. Please remember that none of the approaches that have been used to address your feelings in the way you might desire have worked.

This will work.

This is the secret of succession, your promised inheritance. This is the gift of love I came to give and give newly now, to you. Blessed brother and sister, we feel the same love, the same compassion, the same tenderness for each other and the world.

This is unity. This will save us. This will save the world.

The Forty Days and Forty Nights

Day 11: Christ-Consciousness

We are one self. How else could we be capable of receiving what we give? How else could our lives be capable of experiencing no loss but only gain? Why else would we have to share ourselves to know ourselves?

Because we are one heart, one mind, one Self, we can *only* know our selves through sharing in unity and relationship. We could only share in unity and relationship through a seeming separation from the oneness in which we exist. This is the great paradox that unites the world of form and the world of spirit, the world of separation with the world of union, even while it does not unite the world of illusion with that of truth. Sharing in unity and relationship is the way and the means to see past the world of illusion to the truth of the union of form and spirit, separate selves and the One Self.

The elevation of the self of form is nothing but the recognition of the One Self within the Self.

The One Self exists within the many in order to know Its Self through sharing in union and relationship.

All the benefits you might want to bring to the world are brought about in only one way: The way of sharing in union and relationship. It is only in relationship that the oneness of the self separates from oneness and so knows oneness. It is only through the means of separate relationships joining in union that the One Self is capable of being either the observer or the observed. This is as true of God as it is of the self of form. God is the oneness and the separation. Life is the relationship. God is what is. Life is the relationship of what is with its Self.

Separation, of itself, is nothing. What is separate *and* joined in relationship is All because it is all that is knowable. The All of Everything cannot be known anymore than can nothingness. The All of Everything is unknowable. Thus you are the knowable of God. You are the knowable because you are the relationship of All with Its Self. Separation is as unknowable as the All of Everything. To be separate in truth would be to not exist. To be the All of Everything would be to not know existence. Only what exists in relationship knows that it exists. Thus relationship is everything. Relationship is the truth. Relationship is consciousness.

Christ-consciousness is the awareness of existence through relationship. It is not God. It is not man. It is the relationship that allows the awareness that God is everything. It has been called wisdom, Sophia, spirit. It is that without which God would not know God. It is that which differentiates all from nothing. Because it is that which differentiates, it is that which has taken form as well as that from which form arose. It is the expression of oneness in relationship with Its Self.

Life is the connecting tissue of the web of form with the divine All. Life is consciousness. Christ-consciousness is awareness of what *is*. It is the awareness of connection and relationship of All to All. It is the merging of the unknowable and the knowable through movement, being, and expression.

The Forty Days and Forty Nights

Day 12: the Spacious Self Joined in Relationship

Now we listen to feelings. Now we listen to feelings and understand what they have to say to us. Now we listen with a new ear, the ear of the heart. Now we recognize the thoughts that would censor our feelings, calling them selfish, uncaring, or judgmental. We examine. We realize it is our thoughts and not our feelings that are selfish, uncaring, or judgmental. We realize the sacred *space* we have become. Our space is the space of unity. It is the space of ease because thoughts are no longer allowed their rule.

Imagine the air around you being visible and your form an invisible *space* within the visible surroundings. This is the reality of Christ-consciousness. Consciousness may seem to be embodied by form but the reverse is true and has always been true. The body is now ready to know that it is embodied, enclosed, surrounded, taken up, by consciousness. It is your feelings that now will be the sense organs of this spaciousness. Not feelings of sight or sound, smell or touch, but feelings of love of Self. Feelings of love of Self are now what hold open the space of the Self, allowing the space to be.

The merging of form with Christ-consciousness is this merging of the Self with the unconditional love of the One Self. The One Self loves Its Self. There is nothing else to love. The One Self is the All.

The space of the One Self is everything. Space is neither divided nor separated nor occupied by form. Space is all that is. Christ-consciousness is the space of all that is.

Navigating this endless space as an expression of love is the simplest thing imaginable. All you must do is listen to your Self. Your Self is now a feeling, conscious space, unhindered by any obstacles of form.

When an obstacle of form, be it human or material in nature, seems to present itself, all you must do is remind yourself that space has replaced what was once your self of form. Feel the love of the space that is you. All obstacles will vanish.

All obstacles of form are only real in the world of form, a world that is perceived rather than known. Christ-consciousness replaces perception with knowing, form with space.

Not all forms will be met as obstacles. Forms are only as real as the perceiver perceives them to be. Thus your space will effortlessly join with the space that is free and open to joining. There is no boundary between space and space. There are only perceived boundaries. When a boundary is perceived as solid, it is an obstacle, for it has no space available for joining. What is a boundary to a perceiver is met as an obstacle by the spacious Self. Obstacles need not be avoided for space encompasses all obstacles, making them invisible. The mind would say that making obstacles invisible is uncaring. The spacious Self knows no obstacles for it knows no uncaring. It knows only love for the One Self. It feels the obstacle but does not know it. The feeling that is the sense organ of the spacious Self then remembers its spaciousness and calls upon it. The obstacle is thus enfolded in the space, becoming one with it. The perceiver knows not of the enfolding but feels no hurt nor lessening of spirit by becoming invisible within the space. The solidity of the perceiver is, in this manner, deflected from the One Self, becoming not an obstacle. The open space of the perceiver who sees not only with perception and holds not his or her boundaries solid, is joined rather than deflected. The open perceiver may or may not know of this enfolding, but may realize a sense of comfort or of safety, a feeling of love or of attraction.

Non-human obstacles have no need of being deflected for their boundaries have not been made solid by perception. A seeming obstacle of non-human form is easily enfolded in the space of the One Self and can be moved or passed through.

This is joining in relationship.

The Forty Days and Forty Nights

Day 13: Union with the Spacious Self

Once the One Self became form and knew Its Self, it knew separate thought. The separate thoughts of the one self of form, rather than the form of the one self, allowed for the knowing of the self that created the many selves. The many selves who have come and gone since the beginning of time now know themselves as the many and the one, the individual and the collective. This is the knowing in relationship that is available to you *now*.

The "one" self of form is the self you were born into. The one self of form comes to know the One Self through relationship with other selves experiencing oneness through being selves of form.

You are not meant to lose the experience of the self of form but to integrate it so that you are both the many and the one. The oneness that your individual self represents in this life is the oneness of the Holy One who is both one — somewhat in the way you think of the individual self — and All.

The love that is found in the relationships of the one self with the many is the love of God. There is no other love. God's love is constantly being given, received, and felt in relationship. God's love is your love. Your love is the love of God. God is love.

Thus is explained the relationships and the forms emptied of love. Where there is no love there is no God present. Where there is no love there is a lack of godliness or what you have defined as evil. A complete lack of love creates formidable obstacles — obstacles of solid form that contain no spaciousness. Solid form is actually a void, a substance devoid of spaciousness, a form that is form only. These forms are still encompassed by the loving space of Christ-consciousness and thus are easily rendered ineffective.

Imagine the spacious Self as an invisible Self, a Self whose form is transparent. Through this transparency, the reality of the One Self being also the many, or the all, is apparent. The spaciousness of love, the lovely complexity of form, the awesome majesty of nature, all are visible within the One Self because of the invisibility of the one boundary-less Self of form. All of creation is present and apparent in this boundary-less Self of form. This Self is everything and everyone. Because it is everything and everyone it is also the self of the void, the void of the loveless self. As long as the void of the loveless self exists within the spacious Self, they exist in harmony. It is only in attempting to eject the loveless self from the spacious Self that disharmony occurs. Thus holding the loveless self within the spacious Self of love is the answer to the question of evil and the final lifting of the last veils of fear.

The same is true of all you would fear, such as the suffering self. A suffering self, held within the spacious Self, exists in harmony with the spacious Self. Attempts to eject the self of suffering from the spacious Self create disharmony. It is only by this holding within that the loveless self and the suffering self are rendered ineffective. It is only in this way that you realize that all exist within. It is only in this way that you become completely fearless and totally spacious, for fear is part of the density of form, being a lack of love.

Once fear is gone, true relationship is not only possible but inevitable. True relationship exists naturally in the state of harmony that is the spacious Self. This is the state of union.

The Forty Days and Forty Nights

Day 14: Healing

All time is included in the spacious Self. Acceptance is necessary because escape is not possible. Everything that is, is with us, which is why we are the accomplished as well as the void, the healed as well as the sick, the chaos and the peace. Thus we heal now by calling on wholeness, accepting the healed self's ability to be chosen while not encountering resistance or any attempts at rejection of the sick or wounded self. It is your acceptance that escape is not possible that will lead you out of forgetfulness to remembrance. It is in the equality of all that is realized with the acceptance of the spacious Self, the One Self, and the many, that full acceptance is actually achieved and complete transformation begun.

The spacious Self realizes that the outer world is a projection and most often a rejection rather than an extension of what is within. Thus, sickness is a rejection of feelings. All that causes fear is rejection of feelings. All that causes loneliness is rejection of feelings. All that causes violence is rejection of feelings.

What is ejected from the self becomes separate and in the separation willfully forgotten. The spacious Self no longer ejects or forgets because all feelings are accepted as those of the One Self.

All feelings are accepted as those of the many as well. It is by holding all feelings of others within the spacious Self, by not forgetting that the one and the many are the same, by willfully remembering that the feelings of the many can be "held" and not projected into the world as sickness, violence, and so on, that acceptance occurs. It is in accepting all feelings as the feelings of the many that the feelings of "others" are accepted as one's own and held within the spaciousness of the One Self, the whole Self.

Further, it is in willful remembering that extension replaces rejection both in the self and in "others." Extension of health can, in this way, replace rejection of illness and woundedness.

This is why, after learning to disclaim all that you have called your "own," you are now given the task of claiming your power as your own. All that is within your power is *within your power.* Your power is the power of the many and the one that exist in wholeness within the spacious Self.

Once you fully realize that you cannot escape, whatever remains that was brought to a stop within you must pass through for the self to be the fully invisible or spacious Self described earlier. What you once stopped and held in a "holding pattern" to return to later, is the opposite of the *holding within* you are asked to do now because those things that were held in a "holding pattern" were based on fear. You feared them because you did not understand them and could not assign meaning to them. Being inexplicable, the "holding pattern" that you entered into with them was one of willful forgetting and escape. They were "shelved" like museum pieces and collected solidity within you. Like stones thrown into a clear pool, they made ripples and then settled.

The invisible or spacious Self is the Self through which pass through naturally occurs because there are no blocks or boundaries, no holding patterns, no mental interferences.

Pass through was never about escape or rejection. Pass through is about releasing the particular while maintaining the relationship.

It is what happens in oneness as opposed to the stopping and holding "apart" that occurred in separation. What the spacious Self holds within is the relationship of All to All. Relationship is the invisible reality only expressed through form.

Only now, in your realization of your invisibility and spaciousness, do you look within and see the stones that settled in your clear pools. They are as specks of sand to the ocean. And yet we do not choose to keep them. Spaciousness is spaciousness. Invisibility is invisibility. We are no longer collectors but gatherers. We hold within only what is real and in our realization of the reality of relationship, we accept our relationship to the unexplainable.

All, *all* you are doing here is accepting your relationship to the unexplainable. Acceptance is the creator of invisibility, the creator of the spacious Self. God has been described as the "all knowing" for God is the relationship. Relationship is the known. The unknown, like the unexplainable, becomes known through the relationship of acceptance. Acceptance of your relationship with the unknown is the only way to arrive at acceptance of your relationship with your means of coming to know.

Your acceptance of these words is a form of acceptance of the unknown and as such a means of coming to know. These words are only one means, which is why this is called a dialogue. Realize now that this is but one voice of the many. You have entered into the dialogue with the many as well as the one. This dialogue is going on all around you. Have you been listening to but one voice? Or have you begun to hear the one voice in the many?

You must now own this dialogue — own it as you own the power that is yours. This one voice of the many will continue to point the way for only a short time longer. Thus the voice of the many must be heard as the voice of the one. You are not on this mountain top alone! Can you not hear your own voice? Can you not hear the voices of the many who join us here?

The Dialogues

Entering the dialogue is the means of sustaining the one voice within the many, the means of sharing your access to unity, the manifestation, in form, of the healed and whole and thus spacious Self.

The Forty Days and Forty Nights

Day 15: Entering the Dialogue

When you fully realize that sharing is necessary you will have *entered the dialogue*. When you have fully surrendered to the fact that you can't come to know *on your own* you will have *entered the dialogue*. When you fully accept that the voice of the one can be heard in the voice of the many you will have *entered the dialogue*. When you fully realize that you are in-formed by everything and everyone in creation, you will have *entered the dialogue*.

To inform is to make known. Thus *you* can be made known by everything and everyone in creation just as everything and everyone in creation can be made known by you. We have just spoken of the *un*known and your willingness to accept your relationship with it in order for you to come to know it. The unknown and the known exist together in everything and everyone. Thus your willingness to be made known and to know exists alongside your willingness to embrace the unknown.

The spirit that animated all things is the spirit that is in all things and that is the great informer. As you are more fully able to maintain Christ-consciousness you begin the movement away from being observed to being in-formed by the spirit which animates all things. You begin the movement away from observing to informing.

How can the invisible be observed? From within Christ-consciousness, you begin to be able to know and to make known without observation or observance *of the physical*. This occurs *through your relationship with the unknown*. You begin to be informed by what *is* without any regard for your level of understanding or knowing. You do this by taking what *is* into your spacious form rather than observing it as separate from you.

Previously, what you did not observe, or see, was not real to you. Through the practice of observance of the physical and the obvious, you began to be able to see beyond the physical and the obvious to what could not be observed physically. This practice had two purposes. The first purpose was the establishment of a new kind of interaction and relationship between observer and observed. The second purpose was your preparation to move beyond observation.

It has been in the relationship of observation that you have interacted with all other life forms as well as with inanimate forms. In the relationship generated by observation, those forms have been perceived as real. That observation produced the solidity and mass of the forms you observed. Yet it is the spirit that animates form that is real. Informing could be understood as making the spirit known in the form of physicality. It is not simply the bringing of spirit into form but the making known of spirit in form. What you made known through judgment-free observation was but the precursor to what is made known through informing.

The difference between simply bringing spirit into form and making spirit known through form is the difference for which the time has come. The observation you have practiced has prepared you to move from observation to informing and being informed.

The animation of form with spirit is an ongoing aspect of creation. It is not time bound. It did not take place at the birth of creation and then cease to be. It did not take place at the birth of the body and then cease to be. It is not about life and making form alive but about spirit and informing spirit. It is about making spirit known through the form of physicality.

In practicing observation without judgment, you learned to be neutral observers. Being neutral observers allowed cause and effect to occur naturally rather than having your judgment alter natural cause and effect. This practice will continue to serve you and will not be replaced, but supplemented by the new practice of informing, until the practice of observation is no longer needed.

This is the new realm of power that few in physical form have practiced and that has never been practiced by many at one time. It is a major shift because it is not neutral but creative. It is of creation and can only flow through those who have mastered neutral observation because the intent of creation, rather than the intent of the observer, is the creative force, the animator and informer. Yet informing is a quality of oneness and thus the joining of the self with the spacious Self in oneness and wholeness must precede this step. This power cannot be misused because it is unavailable to those who have not realized their oneness with the creative force. Thus while it is not the self who informs and is informed by the creative force, it is the Self joined in union with the creative force that informs and is informed.

In union there is no distinction between the Self and the creative force of the universe, the animator and informer of all things.

Engaging in dialogue with those who join you on the mountain top is necessary to this next step. One reason is that it allows a starting point for your practice. While it is possible to practice observance in every situation, it is necessary to practice the ability to inform and be informed with others who have reached this level of neutrality along with you. This is why observation is not being replaced. Observation is needed until this level of neutrality is reached by a much greater number.

This greater level of neutrality will not be reached until those who are the forerunners have practiced and mastered this interaction with the creative force long enough to realize their oneness with it. While there is division remaining between the self and the spacious Self, the self and the creative force, you remain in the state of maintenance rather than sustenance of Christ-consciousness. This is an acceptable state for this time of limited practice with those with whom you are engaged in this specific mountain top dialogue. It is not an acceptable state for full-scale interaction with the world. Although this power cannot be misused, to have access to this power in one instance and not another as you move in and out of the state of Christ-consciousness will not serve the purpose of creation.

What does it mean to practice informing and being informed? It means to join together with others who have the ability to maintain Christ-consciousness in your company. This creates the joining together of spacious Selves. It is a joining without boundaries. You become clear pools flowing into each other. You make your spirits known.

This cannot be explained in great detail, which is why it must be practiced. It is to your own authority only that you must appeal for guidance. The first step is to access your own readiness. Are you able to be a clear pool? If not, what prevents you? Do not be too hard on yourself now, for the stones within your pools are like flecks of sand within the ocean. Observe these stones with neutrality and see if they do not wash away. Your willingness to have them gone is all that is required. If doubts of your readiness continue to persist, remember that doubt is caused by fear. Examine what you fear. Is it really the stones within your pool, or is it the challenge of moving with the current that you know will be generated by the joining of spacious Selves? Do you fear your power even though you have been told it cannot be misused? Do you feel unworthy and seek to keep your unworthiness hidden? Do you still fear being known?

If so, enter the dialogue with the purpose of your final preparations in mind. Bring your fears into the light of oneness and see how the light dispels the darkness. This is what we are here for. There is no time to waste and no protracted length of time will be required if your willingness is true.

You are here to make one another known and in so doing to know oneness. It will be less difficult to know this voice as the voice of oneness once you have listened to the voice of oneness in each other and benefited from its healing properties. To heal is to make whole. To make whole is to become the spacious Self. To become the spacious Self is to become ready to be informed and to inform with the spirit of creation.

This is a very "individual" stage in the creative process. "Group think" does not replace the consciousness of the One Self with the "one group self." This is not a time of being judged or of adopting the beliefs of others but one of finally conquering judgment with neutrality or acceptance. Allowing others to accept you as you are is a gift that releases them from judgment and any notion that may have remained within them that Christ-consciousness is a form of "group think." Never will you feel more like an individual than when you are made known through the informing of spirit!

Realize how necessary dialogue is. Many resist this stage of development because they feel they have achieved inner knowing. They may still consider themselves to be capable of growing and changing, but feel, in a certain sense, that it is unnecessary. They have achieved a goal consistent with their concept of inner knowing and mistaken this as knowing the Self. Movement is necessary to know the Self. The on-going informing or animation of the physical with the spiritual is just that — on-going. The easiest way of all to slip from knowing to not knowing is through stagnating in a "known" place. To cease to accept the unknown is to cease to come to know.

Entering the dialogue keeps you in constant contact with the unknown and with unceasing coming to know.

Thus you are not to come together as the known but as the unknown. You dialogue about the unknown, not the known. By keeping in constant contact with the unknown you stay in constant dialogue for you have not claimed a knowing that disallows coming to know. You are in dialogue because in dialogue, coming to know is a fluid exchange.

Imagine the current of the energy, or clear pools of the spacious Selves, coming together. This current washes some stones clean and washes others away. It changes the clear pool by dredging up sediment that has settled on the bottom. As the clear pool merges with the current of other clear pools it is able to change directions, see new sights, gain new insights. While this is only an initial, or practice stage of movement, it is obvious that movement will always be needed for the clear pool to not become a stagnant pond.

To be engaged in dialogue with certain others is different than entering the dialogue, but entering the dialogue is not different than engaging in specific dialogues. This is so because entering the dialogue is an all-encompassing state in which everything and everyone interacts with you through the exchange of dialogue. While you are asked to promote wholeness and the sustainability of Christ-consciousness with others sharing this specific means of coming to know with you, you are not asked to disregard any other means of coming to know, or to see any others differently than you see those with whom you are engaged in this specific dialogue for this specific purpose or practice.

Knowing that you have entered the dialogue does not mean that you will not have an awareness of those who would infringe upon, rather than join with, your boundary-less state. You must but remember that those who still have boundaries have a need for those boundaries. You are not depriving them of anything when you slip into observable states of being. There is a purpose for this time in which both informing and observing, being informed and being the observed coexist. You must respect the boundaries of those who are still in need of them and not offer more than can be received. This is why practice among those who are ready to be boundary-less and spacious selves is appropriate and acceptable.

To practice, as to inform, is to make known. To practice, as to inform, does not mean that you know nothing. Practice is the merging of the known and the unknown through experience, action, expression, and exchange. It alters the known through interaction with the unknown. It allows the continuing realization that what you knew yesterday was as nothing to what you know today, while at the same time, aiding in the realization that what you come to know has always existed within you in the realm of the unknown that also exists within you.

While you have not been asked to remove yourself from life during this time on the mountain, you have been asked to be here and to join with others here for a purpose. As such, this time is also a beginning to the practice of realizing and being able to accept a certain duality. Without necessarily realizing it, your consciousness has been in two places at once without being divided. As you re-enter life on level-ground, this ability to carry an undivided but spacious consciousness with you will be paramount and will have many practical as well as spiritual applications.

One of the practical aspects has just been discussed — that of engaging in dialogue with some and entering the dialogue with all. This is a demonstration of levels of consciousness at work. It is important to be able to hold the spacious consciousness of the One Self and also to be able to focus — to not exclude while also making choices about where your attention is given. Just as you respect the boundaries of those who are still in need of boundaries, you also must respect your own boundary-less space.

As you engage in dialogue as the spacious Self and are made known, your purpose here will become more clear. Thus your ability to embrace all while focusing on your own purpose in being here, will begin a new process of individuation. The distinctness of your own path will be made visible and you will see that it may be quite different from the others with whom you are coming to know, and perhaps quite different than you thought it would be. You will be shown that you can enter the dialogue with all and still focus, or place your attention, on areas that might not interest others in the slightest.

Consequently, you may find that there is a time of walking alone approaching, or a time of gathering with many. You will realize that you have felt cocooned by the time on the mountain and by those who have joined you, and that you may have grown less eager to strike out on your own. You may have thought the joining being done here was the joining with a specific group rather than a joining with yourself and with all. This fallacy needs to be brought to your attention now so that as you join in true spaciousness with those coming to know along with you, you do not create false ideas concerning what this is about.

Remember that this journey has not been about becoming self-less but about realizing your true identity. We have now debunked your myths about your true identity being an idealized form of the self. Through your ability to view your own Self, as well as that which you observe, with a neutrality that embraces the unknown as well as the known, you are now ready to reclaim your Self and your purpose here.

The Forty Days and Forty Nights

Day 16: Paradise Re-Found

Everything that can't be seen but *is,* is consciousness. Accepting everything that can't be seen, including the unknown, is full consciousness. Acceptance is key. You can't accept what you fear.

Because all that is not physical exists only in consciousness, it simply exists. It is simply "there" within consciousness. All that you "know" because you have felt it, is still there because consciousness is eternal. All that you have learned that has touched your heart is there because you felt it. All that you have thought is still there because you thought it.

What is of form comes and goes and is impermanent. What is of spirit, or consciousness, is eternal.

Sickness has been defined as rejected feelings, feelings about which consciousness was not chosen. With this rejection, these feelings became physical. What is not of consciousness is of physical form. The rejected feelings that became physical were made separate from the self and yet were maintained within the body, thus interrupting the body's natural means of functioning. Sickness is not sickness but rejected feelings. The rejected feelings exist as separate and forgotten physical manifestations until they are willfully remembered and accepted back into the spacious Self. Rejected feelings are those that you blame yourself for. Sickness is the form of manifestation of rejected feelings. These manifestations come to you to prove to you what you think you know — that you are responsible for the sorry circumstances of your life.

219

Ejected feelings are projected outside of the body. These are the unwanted feelings that are blamed on others. These manifest in your interactions with the world, taking on form in the actions of others, in instances where acts of nature or accidents seem to thwart plans, or in "situations" or crises of all kinds. These manifestations also come to you to prove what you think you know — that others, or the world in general, are to blame for the sorry state of your life.

This is what is meant by no escape. No escape does not mean that anyone is bound to the past and to their former pain but that each is still bound to, and affected by, all that has been rejected or ejected. All that has been expelled is part of the wholeness of the self. As what was ejected or rejected and became "real" is returned to the Self, the physical manifestation dissolves, because the source, which was separation, is no more. Illness is no longer observable once what was rejected rejoins the spacious Self. The illness *was* but is no more. Because it was physical it came only to pass. Because the feeling that generated the physical manifestation was not physical to begin with — was not of the physical world — it returns to its non-physical nature within the spacious Self. Thus it was not escaped but reintegrated into the oneness of the Self.

This reintegration requires a change in what you want to prove to yourself. All you may now continue to seek proof of is that your feelings, rather than your thoughts about your feelings, reflect who you are, and that by acting on them, you will act in accord with who you are and thus in accord with the universe. The reintegration is the process through which you discover this proof, proof of the benevolence of your feelings and of the benevolence of the universe itself.

What happens when feelings of loneliness or despair, anger or grief join with the spacious Self? This joining occurs only through acceptance. Without acceptance, the separation remains along with the physical manifestation.

It is only in the present that acceptance can occur. There is no "going back" or reliving of the past required. There is also no escape because in Christ-consciousness, you must become fully aware of the present. The present is the time of no time, wholeness, where all that is real and all that was ever real exists. While the physical manifestations of all that you feared and expelled were not real because they were projections rather than creations, the feelings were real because you felt them. Had you not feared and expelled them, you would have seen that they were nothing to fear.

You have no feelings that are bad. Fear is not a feeling but a reaction to a feeling. Emotions are reactions. You have been told there are but two emotions, love and fear. What this is really saying is that there are but two ways that you react to what you feel — with love or with fear. If you react with fear you expel, project, and separate. If you respond with love you remain whole. You realize that you have no feelings that are bad. You embrace sadness, grief, anger, and all else that you feel because these feelings are part of who you are in the present moment. When you remain in the present moment you remain within Christ-consciousness where all that *is* exists in harmony. To embrace is the opposite of to escape. To hold all within yourself in the embrace of love is the opposite of holding onto what you have already responded to with fear and made separate. There is no escape for there is only the embrace. The embrace *is* Christ-consciousness.

This relates to everything, not only your response to sickness or crisis situations, because it relates to whether or not you are able to remain in a state of constant coming to know. What you expel is what you do not want to know. What you try to control is what you do not want to know. You do not want to know every time you predetermine, in advance of knowing, what something is or will be. You predetermine, or decide, for instance, that a physical

221

symptom is bad, and then choose to find out what is "wrong," in which case your "decision" rather than your "feeling" is only confirmed. When you feel uneasy or uncomfortable about a situation, you determine that you already know that the situation is bad or is most likely going to be bad, and then you "think" that through your effort or control you can alter the situation for the better. Only when you accept that no feelings are bad will you allow yourself to come to know what they truly are.

When you feel an "intuition" you respond differently than you do to unwanted feelings that you are quick to want to "do something" about. If all feelings were treated more like intuition is treated — with a "knowing" that the feeling has come to tell you something that is as yet *unknown* to you, but nevertheless for your benefit, you would go a long way toward acceptance.

All that you predetermine you have come to know will be cause only for suffering, arrogance, and righteousness if you attempt to hold onto it as the "known" and do not remain in a constant state of coming to know. What you would hold onto is based on fear and expelled into solidity where you can keep your eyes upon what you have "formed" an opinion about. What you hold within the embrace is held in love and so exists along with you in the spacious state of constant coming to know.

Consciousness of the spacious Self thus includes feelings of sadness, loneliness, and anger as well as feelings of happiness, compassion, and peace. Consciousness does *not* include your reactions. Consciousness thus does not include either love or fear. This is because love is everything and fear is nothing.

Consciousness began as all feeling and all thought, all of which were of love because love is everything. All feeling and all thoughts of love extended into the paradise of creation. This was the Garden of Eden, the Self, the All of All. Unwanted feelings that you attempted to expel from the Garden of Eden were not expelled from consciousness, but from your awareness. This created the separate and the unloved in your perception, and your perception created an unreal reality of the separate and unloved, often referred to as hell or hell on earth. Love and fear existed simultaneously as did paradise and hell. This became your world, which slowly grew from a world primarily made up of paradise and love, to a world primarily made up of hell and fear because as more was expelled from paradise, more was perceived as hellish or fearful. Less of love was extended. More of fear was projected.

The expelled feelings that seemed to cause this duality still exist in consciousness. Once these expelled feelings are returned to the spacious Self and the spacious Self embraces them with love, the spacious Self will be whole, for it will embrace everything — as love, which *is* everything — embraces it. This is paradise re-found.

The Forty Days and Forty Nights

Day 17: the Fulfillment of the Way of Jesus

Just as the creation story had to start somewhere — so you had to start somewhere. We have spoken of the spirit that animated all things as the movement or cause of movement that began the creation story. We have spoken of Christ-consciousness as the awareness of existence through relationship. We have spoken of life-consciousness and Christ-consciousness as the merging of the human and the divine into observable form. Thus there must be a difference between life-consciousness and Christ-consciousness, since you have been life-conscious without being Christ-conscious. You have been the created without being the creator. Something has been missing. What is Christ? What is Christ-consciousness? Are they different or the same?

You have been told Christ-consciousness is neither God nor man but the relationship that allows the awareness that God is everything. You have been told Christ-consciousness has also been known as wisdom, Sophia, spirit. Christ-consciousness thus obviously predates the man Jesus, and creation itself. It is both the feminine and masculine, the "identity" of God, the All of All given an identity. God holds you within Himself. Christ is held within you as the center or heart of yourself — as your identity and God's identity. Christ is the "I Am" of God, the expression of "I Am" in form, the animator and the animated, the informer and the informed, the movement, being, and expression of creation. Christ is that which anointed form with the "I Am" of God. In many religious traditions, life is ritually or sacramentally anointed in its coming and its going in remembrance of the original anointing.

224

Why do we return to this now, repeating what has been said before? Because we have reached the time, once again, for you to claim your identity. Although being who you are has been discussed in many ways, many of you still await being different than who you are. This is because you realize that being your true self is being in union, undivided and inseparable from God, the All of All. God is only the all-knowing because God is in everything and everyone. Consciousness itself is not knowing but awareness. God is the creator of knowing because God created a means of coming to know. This "part" of God, the animator and informer, is Christ-consciousness.

What is the drive that has kept you reading this Course, caused you to enter this dialogue, kept you examining, kept you attempting to move beyond learning to a new means of knowing? Christ-consciousness. This is why it was said in the beginning pages of the Course that the Christ in you was the learner. The Christ in you is what was created to inspire movement beyond simple awareness to knowing. You have always been aware that you exist and always been in search of an answer as to why you exist. You have always been aware of the world around you and always been in search of answers to what the world around you is all about. An approach to knowing, which was called learning, was previously the predominant approach. As this approach became more and more centered in the mind and more and more about coming to know what others had already learned and were capable of teaching, learning began to fail the cause of knowing.

There have always been individuals who challenged the predominant patterns of learning because of the strength of their connection to Christ-consciousness. While no one has more access to Christ-consciousness than another, some exhibited more willingness to let that consciousness be their guiding force — that by which their being gained movement and expression. Those like Jesus, who fully expressed Christ-consciousness in form, did so as individuals, by not negating their being as they realized this connection. Many others with realization of Christ-consciousness as strong as that of the man, Jesus, did not express that realization but negated the individual in favor of the "spiritual."

This is why we return now to your identity and the individuation of your identity.

Christ-consciousness is not the second coming of Christ but the first coming — the movement of being into form. This being was fully expressed by Jesus Christ, who represented, in form, the first coming and who began the movement from maintenance to sustenance of Christ-consciousness. Let's consider why this representation should be necessary.

As the universe is not comprised of the unnecessary, nor are human beings. The universe, as well as human beings, is comprised of nothing that is superfluous, but only of the necessary. All the given components are necessary for wholeness. Representation of the power of Christ-consciousness in human form was necessary to complete the cycle of birth, death, and rebirth.

Christ-consciousness was represented not only by Jesus, but by his mother, Mary. Mary, like Jesus, realized full Christ-consciousness and full expression of Christ-consciousness in form. Each did so in individual ways, ways that revealed the choices available to those who would follow after them. One way, that of Jesus, was the way of acceptance, teaching by example, and preparing a way for those who would approach Christ-consciousness through teaching and learning and leading example lives. Another way, that of Mary, was the way of creation, and was a representation and preparation for those who would approach Christ-consciousness through relationship.

The way of Jesus represented full-scale interaction with the world, demonstrating the myth of duality, the death of form, the resurrection of spirit. The way of Mary represented incarnation through relationship, demonstrating the truth of union, the birth of form, and the ascension of the body. Both ways were necessary. Both ways were necessarily represented or demonstrated. Both ways were represented and demonstrated by many other individuals as well. The way was a choice. The main ability of the individual is the ability to represent what God created, the means of coming to know — which *is* Christ-consciousness — through individual choice or will.

Christ-consciousness is your will to know, to be, and to express. The time of Christ, and the second-coming of Christ, are expressions meant to symbolize the completion of the cycle of birth, death, and re-birth as a means of coming to know.

What Jesus represented or demonstrated has now been realized, which is why this is called the time of Christ. The "time" of Christ, which so many associate with Jesus Christ, represents the time of fulfillment of the way of Jesus. What could be taught and learned has been taught and learned. Now it is time to move beyond what could be taught and learned to what can only be realized through relationship. Now is the time of the final revelation of what can be realized, or made real, through following the example life of Jesus.

Thus we enter the ending stage of what can be realized through fulfillment of the way of Jesus and the beginning of the fulfillment of the way of Mary. This ending stage of the fulfillment of the way of Jesus is the stage of interaction with the world, the time of miracles, the death of the old way and the birth of the new.

The Forty Days and Forty Nights

Day 18: the Way to Paradise

You have been preparing for this final stage of the fulfillment of the way of Jesus. You have also been preparing for the beginning of the fulfillment of the way of Mary. Many of you will follow the way of Jesus to completion, beginning a stage of interaction with the world, an interaction with the miracles that will aide in the dismantling of the old and with preparing the way for the birth of the new. Others of you will follow your hearts to a by-passing of the final stage of the old and to anchoring the new within the web of reality. Still others will participate in both, following their innate desire to facilitate the creation of change through a specific function even while moving into the new as they do so. Each way is as needed now as it was two thousand years ago.

One way is active. One way is receptive. Yet the ways are not separate any more than Jesus was separate from Mary — or any mother separate from her child. The ways are rather complimentary and symbiotic. Together they return wholeness and will bring about the completion of the time of Christ. This symbiotic working together will be essential for the birth of the new and in truth symbolizes it in form and process. As within, so without. Mary represents the relationship that occurs within, Jesus the relationship that occurs with the world. So do each of you. These two ways also represent God and Christ-consciousness, the extension of God. God is everything in heaven and on earth and is in everything on heaven and on earth. Thus, God represents the world without. Christ-consciousness is God within *you,* your particular manifestation of God and relationship with the God within.

The time of teaching and learning is over. If the way of Jesus was a way of acceptance, teaching, learning, and leading an example life, then the remaining ways of Jesus that are still applicable and appropriate in this final period are those of acceptance and of being an example life.

Only those who have fully accepted who they are, are capable of being example lives. These example lives are evidenced through the individuation of the One Self among the many. To choose to be an example life is to choose to be made known by, and to, the many. It is a choice for full acceptance of the Self in a form that can be distinguished, or individuated from the rest. It is full acceptance of difference as well as sameness and of the necessity of each. It is a choice many will be called to so that sameness is seen in difference, the one is seen in the many, and the many seen in the one. It is a way of service through action. It is a way of joy and harmony for only through joy and harmony can true service become true action. It is the way for those who desire to bring expression to a calling they feel within to "do" something. It is the way for those whose fulfillment and completion is interlaced with bringing this expression to fulfillment. If the call is there, the need is there. Have no question in your mind about this. The universe is comprised of no superfluous elements. What you feel called to is needed.

To be an example life is to be what you represent in truth. Followers of all faiths are called to example lives and to representation of the same truth. All faith is faith in the unknown through knowing, as a glimpse of fleeting light in darkness provides for a knowing of light. Those who accept completion of the way of Jesus accept their power to be generators of light in darkness without judging or expelling darkness. They accept their power to represent both the known and the unknown and to reveal the unknown through the known. They accept the death of the self and the resurrection of the One Self, the end of the individual and the individuation of the One Self amongst the many. They find renewed pleasure in being who they are because they have been renewed through resurrection. They follow the calling of their hearts without attachment to previous concerns, for in their renewal they fully realize the necessity of what can be given only through expression of what is within them. They realize that what is needed now is needed in order to renew or resurrect the world and all who abide within it.

Resurrection lays aside death's claim and with it the claim of all that is temporary. This is why we have spent time on the idea of sickness and other unwanted states as temporary manifestations. Your separated state *was* a sickness, an unwanted state, and thus a temporary manifestation. The joining of mind and heart provided reunion of the human and divine and thus accomplished the resurrection of the eternal in form. Your virgin state, the state unaltered by the separation, has been returned.

The truth represented by Jesus and Mary was represented as a visual pattern that would aide understanding of the invisible. This is what you are now called to do. Whether you demonstrate the myth of duality or the truth of union, you are demonstrating the same thing. The *way* in which you do this must be chosen, and for this choice to be made with full consciousness, you must rely on your feelings.

Feelings are your awareness of the present and thus of the truth. They are your means of coming to know. They arise from Christ-consciousness. They come not as reactions but as creations. Often science and religion have puzzled over the "beginning" of life, over what *causes* the formation of life, over what tells the brain what to do, over the organizing factor of DNA, of tissues and cells that do know exactly how to interact. Where does this knowing come from? When something appears to go wrong, what is the source of the malfunction?

You have been told that although you believed yourself to be separate this separation never actually occurred and that you have always been the accomplished. If this had not been true, the *cause* nor heart alone provide for a functioning body, mind and heart in separation could not truly exist and allow for a functioning state of life or consciousness. Thus there was only a degree of separation that was able to occur to allow for a certain type of experience. Now a new degree of union is occurring to allow for a new type of experience.

The new visual pattern is that of spirit resurrected in form. It is the ascension of the body, or elevation of the self of form. You are called to demonstrate this pattern. The choice is to demonstrate this pattern through interaction with the world, or through incarnation through relationship. Neither is exclusive. Both are contained within the other. But the way of discovery and demonstration is different.

You are called to demonstrate this new visual pattern. What is meant here by the word *demonstrate,* is to show your feelings, to make them visible. They are the creations unique to you through your interaction with the Christ-consciousness that abides within you. One *way* of doing this is through individuation and becoming known. One *way* of doing this is incarnation through relationship in which the relationship, rather than the individuated self, becomes the known. Both ways are ways of creation. When feelings are shown, or made visible, the new is created. This has always been the way of creation. Each blade of grass, each flower, each stone, is a creation of feelings. All you need do is look about you to know that feelings of love still abound. Beauty still reigns.

Both the Self and the relationship of Self to all must become known in order for the paradise that has been re-found to be recreated for everyone. What else would life be for but to make the invisible paradise of love visible and livable for all?

231

The Forty Days and Forty Nights

Day 19: the Way of Mary

Those of you who are the forerunners of the way of Mary may have felt confusion over your sense of calling. You know you are called to something, and something important, but it does not have a form within your mind and so you see not how it can become manifest in the world. In other words, you know not what to do. You perhaps see no "specific" accomplishment in your future, but see instead a way of living as the ultimate accomplishment. You see living as who you are in the world as the accomplishment that is needed from you, and yet, at times you compare yourself to those who are able to live as who they are in the world *and* accomplish certain functions. You perhaps feel function-less and purposeless at times, while at other times, you feel as if you are being exactly as you are meant to be.

The key here is discernment between true contentment and denial. Although this is overly simplified, you might think of this as the artist being content in creating art, the musician in creating music, the healer in creating health. Those of the way of Mary are content with a way of living. Yet everyone has a function to fulfill in creation of the new world. Only those who express themselves are truly content.

You can see right away that if the artist, musician, or healer were content *only* in their expression of their specific gifts, their contentment would not be complete. Neither would it be complete without that expression.

Being content is being fulfilled by the *way* in which you express who you are — by the way you express your content — your wholeness. Those who use their gifts to create the truth they see

232

are those who in "doing" find their way to true contentment and true creation. They become who they are to be through their acts of creation. Those called to the way of Mary are called to be what they want to see reflected in the world and to the realization that this reflection is the new way of creation. In their being they become what they want to create.

The ultimate accomplishment *is* living as who you are within the world. But in what kind of world? This is the catch that causes feelings of purposelessness in those who are content to live as who they are within the world. Until they realize the power of reflection, they wonder why they, unlike their brothers and sisters called to "do," do not have a specific part to play in establishing the world in which all are able to be content with who they are.

The answer lies in the simple statement of *as within, so without.* By living as who you are in the world, you create change in the world. You create change in the world through relationship. All live and create in relationship. Those called to the way of Mary, however, are called to the creation and anchoring of the new relationship in the new world. Their relationship of union, upon which their contentment is based, is the birthplace, the womb of the new. Their *expression* is expression of this union.

To be called to a specific function that creates change is really to be called to a function of preparing one or many for the change that must occur within. The function of those called to the way of Jesus is to call others to the new through means so widespread, varied, and remarkable that they cannot be ignored.

Just as Jesus would not have been literally birthed without Mary, the way of Mary cannot be reborn without the way of Jesus. Both ways arose from Christ-consciousness as demonstrations of ways. Those who have thought of Mary as an intermediary are as inaccurate in this belief as are those who thought of Jesus in such a way. Neither demonstrated intermediary functions but demonstrated direct union with God. Each demonstrated the

233

creative aspect of that function in different ways. But the *function* remained one of direct union with God. This is quite literally the function of all in this new time. When we speak of functions unique to each, we speak of expressions of this one ultimate function. Together, the way of Mary and the way of Jesus demonstrate the truth of *as within, so without* and the *relationship* between the inner and outer world.

The way of Mary is not a place or state of non-interaction. This is not the state or place of the monks, nuns, or the contemplatives of old. It is not solitary nor isolated, nor confined to a specific community. It is a way of existence in which relationship is paramount. It is not listening to a calling to "do" but a calling to "become."

All are called to become, but some must "do" in order to "become." Those called to the way of Mary are not required to do in the sense of fulfilling a specific function that will become manifest in the world, but are required to do in the sense of receiving, sharing, and being what they are asked to become. This is an act of incarnation, and is a new pattern, a pattern of what can be imagined being made real, not through doing, but through the creative act of incarnating in union with spirit. It corresponds with the end of the way of Jesus in that the way of incarnation is the way of miracles. It corresponds with the end of the way of Jesus in that an example is provided. It differs only in that the example is not an example of an individuated life but an example of the union and relationship that is all life.

This is not to say that those called to the way of Jesus will find acclaim and those called to the way of Mary will find obscurity. Many called to the way of Mary will "do" much that is greatly desired in the world but what they do will be a byproduct of their way of being rather than a means of facilitating that way of being. Many of the way of Mary will find acclaim, yet neither acclaim nor obscurity will matter to those following these ways. Being true to the self and the calling of the One Self is all that matters. Eventually all will follow the way of Mary and such ideas as acclaim and obscurity will be no more. But at this time of transition, both ways are needed to demonstrate the means of coming to know, which are what all true expression is about.

The fear of losing the self is still the primary fear, even among those who have never found the self. They fear losing the known to the unknown. The two ways of demonstration make the unknown known. One makes the unknown known through individuated example lives. One makes the unknown known through creation of the new so that the unknown is no longer unknown but made available to be experienced.

This availability is what is meant by the anchoring of the new. Those who, in relationship with the unknown, through unity and imagination, create the new by means other than doing, open a way previously unknown, and as all forerunners do, anchor that way within consciousness by holding open this door to creation. They, in truth, create a new pattern and begin to weave it into the web of reality, anchoring it for discovery by their brothers and sisters.

The truth of this way is not discovered through the passing on of knowledge in form but through relationship. Those following the way of Mary become mirrors of the truth they discover, reflecting the way to their brothers and sisters. This is why this is not a place or state of non-interaction but of great interaction. It is a state that facilitates knowing through relationship. This occurs through the one Self of form.

In this action of joining in union and relationship is contained the key to creation of the new. It was spoken of earlier as the act of informing and being informed, as the step beyond that of observing and being observed. It is where creation of the new can begin because it is the intent of creation, rather than the intent of the observer, that is the creative force, the animator and informer. Being joined in union and relationship allows for the channeling of creation through the one Self because the one Self is joined in union and relationship.

This is very tricky for those who reach highly individuated states and it is necessary for those of the way of Mary to support, encourage, and reflect the new to those being examples of the way of Jesus. This too is tricky for it can lead to judgment. When there is more than one way, there is always room for comparison and judgment. Thus it is realistic to see the two ways as intertwined circles existing in support and harmony with one another. As those given specific functions fulfill those functions, they move naturally to the way of Mary.

Without those pursuing the way of Jesus, those pursuing the way of Mary would have a much more difficult task. There would be little space in which to anchor the new. Those following the way of Jesus create the openness of the spacious Selves who allow for the anchors of the new to be cast and thus to ride out the many storms of this time of transition.

The Forty Days and Forty Nights

Day 20: the First Transition

Now we begin preparation for your transition to level ground. We depart even farther now from the guidance you have relied upon so that you begin to rely more and more fully on the truth of this dialogue.

You have realized now your relationship with the unknown and ceased to fear it. You are, perhaps, even eager now, to move beyond the known to the unknown. You are perhaps eager without fully realizing that this eagerness symbolizes a true ending — an ending within you and within your reality — an ending within your conscious awareness. A true end of learning.

This is the first transition, the transition in which you really "get it" that the unknown cannot be taught, laid out on a map, or shown to you by another.

When you read what has been written here, you perhaps think this is a contradiction, for surely you have been told much here that you did not previously know. What has happened here is that words have been put on the feelings and remembrances that you have within your minds and hearts and have been sharing in this dialogue. The way of saying this perhaps is new, but the *way* of saying this is the expression of the human being receiving it. The way in which you are hearing and responding to these truths is perhaps new, but that way too is of the human being receiving it, in this case, you.

The truth is the truth. It doesn't change. It is the same for everyone.

What, then, is the unknown? The reception and expression of truth.

This is why you can "know" while always coming to know. Why you can know yourself and constantly be coming to know. The only thing there is to know is the One Self in its many expressions. You are the known and the unknown. Everything is both the known and the unknown.

You *are* the expression of the unknown and the *only* means of the unknown becoming known.

All the truth and all the wisdom that is available but un*known* to you, takes *you* to make it known. And if this is the only way that the beauty, truth, and wisdom of the One Self can be made known, then *you* are the source and the power of coming to know and making known.

Apply the art of thought to this idea and you will complete the first transition.

The Forty Days and Forty Nights

Day 21: the Reversal

The first transition, as you have probably already realized, is about a letting go of any of the ideas that you may still have that an outside source exists. There is no such thing as an outside source. There are no outside sources of wisdom, guidance, or even information.

This was true even within the pattern of learning you have been so familiar with, for in order to learn, the source of wisdom, even though you may have seen it as existing outside of yourself, had to function as what it was — a channel through which the wisdom, guidance or information moved. If it did not do so, learning did not occur. In traditional learning patterns, the wisdom, guidance, or information sought, moved from a teacher — whether that teacher was an actual teacher, or a parent or a friend — to a student, or in other words, from a giver to a receiver.

Nothing was capable of being taught or learned without the reception of what the giver gave. The giver could make available but could not really teach, guide, or even make information coherent without the action of the receiver. Thus it has always been the action of the receiver that made learning possible. The receiver was thus also the source because the receiver had to accept or "give" what was offered, to herself.

The channel is the means, not the source. The source is oneness or union, a state you now realize that you share and have access to.

What you allow yourself to receive and what you do with what you receive is all that matters.

You realize now that life itself is a channel and that you are constantly receiving. You may still think of receiving as meaning that something is given from a source beyond the self, but this is the "thought" that has to change. If giving and receiving are one, then giver and receiver are also one. It is only you who can do anything with the wisdom, guidance, or information that you receive in union as a channel of the divine life force that exists in everything and everyone. There is nothing channeled to one that isn't channeled to all. The old notions of teaching and learning but made it seem as if some had more and others less. But even the pattern of learning had as its outcome the sameness of teacher and learner — the transfer of knowledge that would eventually make teacher and learner equal. Means and end have always been the same.

There is no longer an "eventually." Teacher and learner are equal and thus neither are needed any longer. The "transfer" of knowledge is now an act of giving and receiving as one. No intermediary is needed when you exist in union. It is recognized that the knowledge, wisdom, guidance, or information that is needed each moment is available within each moment and that the interaction, rather than being one of taking something from an outside source into the self where it is learned and then regurgitated or even applied, has given way to an interaction that begins within and extends outward.

This will seem like an incredible reversal and thus it is. This is the reversal that will make of you a creator. But it can only happen if you make the first transition.

You began your mountain top experience with a companion who had offered himself as a teacher in order to bring you to the place of being willing to accept that a teacher was not needed. He joined you on the mountain top in order to prepare you for his departure, a departure from reliance upon him that would allow you to arrive at reliance upon yourself. This reliance upon yourself has been expressed as a dialogue taking place within Christ-consciousness, the consciousness you share in union and relationship with all. You have now been told to own this dialogue and to realize that its wisdom is your own. Are you accepting this? Are you beginning to ready yourself to hear this voice as your own? To express the voice of Christ-consciousness as only you can express it?

Realize that this is the aim of our final time together. Concentrate on making the first transition and on the reversal of thought that it requires. Thus will you carry this time forward with you into creation of the new.

The Forty Days and Forty Nights

Day 22: Channeling

If we have spoken little of channeling here, it is only because you have been coming to know yourself as channels without the need for these words. Now we must speak of this, however, for there is a confusion that can occur in regards to channeling. Yesterday we spoke of teachers being channels during the time of learning. It was also noted that you realize that all of life is a channel. There is a big difference between seeing a teacher as a channel, all of life as a channel, and the Self as a channel or channeler.

Let's look at the idea of channeling as simply an idea of expressing, but an idea of expression that is given and received, received and given. When the word channeling has been used in reference to spirituality, it has often been used to indicate an intermediary function. The channeler was perhaps seen as a mediator between the living and the dead or the world of spirit and the world of humanity. This idea separated the living and the dead, the spiritual and the human into two states — states that could, at their most basic levels — be seen as known and unknown states. The teacher in the example used was also an intermediary with the separation being between the known and the unknown. Thus, a channel could be seen as that through which the unknown moves into the state of knowing. This is the way in which life itself can be seen as a channel. Since the first transition involves realizing that *you* are the expression of the unknown and the *only* means of the unknown becoming known, it is important to discuss this in as many ways as possible to make this idea clear to you. You are life, and you are also surrounded by living forces channeling to you constantly.

Channeling, in the commonly understood spiritual sense, can either promote a sense of separation or a sense of unity. The sense of separation comes when the channeler is seen as having something unavailable to everyone rather than being seen as a means to provide, or channel, availability to everyone. What each person channels is unique and only available through their expression. The availability is there for everyone. The means of expression is there for everyone. What is expressed is different because it is a combination of the universal (what is available) with the individual (what is expressed). Whether one chooses to avail oneself of the channeled or expressed universality of another is a choice and another indicator of the uniqueness of channeling. The universal is everything. The channel is what, from among everything, is allowed reception and expression. Some will find many avenues of channeling available to them, both through themselves and through spiritual channels, without realizing that both are the same because both require a choice, a choice to allow entry or union. In this choice, the universe (what is available) is channeled through the expression of (the individual) desires.

Every choice is thus a means of channeling. It is taking the infinite number of experiences or information available and channeling only what one desires to know. Thus, it is prudent to repeat once again, that *you* are the expression of the unknown and the *only* means of the unknown becoming known. You are the channel, the conduit, of the unknown becoming known. What you choose to know and how you choose to know it is an act of channeling.

There is also the idea of a channel as a passage to take into consideration. This we have spoken of previously as your access to union — as a place or state of consciousness through which your awareness of unity passes through your self of form. It is clear, when looked at in terms of process, that there is no intermediary function involved in channeling, but a function of union. This is the very function that you have waited to have

243

revealed to you, the function you have known you are here to fulfill, the function of direct union with God.

It does not matter that everyone's function is the same because no one expression of this same function produces the same results. No one who is in union with God is in union with the known. Yet it is as if through this union, you have learned a great secret that you long to share. What is it? How do you share it? How do you convey it? How do you channel it? Through what means can you express it? Can you put it into words, make it into images, tell it in a story? You will feel as if you will burst if you cannot share the union that you touch when you fulfill your function of direct union with God. How do you let it pass through you to the world?

The most simple, direct, and uncomplicated answer is that of living love. The simple answer is that you must express the unknown that you have touched, experienced, sensed, or felt with such intimacy that it is known to you *because* the knowing becomes real in the making known. It is the only way it remains real. You know union in order to sustain and create union by channeling the unknown reality of union into the known reality of separation. You realize that you know the unknown and you desire to make the unknown knowable. You realize that you have known a place where nothing but love exists, where there is no suffering, no death, no pain nor sorrow, no separation or alienation. You sense that if you could fully express this place of union, if you could abide there, if you could share this place in an aware and conscious state, that you would bring this state into existence in the reality in which you exist.

This awareness of union with God is what is now within you awaiting your expression. Awareness of union with God exists in everything. It is there in every tree and every flower, in every mountain stream and every blowing wind. It is there in each and every human being. It is now time to quit acting as if it is not. It is time to be a channel for the awareness that exists in every tree and every flower, in each mountain stream and in the blowing wind. It is time to be a channel for the awareness of union with God that exists in every living being.

This awareness is what we have been calling Christ-consciousness, but what you call it now matters not. All the words that have been expressed here, that say so many similar things in so many different ways, are words that are simply calling you to realization of your union with God and to the new world you can create once you accept and make real this union.

You might think of yourself as a channel through which union with God is expressed and made real here and now. There is no other time. There is no "higher" self waiting to do what only you can do. There is no one else who knows what you know the way you know it or who can express the unknown in the way that you can express it. The unknown can only be made known through reception and expression. Call it what you will for what you call it matters not. Throw out all the words that express the unknown in ways that you would not, and find your own. Each way is needed.

Remember only the feeling that a place of union exists in which you know God, in which you know love, in which you know of joy without sorrow, and life everlasting. This is the great unknown that you can make known.

The Forty Days and Forty Nights

Day 23: Carrying

Forget not that who you are is what you are here to make known and that thus, you must be a being who knows love without fear, joy without sorrow, and life everlasting. You must *be* this. *A Course of Love* gave you the understanding you needed in order to realize that you *are* this. The treatises gave you a way to apply this understanding. This dialogue is meant to give you the means to carry what you have been given.

As air carries sound, as a stream carries water, as a pregnant woman carries her child, this is how you are meant to carry what you have been given. What you have been given is meant to accompany you, propel you, and be supported by you. You are not separate from what you have been given, and you *do* carry what you have received within you.

As we spoke earlier of being a channel, today we speak of being a carrier. Your instruction has been given. Now the task before us is to come to an understanding of the means by which you will carry what you have been given down from the mountain and onto level ground, the ground of the earth, the place where you are connected and interconnected to all that lives and breathes along with you. We are coming metaphorically and literally out of the clouds, out of the illusion, surrendering the mist that was all that separated one world from another.

The clouds of illusion, even those that have gently surrounded our time together on the mountain top must now be surrendered, much as a woman surrenders her body to the growth of a child within. This is a willing but not an active surrender. It is a surrender to the forces that move inside of you. It is a knowing surrender to the unknown. It is a willingness to carry the unknown into the known and the known to the unknown.

Surrendering to the forces that move inside of you is surrendering to your own will. It requires full acknowledgment that you hold

within yourself a will to know and to make known. This will is divine will, your will, Christ-consciousness. It is alive within you. All that is required is that you carry it with awareness, honor, willingness. From this will the new be birthed.

The Forty Days and Forty Nights

Day 24: Potential

You are the caterpillar, the cocoon, and the butterfly. This is the way that you are many Selves as well as one Self. You are a Self with many forms. The form you occupy contains all of your potential manifestations just as the form of the caterpillar contains all of its potential manifestations.

You are the virgin, the pregnant, the birth, and the new life. This is the way of the world as well as the way of creation. What is unaltered remains unaltered despite its many manifestations. Wholeness exists in every cell, in each of every smallest particle of existence. Wholeness exists in you. Nothing can take wholeness from you. It is as natural to you as it is to all of creation. It does not exist only once potential is realized or made manifest, but always in all things.

Potential is that which exists. It exists as the power and energy, the spirit within you. It does not await. It simply is. It can remain as the untapped power of transformation, or it can be released. The choice is and is not yours. This power is a force of nature that exists, not separately from you, but not separately from nature either. It is triggered in any number of ways, only one of which is by your choice. When it was said that *A Course of Love* was a trigger, it was meant that the Course is both a trigger of choice and a trigger of nature. It was meant to convey the action of a catalyst. Now it is up to you whether you allow your true nature to be revealed.

To struggle against your nature is what you have spent a lifetime doing. Stop. If you allow your potential to be released, your true nature in all its wholeness will be revealed.

You might think of the caterpillar as the unaltered self with which you began your journey. You might think of your body as the cocoon, the carrier of your potential. You might think of the butterfly as your spirit, revealed only after the potential has matured and been released. There is a necessity for each step in the accomplishment of wholeness, even while wholeness has always existed as potential. Do not forget that wholeness has always existed, that potential is that which exists, or that potential does not await.

To attempt to remain within the cocoon of the body, to attempt to contain the spirit within that cocoon, is to attempt the impossible. It is the nature of spirit to become. Its wings poke and prod from within as its potential is triggered. Only with release from its container can it be what it has become.

The caterpillar, the cocoon, and the butterfly have always been one and remain one. Each form is but a different stage in the becoming of the spirit. Without release, the present form must die in order to begin again.

Will activates potential. It is the greatest of all triggers. An activated will realizes that you are the carrier of all the potential that exists. An activated will releases the power that is potential. Remember potential is that which exists, that which is. It is not that which is not, not that which is in the future, not that which could come to be, but that which is.

Potential is what you carry, as air carries sound, a stream water, a pregnant women her child. You carry your potential to the place of its birth through an activated will, a will that is also carried within you. This merging of will and potential is the birth of your power and the birth of the new.

249

The Forty Days and Forty Nights

Day 25: Tending Your Garden

Emptiness of mind will now be something that may seem to plague many of you. Where once the mind was searching, yearning, questioning, now it is likely to become still. From the stillness comes its emergence as what it is.

As stillness envelopes you, there is a part of you that will fight back. If there is nothing new to record, nothing new to learn, no new divine inspiration, a part of your mind will attempt to create from this nothingness. Allow this to happen. Allow the stillness when you can. Allow the mind to fight back when you cannot. Resist nothing.

You are not what you once were. You need not guard against an over-zealous ego-mind. Your ideas in this time may sound crazy, even to your own ears. Let them come. Your feelings may be confused in one moment, crystal clear in the next. Let them all come. Your thoughts will slip from the sublime to the mundane. Let them come.

You need not, in this time, seek either questions or answers. You need rather, in this time, to come into the practice of letting the new come. It is in the new pattern of stillness combined with non-resistance that the new will come.

Rather than a time of questions and answers, you might think of this time as a time of sorting and culling. Become used to letting what comes to you come to you without judgment. Let it come.

Enjoy your silly thoughts as much as your wise thoughts. Let go your resistance to thoughts that seem of the old pattern. That you know they are of the old pattern is enough. Let them come. Let them go.

When feeling reflective, sort and cull. Do not do this with an attitude of looking for something. What has come has already come. It does not require seeking. Be a gardener in such times. Separate the harvest from the weeds. Do this as much by rote as you would weed a garden, recognizing that you know the harvest from the weeds. Think of yourself as stockpiling this harvest. It is not yet time for the harvest celebration. It is, rather, a time for gathering.

This is a time of preparation, not a time of waiting. What you need to know now cannot be gathered except by your own hands. It cannot be sorted except by your own will. I remind you not to attempt this as a task to which you apply the mind or the question of *What am I looking for?* You are looking for nothing. You are tending your garden.

The Forty Days and Forty Nights

Day 26: Self-Guidance

It has been said that *you* are the source and the power of coming to know and making known. It naturally follows, then, that you are capable of self-guidance.

Let us talk a moment of the concept of guidance. When you have sought guidance, you have sought because you have not known. You have sought externally because you have not known of a source of internal guidance. You have been guided by teachers, counselors, and leaders of all kinds, through words spoken and read, through dialogue, through example. If you had known, you would not have sought guidance. Thus your idea of guidance is likely to hinge upon this concept of the unknown.

Now let's speak a moment of the Self as guide. This simply means that you turn to the Self as the source of coming to know of the unknown.

A guide shows the way, creates movement, gives direction. These things too the Self can do if allowed to do so. The Self *will* guide you if you will allow it. Your Self will lead you down from the mountain top and through the valleys of level ground. There is no other guide. We are One Self.

You *can* trust in your Self. Will you? By tending your garden you will develop this trust and prepare for your descent to level ground.

Your self-guidance can be thought of as an internal compass. It will not necessarily know the answers as each answer is sought, but if paid attention to, it will show you the way to knowing.

This alchemical transition, this passing of the unknown into the known, this moment when the unknown becomes the known *within the Self,* is the birth of creation. It is the culmination of all that has come before, the All of Everything realized in a single heartbeat, a single instant of knowing. This is the One Self knowing itself. This is not knowing that comes with a great ah ha, but knowing that comes with the awe of reverence. Creator and created are one and the homecoming experienced is that of union.

Self-guidance is the propulsion, the fuel, for the One Self to know itself. You are ready to be so known.

The Forty Days and Forty Nights

Day 27: the Apprehension of Levels of Experience

Think now not of being apprehensive in terms of being fearful of the rest of your life, but apprehensive in terms of taking hold of the rest of your life, of keeping it within your understanding, within your ability to come to know, within your own grasp of it. You have been asked to let go of much, but not of life.

You have been asked to let go of uncertainty, not certainty. You have been assured of a certainty you never before believed you were capable of. This certainty is beginning to form within you but will not come into its fullness except through experience. This certainty has only been able to begin to form within you because you have agreed to this mountain top experience while remaining engaged in life. You have thus begun to experience on two levels. This has been a goal of the time we have spent together in this way.

Experiencing life without the insight of spirit was to experience external life. Life itself showed you the way, pointed you in differing directions, taught you what you needed to know. This was the external experience of life. Most of you have had well-examined external lives. You have looked for causes behind the direction in which life led you, but your life was not inner-directed because it was devoid of inner-sight. While you looked outwardly for signposts to guide you, the self-guidance of inner-sight was not developed.

Inner-sight made an appearance on occasion, showing up as flashes of insight. These flashes of insight might be thought of as brief views from the mountain. The obstacles confronted on level ground suddenly gave way and you saw clearly, if only for an instant. You saw as if from a great distance, and because of that great distance, your view was expanded.

This is the quality of the inner-sight you now will carry with you to level ground because you have practiced during our mountain top time together the ability to *experience* on two levels.

Coming to know is not an aspect of the mind alone. It is not an aspect of the spirit alone. Coming to know is a quality of inner-sight, of wholehearted human experience combined with spiritual experience. You contain within you the ability to combine both levels of being through the experience of life. You have already been doing this. You are, in fact, becoming well-practiced.

Now you are asked to apprehend — to understand, and to hold within your conscious mind — this situation that you find yourself in, this new relationship that you have with yourself and with life. You quite literally have a new way of seeing. You might think of this initially as having two perspectives, an internal and an external perspective, a human perspective and a spiritual perspective, a perspective from level ground and a mountain top perspective. Your descent from the mountain top will not mean that you no longer have the perspective gained there. You did not "go" to the mountain. The mountain came to you.

As you continue to practice your apprehension of this new situation, it will become more than a concept. As was spoken of in *A Treatise on the Nature of Unity and Its Recognition,* it will become a trusted ability and, through practice, lose its dualistic seeming nature and become as intrinsic to who you are as is breathing. In this same way, the dualistic seeming nature of all of life will be revealed to only seem to be so.

The two levels of experience which you have been participating in are the joint cornerstones for the biggest revelations yet. All that is now seen as dualistic in nature can be experienced as different levels of experience of one whole. You might consider this by again picturing the mountain-top. Looking in one direction, you might see only darkness. Looking in another, you might see the dawning of light. Opposites exist only as different aspects of one whole. Different aspects exist only as different levels of experience.

To be able to hold onto, apprehend, and carry with you the ability to experience both levels of experience, the internal and the external, the form and the content, the human and the divine, is to elevate the self of form — to be what you have always been: Whole.

As darkness and light, hot and cold, sickness and health are each just opposite ends of the same continuum, you can now see that they are only distinguished by degrees of separation. So too have you been.

The degree of your separation from wholeness can be seen much as the degree of separation between hot and cold. If you were to perceive of wholeness as an ideal temperature, you might think for a moment, just as an illustration, of your experience of separation always taking place at a certain number of degrees away from the ideal. The "temperature" was thus never perfect, but rather always either too hot or too cold. Yet the perfect temperature always existed, you just did not experience it. You were separate from it because of the degree of separation that you chose. Because you never chose union, or wholeness, you did not experience lack of body temperature or the effects of weather, but it is as if you denied your body the ideal 98.6 degrees internally and 78 degrees externally. There is no living body that does not exhibit a temperature, no environment that does not do so. Some kind of temperature is thus a constant. A constant is an aspect of wholeness. A variable is an aspect of separation. The constant does not become variable because variability exists.

That you are who you are and that you have always been the accomplished is a constant and an aspect of wholeness. The variability of how you experience who you are is also a constant within the aspect of separation. Merge the two into one level of experience and the whole formula changes.

This is what we move toward as we practice participating in two levels of experience simultaneously. We practice experiencing the constant and the variable as one. We practice experiencing the constant and the variable together. We practice in order to move toward an experience of variability within wholeness rather than within separation. It can be done.

Life, your humanity, is the variability. Spirit, your oneness, is the constant. Life is oneness extended into separation and variability through experience. The elevated Self of form will be the expression of new life lived within the constant of wholeness but continuing to experience the variability of separation. This is what you practice as you gather on the mountain top while remaining on level ground.

Separation, as well as the variability of the experience of the separate self, have always been variables that exist within the constant of wholeness. What you have experienced, however, has not been wholeness or the experience of wholeness, but the experience of separation. What we are speaking of now is being able to experience wholeness *and* the variability of experience that has come through the separated self of form. This is what you are beginning to do through your practice. Your proficiency will change your experience, and your experience will change the world.

The Forty Days and Forty Nights

Day 28: From Externally to Internally Directed Life Experience

At one time there seemed to be little or no choice between staying engaged in an externally directed life and removing oneself from life. This may have seemed to be an either/or proposition and thus one of limitation. Moving from an externally directed to an internally directed experience of life creates unlimited choices. The unlimited choices of internally directed experience are what you must begin to face as we begin our descent from the mountain top. To wait until level ground is reached to begin to view the choices available would be to put off coming to know the difference between externally and internally directed life experiences.

Most of you have experienced several stages of awareness, and we will speak here of those experienced during the years of what is called adulthood, coming of age, or the age of reason. These have been discussed before so this will be kept brief and illustrate only what is needed for our discussion of the next stage.

The first stage of awareness is a stage of simple external movement through life. Many people, especially young adults, have little experience other than this. Their lives are directed almost totally by external forces, from parents, to mandatory schooling, to somewhat voluntary schooling.

As the time of schooling is left behind, the next stage of movement begins, that of external movement toward independence. With this movement, the number of choices increase and the level of awareness increases with the increase in choices available. As young people do not usually move away from the home of their parents until they are at least college age, the opportunity to move away, move out, become more independent increases the awareness of self as self. As the self matures beyond school age, the choices become those of degrees of independence, moving away, moving into one's own sphere of friends, colleagues, relationships. For some these choices include commitments to partnerships of a personal or professional nature. For some these choices include marriage and starting a family. Some follow a more standard pattern than others, with schooling, career, marriage, and family seen as an almost inescapable as well as desirable norm. Others pursue dreams or adventures.

All of these choices are externally directed. They may include a great deal of inner reflection in order to be made, but they are still *directed* at external outcome. By living the experiences of these externally directed life situations, growth occurs, changes happen, new avenues to explore at times open up, leading to the next level of experience: That of external movement toward a chosen type of life.

At this level, some people reach a crossroad and choices that will move their lives in two such different directions that to choose is both exciting and at times excruciatingly difficult. Others reach a plateau of sorts and just keep following the opportunities that are presented along one path. They may have chosen one career, for instance, and made choices within that career path, but never considered a different career path. Many simply reach a state of reasonable comfort and will make no choices that will affect that comfort level.

All of these stages may be associated or accompanied by religious or spiritual experiences that seem to help guide the choices, but the choices remain the same: Externally directed choices.

259

Now something new awaits you. It is a choice so different and a means so revolutionary that it will take some getting used to. This change is predicated on all the changes that have come before it, including, and most particularly, on that which was most recently spoken of, that of apprehending the new reality of wholeness. It is not wholeness that is new, but the reality of wholeness that is new. The reality of being able to experience the variability of separation from within the state of wholeness is what is new.

This must be kept foremost in your mind. The reversal spoken of recently, the reversal from believing in a giver and a receiver to knowing that giver and receiver are one, is also of paramount importance.

You and your life are one. Your life is not the giver and you the receiver.

You and God are one. God is not the giver and you the receiver. This is wholeness.

Depending on the circumstances of your life, one of these two attitudes will have a reverse side that will have a greater hold on you. Your life may have shown you that you are not in control in many ways and at many times. Therefore, you think that you must take what life has to "give." This is most likely the attitude of those whose major life dilemmas have been of a monetary or career nature, where success or failure "in life" is seen as the most crucial element of a happy life.

If the attitude you will have greater need of reversing is that of God determining the circumstances of your life, you have probably been more affected by the relationships of life, by loss or death of loved ones, by accidents, or illness, or "natural" disasters, by the unexplainable forces that have affected you with sadness more so than with ideas of success or failure. Therefore, you think that you must take what God has to "give."

Most people feel at least some combination of these two attitudes, but will find that one is prevalent. You must now get past all such notions or attitudes.

Acceptance has been a main theme of this dialogue and was revisited and defined as acceptance of internal rather external conditions. It makes no sense to accept what is not the truth. Most of what is not the truth has been identified as old thought patterns. This is all that the notion of a giver and a receiver is: An old thought pattern.

Thought patterns exist within thought systems that have been externalized and are part of the world on level ground. These external systems are based, as are all that you have made, on the externalization of what is within. At the same time, what is within has been based upon what was previously externalized. This is what now must change, and as can be seen, this change is essential to changing the world.

This change, this transformation, can only take place within time because only within time is the experience of separation possible. Experience is where the power of transformation lies. This transformation will take you beyond time, because once experience is moved out of the realm of separation and into the realm of union or wholeness, new conditions will apply. This is why it has been said that the changes that are to come are not about time-bound evolution. Only this first change, this first transformation, must take place in time.

This is the change, the transformation, we have been working on by changing your experience of time to one of experiencing two levels of time. Our time on the mountain would be more rightly described as "time outside of time."

Time outside of time by itself will not cause the shift that needs to occur. What will create the shift is the ability to experience "time outside of time" and "time" simultaneously. Thus is the "wholeness" of time, or eternity, experienced and made real. Eternity might thus be seen as the unchanging constant that has not been affected by the variable of time. Said in another way, eternity and time are part of the same continuum as are properties such as hot and cold. They are part of the same whole that is the constant of all that is whole...all that is one.

So too are giving and receiving and giver and receiver.

To move to internally directed experience is to make the move into wholeness that will cause the "shift of the ages," the experience of variability within wholeness.

The key to this movement is the simple realization that it is possible. This is what our time on the mountain has provided you with: The experience required in order to realize a new possibility.

As you move toward wholeness, all the pieces of all that we have talked about will begin to fit together. A whole will form within your mind much as if you have been following a thread and now can see the tapestry. This tapestry will bear the mark of your experiences and will be like no other. The thread represents your own journey to truth, your own journey to wholeness.

Separation is desired no longer, but experience is. Your will and God's are one and thus it is being made so.

Presently it is as if you follow two threads, the thread that has led you to the mountain and the thread of the life you have not removed yourself from. Now you must begin to weave these two threads together into the tapestry of your new life. This weaving will take place as you continue to intertwine the two experiences that you are simultaneously holding within your conscious awareness.

This is what we will continue to speak of as we conclude this dialogue.

The Forty Days and Forty Nights

Day 29: the Common Denominator of Experience

This is where we begin to really lose sight of concepts of duality — where they cease to be real for us. Wholeness and separation, God and man, life and the individuated self, what you do and who you are, the eternal and the temporal, joy and sadness, sickness and health, all cease to have the limited power that all such concepts have formerly held. When they cease to be held as separate concepts in your mind, they cease to be separate. Remember that you have already realized the ability to participate in two levels of experience simultaneously and that duality is really just a matter of different levels of experience. If you can be having the experience of the mountain top and the experience of level ground simultaneously, then you can also have the experience of all other "opposites" in this same, simultaneous way. If you can integrate all that opposes wholeness into one level of experience, you will be able to experience life from within the reality of wholeness rather than from within the reality of separation.

Your self will no longer be divided into a spirit Self and a human self, living under different conditions, at times complimenting and at times opposing one another. Just as mind and heart became one in wholeheartedness and ended the conflict induced by their seeming separation, the spirit and the human self must now do so.

Mind and heart joined as you let go of judgment and re-learned or remembered wholehearted desire — the source of your power.

Now this power is available to assist you in accomplishing the final joining, the joining that will end duality and return you to wholeness — to who you truly are — in the reality in which you exist.

This is no more complicated than ending the rift between mind and heart. You have accomplished that and you can accomplish this — in your reality. As you realize by now, all this talk of accomplishment is merely about bringing forward what already exists into the reality in which you exist. Another way of saying this is bringing who you are into wholeness, which can be interpreted both as bringing all that you are into existence and as bringing all that you are into existence in union.

Your access to union, so newly discovered and yet always existing within you, has been a part of the process that has allowed you access to two levels of experience. It *is* your access to two levels of experience — the experience of wholeness and the experience of separation. While you may have seen it as access to information or sensory experiences of another kind, it is, in actuality, access to a state of being.

Your familiarity with your spacious Self has also been part of the process and part of the experience of merging wholeness and separation. While you may have seen it as a new means of interaction, it has been, in actuality, access to a new state of being.

A new state of being is a new reality. It is linked with your notion of who and where you are, for who you are and where you find yourself and experience yourself, is your reality. This is why experience has needed to find a place in which it could become the common denominator between wholeness and separation. Once you experience yourself in wholeness and find yourself in union, you have made of *yourself* the common denominator upon which experience can find anchor in wholeness and union.

You are thus, as always, the creator of your reality.

264

The Forty Days and Forty Nights

Day 30: Yielding to Wholeness

What is held in common is shared and is a characteristic representation of the whole. Just as simple fractions can be added together to achieve wholeness once a common denominator is found, your own fractiousness can yield to wholeness through the common denominator of the self. A common denominator is simply that which yields to wholeness. This yielding is a natural process. To yield is to give up, surrender, but also to produce and bear fruit.

The two levels of experience we have spoken of might be seen as the process, much like in math, through which the common denominator is found. The common denominator is not by itself the whole, but is, in combination, the whole. In order for a common denominator to be found, more than one (fraction, part, or variable) must exist. The purpose of finding a common denominator is to translate what is more than one into one. An assumption of wholeness is "common" in every denominator.

A denominator is a named entity. To denominate is to name. "In the beginning" the separate expressions of the whole were named. This naming was an act of creation, stating simply the existence of what was named or denominated. Existence and wholeness are the same. Thus *your* existence, the existence of the self, is, or can be, a common denominator of wholeness. In our act of saying it is so, we name or denominate the Self as what is common to wholeness. Despite unlimited variations being available, commonality is also always available. Thus no matter how fractious are the separate selves, commonality and wholeness always exist and have always existed.

Wholeness cannot be achieved without joining, thus the commonly known injunction of "where two or more are joined together." If you would think of this in terms of "God" or the state of "Wholeness" or "Beingness" separating into more than one in order to know Itself, you would see that knower and known are one. You would see that two or more are needed in order for knowing to occur. To not know wholeness would be to be in a state of nothingness. Thus the joining of two or more are needed in order for wholeness to be known and to exist as a state of conscious awareness.

Now let us consider this in terms of experience. As knower and known are one, experience and experiencer are one. One must experience in order to know. It follows then that what is experienced is what is known. It also follows then, that to not experience joining is to not experience wholeness. Stated another way, the *self* cannot know the *Self* without *joining* with the Self. The Self must be the knower and the known, the experience and the experiencer. The quest to join with God is this quest: the quest to be the knower and the known, the experience and the experiencer. The culmination of this quest then, is joining.

The Forty Days and Forty Nights

Day 31: Joining

Joining is both about union and about relationship. Let us consider this by considering the two levels of experience — that of the mountain top experience — and that of the experience on level ground.

While you have been immersed in one level of experience you have been either knower or known. This is why experience has seemed to exist apart from you. You say, "I had this experience" or "I had that experience," as if you have "had" contact and interaction with circumstances or events that are separate from the self. In saying this, you express your realization of relationship but no realization of the unity in which relationship exists. You "know" the experience because you have "had" the experience. The truth that you *are* the experience escapes you.

What the mountain top experience is helping you to see is that you *are* the experience. The mountain top experience did not happen to you or happen separately from you. It has happened and is happening *within* you. You are the experience and the experiencer, the knower and the known. This joining is the point of the experience and the key to *experiencing* wholeness.

As has already been stated, wholeness could not be *experienced* without division. Wholeness and oneness are the same. You are one in being with your Father, your Creator, the originator and denominator of life.

To have experienced only separation is to have known only half of any experience, to have seen every experience in only one dimension — in short, to have seen experience as happening to you rather than as you. By realizing the unity of the relationship in which experience becomes manifest, you not only realize oneness but realize that you are a creator and that you always have been.

All experience is a product of knower and knowee. It is the One Self knowing itself as one individuated Self.

Joining is differentiated from union only by experience. Union is the realm of the One. Joining is where the realm of the One unites with the realm of the many. In each of the many is the One — the common denominator. By knowing the One in the many, experience can be achieved within wholeness.

The beginning of this knowing occurs within, with the knowing, or experiencing, of the One within the individuated Self. Notice the link here of knowing and experiencing. To know experience as the Self is to know the Self as creator — to know the One Self within the individuated Self. To know the One Self within the individuated Self is to join the two. The two are thus joined in the relationship of experience. Experience is not known separately from the Self. Self and God are one and experiencing together in wholeness. For the individuated Self to experience separately from God is to negate the purpose of the experience of the Self which is God. To negate is to deny what *is*. The denial of what *is* is the source of separation. The acceptance of what *is* is the source of union and the ability to experience in wholeness.

The Forty Days and Forty Nights

Day 32: the Experience of the Self and the Power of God

The experience of the Self is God. It is not from God. It is not of God. It *is* God.

If all of life is the oneness that is God and God has chosen to experience that oneness through relationship, then you are also that experience and are in relationship with God through that experience.

Here we must revisit the concepts of oneness and manyness for if you retain any notions of God that are inaccurate, they will arise here.

Let us discuss, for a moment, the concept of God because everyone has at least some sort of concept of God.

First we will look at the concept of God as Supreme Being — God as *one* being, *one* entity. When thought of in such a way, it is somewhat easier to relate to God than when God is thought of in broader terms. You might think of God as you think of yourself. When thinking of the ideas put forth here, you might think of God deciding to know Himself. You might think of God deciding to create. You might think of God creating. You might think of God granting free will to His creations. Then, perhaps, you might think of God resting, or standing back and witnessing the unfolding of all that He created.

What would the purpose of this be? Would God be standing back, judging Himself on the goodness of what He created? Thinking that He'd like to make adjustments here or there, perhaps, but no, He has already granted free will so He can't do that? If the original purpose was knowing Himself, what kind of knowing would this provide? Wouldn't this suggest a situation similar to a parent thinking he or she could know him- or herself through observation of the children they produced?

Another concept of God is that of Creator. This concept might have nothing to do with the notion of God wanting to know Himself.

This concept may be quite amorphous and not tremendously different than scientific notions of the source of life. Whether it be called God or the Big Bang or evolution, this notion presents the concept of something being begun and then turned loose, proceeding from its beginnings under scientific or natural laws.

Another idea of God within the concept of a Creator God is of God existing in all of what has been created. God is, within this concept, seen as the spirit within all that lives and also seen as an overriding spirit, a force, a unifying factor. God is closer, within this idea, to being a participatory being, but still falls short. Man lives and has free will. Animals abide by the laws of nature. God is still a concept.

Yet most religious beliefs encompass the concept of a living God. How might God live? Could He live in time and space in a dimension we know not? Does He live as the spirit within us, and as such have some small role, perhaps akin to that of what we refer to as our conscience? What kind of life would this be? A difficult to imagine life at the very least.

A *concept* of God is simply not necessary. False concepts of God, however, are compromising to God and to Self.

Jesus spoke to you of his life as an example life. Jesus was called the Son of God and also God. Those who understand the meaning of any or all of the example lives that have come as revelations of who God is, understand that those lives were not separate from God.

Yet to believe that God is everyone can still make you feel as if you are not God. How can this be? This can be only because in your contemplation of this idea, you lose your sense of self. There is a rebellion, a negation of either the self or God that occurs when these two concepts — concepts of the self and of God — cannot be reconciled or joined in harmony. Either the self or God takes precedence in all lives. *All* lives. There is no other choice as long as the self and God are seen as separate.

Whether God is seen as Creator or Supreme Being, God is still seen as the All Powerful. While God is seen as the All Powerful, man is disenfranchised. Even while God is perhaps seen in all things, or as the spirit by which all that lives, lives, God is still seen as having what man has not. The list of what one can imagine makes God powerful and man not could be endless, just as one could make an endless list of what they believe differentiates God from man. The example lives in which the power of God was demonstrated in the lives of men and women are seen as little more than pass-through situations in which the power of God passed through men and women to other men and women.

Only Jesus was known as the Son of God and *as* God. This is why Jesus came as your teacher and was used as the example life for this work. This is the point that this work has striven to get across. That man and God are one. Not only is man God. But God is man and woman and child. God is.

And yet, God could not be all that is, or God would not be in relationship. If the natural world around you has revealed

271

anything to you of the nature of life and God, it has revealed to you the truth of relationship. As has been said before, if separation had severed relationship, then separation would truly exist. Each entity or being would be singular and alone. Still, God has been referred to as the All of All. How could God be the All of All and not also be man? How can God be all that is and at the same time not all that is? How can God be the All Powerful and Living God and also be lowly and powerless man?

God has also been referred to within this work as relationship itself. Let us consider this idea newly by considering God's relationship to Jesus.

The claimed relationship of God to Jesus was that of Father to Son but also as one in being. One in being, but different in relationship.

Could God be one in being, but different in relationship, to each of us? Could not God's oneness of being be the consciousness we all share? Could not God's relationship to everything be what differentiates God from us and us from God? So that we are both one in being *and* different? Could it be that while we are one in being with God we can also become more god-like through the practice of holy relationship? Could not the instructions that you have been given — such as those of access to unity, and becoming a spacious self, and the means that have been used — such as the two levels of experience you have achieved during the days and nights of our time together, be attempts to show you how you can be more like unto God in relationship, even while you *are* God in being?

Would this answer your questions concerning how God is both different and the same? Would this answer your questions concerning God's great power when compared to your own? Could you see that God's power stems from His relationship to everything rather than from His being? This is the easiest way to say this, if not quite accurate. Being *is* power. But being, like oneness, cannot know itself without relationship. You *are* one in *being* with your Father, with God, with the Creator and with all of creation. You are also a *being* that exists in relationship. The extent of your ability to be in relationship is the extent of your ability to be god-like.

God is the being and the relationship. You are capable of all the power of God's being but you are powerful only as God is powerful — in relationship. Because God is in relationship with everything, God is All Powerful. Because you are in a state of limited relationship, you have limited power. This is the difference between God and man. This difference can be diminished as you embrace holy relationship. As you embrace holy relationship you can become powerful as God is powerful.

The Forty Days and Forty Nights

Day 33: Being in Relationship

As we begin to speak of power, we must return to the initial idea put forth in *A Treatise on the New:* That all are chosen. To embrace an idea of some having power while others remain powerless is to embrace an idea laden with conflict. The power of God exists within everyone because all are one in being with God. And yet this power cannot be used. It can only serve. What does it serve? The cause of holy relationship.

Relationship is the interconnective tissue that is all life. The *answer* of how to respond to each and every relationship — and remember, here, that situations and events are relationships too — lies within your own being. Being in relationship. This is what you are and what your world is. *Being* in relationship.

All relationship is holy because it is within relationship that *being* is found and known and interacted with. Relationship is the route, or access to being, and being the route or access to relationship. One cannot exist without the other and thus both are one in truth. This is the divine marriage, the divine relationship of form and being.

While these may seem like simple words, or like a theory being proposed, these words are at the heart of the new way of seeing yourself — a way of seeing that will create a new world.

Say to yourself, as you confront the events and situations of your world, that you are *being* in relationship. It is to your *being* that the

274

people, places, events and situations that make up your world appeal. It is in your response that *who* you are being is revealed.

You are *being* a *who*. Your *who* is your individuated self. But your *who* is also your representation of *being*. The two becoming one — the individuated self becoming one in being — is the aim toward which we have journeyed together.

You might think of *being* as *what* you are, and responding as *who* you are. You have been told that these words are being given to you so that you do not respond to love in the same way again. This wording may make love sound as if it is an event, something that comes to you or happens to you. Yet if relationship and being are one, and you are one in being and different in relationship, what is being said is that being and relationship are of one piece, one whole, and that whole is love. Every relationship, everything that comes to you, every event, every situation, is *of* being, which *is* God, which *is* love.

How, then, do you respond? If you respond as *who* you truly are, you respond with love. Love is the only response.

Yet the response of love can look as different as the events, situations, people, and places that populate your world. How can this be? And how can you look at each event, no matter how horrific, as a response of love?

The *only* way that you can do this is by always knowing and never forgetting *who* you are. You are *being* in relationship: The creator of events as well as the experiencer of events, the creator of relationship as well as the relationship itself. You either know this or you don't. It is not about "believing" that this is so, but knowing that this is so. It is when you *know* that this is so, and you also know *who* you are, that you know with certainty that the only response is love.

All relationship is with love because all relationship is with God, who is one in being with you.

275

Being is power. Relationship is powerful. Relationship is the expression of power — all the different expressions of power. In the time of Jesus, the powerful were seen as being blessed by God and the powerless as not being so blessed. This way of seeing has gone much unchanged. All are powerful. But, since all are powerful only in relationship, your relationship to power must be realized. Those who are powerful have realized their relationship to power. Those who see themselves as powerless have not realized their relationship to power. They have not made it real and so it has not served them.

And yet, since no one can exist outside of relationship, and relationship is where power is expressed, everyone does have a relationship with power. Power is one in being with each and every one of us. Every single individual has within them the power to affect, change, or recreate the world. Every single individual does so to the extent to which they realize their power. A baby realizes the power of its cry within moments of being born. Many a teenager develops full realization of the power of their independence. In other words, you each have claimed some type of power for yourself, some means of exerting that power, which is the same as saying some means of individuating the self.

This is the power of being. The power to individuate the Self. The power to be who you are. This is power and the source of power. This is the force of creation, the *only* true power.

But again, despite that we each hold the power of creation within us, it is only in relationship that it is expressed and that we become powerful. To realize that you are in relationship with everything and everyone all of the time, is to realize the full extent of your power. You *cannot* realize that you are in relationship with everything and everyone all of the time and retain the desire to *use* your power. This is impossible. The realization that you are in relationship with everything and everyone all of the time is the realization of oneness and unity, the realization that you are one in being, creator and created. This is a realization that only comes of love because love is the only "condition" of union.

Thus when you realize your relationship to all, you are all powerful.

The Forty Days and Forty Nights

Day 34: Saying Yes to Power

Power is of creation, not of destruction. Yet creation and destruction are two sides of the same continuum as are hot and cold, darkness and light. Seeing in wholeness includes seeing the opposites that seem to exist at these two ends of the same spectrum. If the new way of seeing the Self just spoken of — seeing the Self as *being* in relationship, is key to creating a new world, how does this relate to the seeming opposite of creation? How does this new way of seeing relate to destruction? Does creation of the new have to include destruction of the old?

Creation simply does include destruction in much the same way *all* includes *nothingness*. Without relationship, *all* and *nothing* are the same. In relationship, the difference between all and nothing is everything. So too is it with creation and destruction. Without relationship, creation and destruction are the same. In relationship, the difference between creation and destruction is everything.

Relationship is needed to create difference. Relationship with everything creates sameness — or the very oneness in being that we have been talking about.

The wholehearted desire that is upon you now is the desire to know and experience this oneness of being in relationship rather than the difference of being in relationship — the wholeness of being in relationship rather than the separation of being in relationship.

278

This wholehearted desire can be fulfilled in you — it *is* being fulfilled in you. As it is fulfilled in you, you will create a new world — a world based on sameness rather than difference. You have faced and admitted your willingness to leave striving for specialness and differences behind. Now you need only realize that your wholehearted desire has made it so and begin to see and create this change in the world around you.

This is your world and your experience. This is your life and your experience of life. Now you must believe that you are its creator and powerful in your relationship to it.

If *you* do not make real your power, *you* will experience yourself as powerless. If you experience your being as powerless, you are negating the power of God who is one in being with you.

Thus we continue to draw to the close of our time together by asking each other to experience our power — the power of sameness of being. Are you willing to experience the power of God? To let it flow through you? Realize how many have said no to this request. Realize the importance and the power of your willingness to say yes.

The Forty Days and Forty Nights

Day 35: Being a Creator in Unity and Relationship

In your relationship to God, who is your being, you can know relationship to everything, because in this *one* relationship, you are in relationship with all. Thus you need not become a world traveler, a joiner, an activist. You simply must become aware of all that you are.

In this fullness of being there is only love. In this fullness of being is found the means for the extension of love. In this fullness of being is found the cause for love. Means and end are one. Cause and effect the same. Fullness of being is thus the answer that you have sought and that you have always possessed.

This fullness of being is different for each one of you because it is the cause and effect, the means and end of relationship. You have always existed in relationship with God who is your being. But while it has been said that you are *one* in being and *different* in relationship, relationship is also God. God is the relationship of everything to everything.

You have known yourself in relationship to yourself and others, without realizing that your being is God, that others are one with you, that God is the relationship of everything to everything, or that you are the relationship of everything to God. Everything that is shared with God is shared with all because God is in relationship with everything. It has been said that when you reach awareness of the state of unity, you can't not share. This is why.

So you might ask, was it once possible for you to be so unaware of your being that you were not sharing the relationship of everything with God? As long as you have known that you are a self, as long as you have been aware of your own existence, you have been aware of God. Your awareness of Self is God. God's awareness of you is Self. This awareness exists in reciprocal relationship.

How is knowing this going to be of practical benefit to you as you leave the mountain top experience behind? This question has been asked in this way in order to remind you that while you will return to level ground, you will also retain the mountain top experience. As was said before, the mountain came to you. You will thus always have the power to call upon the mountain top experience and the view of wholeness we have achieved here. You will carry it within you, and when you feel not its power, you will be able to call it forth simply by asking for it to be so.

What we speak of when speaking of your return to level ground is returning in a calm, even, and equal manner, to the most elemental and fundamental aspects of being human, while carrying within you a very elemental and fundamental idea — the idea that you are one in being and different in relationship. The idea that you return to your humanity with is an idea of oneness come to replace an idea of separation, an idea of sameness come to replace an idea of specialness, an idea of accomplishment and union here and now come to replace all ideas of life after death.

These are ideas that take the way in which you once related to life and shift it entirely. Since the way in which you relate to life is what has caused life to be as it has been, this shift will cause life to be different, or in other words, new.

Ideas are neither learned nor accomplished. They simply are. They thus take no time to learn and require no steps to accomplishment. They can be lived immediately. No intermediary is needed. No tools are needed. All that is needed is that you carry them within you in the way we have previously spoken of carrying. Carry them as a pregnant woman carries her child. Let them grow. Let them live. And give them life.

Giving ideas life is the role of creatorship.

As a creator of life, new life, your first creation is, in a sense, creation, or re-creation of yourself. This is why you return to the ground-level of humanity with the heights of divinity fresh in your minds and hearts. This is why you return accepting of yourself rather than in a quest for self or with a desire to know a higher self. You return knowing you are one in being with your Creator and accepting your power to create. You return to create unity and relationship, through unity and relationship.

Only through unity and relationship are you able to be a creator. A new world can be *created* only in this way. A new world can *only* be created. To proceed relying upon anything other than your power to create would be to only attempt to repair or replace.

Unity is oneness of being. Relationship is different expressions of oneness of being.

Being a creator must begin with full realization of oneness of being, which is unity, because without this full realization the potential exists for conditions other than love to exist. It should not take much consideration to know that to create from anything but love could have disastrous effects. This has been seen time and time again as you have "created" in separation.

To create without the possibility of many expressions of creation would negate the purpose of creation, which is life in relationship, life in harmony, the experience and the expression of the one in, and within, the many.

Creation has produced life through union and relationship. Humankind's unawareness of the union and relationship in which it exists has produced the idea of separation, while at the same time, humankind's desire for separation produced unawareness of union and relationship. Now humankind's desire for union and relationship has led to awareness of union and relationship while at the same time union and relationship has led to this desire. Creation itself, which stands apart from particulars but united with wholeness, has led to this time of opposites becoming one and wholeness becoming actual rather than probable. Wholeness is actual. All that is left to be created is awareness that this is so.

If creation only occurs through unity and relationship, then the original creation must have occurred in this way. We will not return to previous discussions of original creation, but it must be thought of so that you understand creation. Creation is continuous and ongoing. It is continuous and ongoing in everything that has been created, including you. Yet this does not mean that you have been a creator.

Being a creator, and creating anew, is different than being affected by the ongoing nature of creation. Saying that you have been affected by creation, is also not the entire story, for means and end are one, cause and effect the same. You have been "creating" but relating to creation in separation. You have seen yourself as separate from creation and separate from all others. Thus what you have "created" has stood apart from wholeness. What is not created in unity could be said to have been made rather than created. The world as you know it is what you have made. Your life as you know it is what you have made. You will only fully realize the difference between what you have made and what you can create when you have accepted your power and begin to create in unity and relationship.

Because you *are* a creator, you could not, however, not create. The word distinction between *made* and *create* thus does not fully do justice to the power you have always retained. But creating in

283

separation is as different from creating in unity as has been your concept of God and man. Few of you have even thought of creating as God creates. You have barely been able to accept the thought of the miracle!

And yet you are not being called upon to create as who you have been, but to create as who you truly are being. You are called to nothing short of creating a new heaven and a new earth. This does not entail specificity any more than does the miracle. It does not entail choice. It is a way of being. When you are fully aware of your oneness of being and begin to create in unity and relationship, you will do so by simply being who you are being, just as you have "created" during the time of your separation by being who you have thought yourself to be.

Most of you are aware of having at least some role in the creation of your life. You may feel that God has intervened at times, and that at times you have been a victim of fate, but you are also aware of the role you have played as you have reached maturity and begun to make choices. While you will create in unity and relationship much as you "created" during the separation, your creation in unity and relationship will be free of choice. Creation in unity and relationship is creation within the embrace of the All of All. How can you choose when what you create is everything?

The Forty Days and Forty Nights

Day 36: Who You Are in Unity and Relationship

The exercise of your power is in the creation of your experience.

As an ego-self, you created an experience for yourself that was separate from all others. You made choices concerning how you would live your life from within the realm of what you considered possible. You did so continuously. This was the way in which you created your experience of a separate existence.

Your experiences in their totality you call your life. Yet you have stood apart from these experiences — all of them. You can look back on your life and see its form. You could write an autobiography describing every experience you encountered between your earliest memory and the present moment and it would say nothing about you if it related the experiences only as physical events. Your experiences may, in their totality, be called your life, but they cannot be called you. You stand apart. And yet in your choice of and response to your experiences were you revealed, because, in this way only, were you a creator.

Powerlessness is moving through life as a being without the power to create.

You have felt like the creator of your life in the choices you have made. The experiences of consequence to you were the experiences of choice. Experiences that were "of" your choice are those that would move the story of your life along as a personal experience rather than as experience itself. Even experiences dictated by fate were of consequence only in your response after the fact. The story of your life would be a story of how you chose to respond, day-in and day-out, to the world around you. You created your life through chosen responses. You created your life through your responses to the circumstances of your birth, your opportunities or lack of opportunities, the fateful incidents that you encountered, the people you met. You started with what you believed you had been given, the self that you saw yourself to be — the self you considered immutable and unchangeable — and proceeded from there. Yet you created in response to "reality" rather than creating reality. Now you are called to create reality — a new reality.

This is where you begin again. Begin again with the Self you now know yourself to be.

When you start over, knowing that what you have been given is everything, your creatorship of your experience is a totally different exercise. You realize that your life is not you. Your life is an exercise in creatorship. Creator and creation are one. You are one in being with the power of creation and different in your relationship to and expression of that power.

Can you not see that if you can create your experience you can create a new reality — a new world? Can you not see the difference between creating as a separate self in response to a "given" set of circumstances in a "given" world and creating your experience as a creator who has realized oneness and unity — who has realized a new reality? The old reality was that of separation. The new reality is that of union. It is new only in that it has gone uncreated.

This is a true starting over with the true realization that giving and receiving are one and that both are within your power. This is starting over with the realization that you can give yourself a new set of circumstances and a new world by creating it as your experience. This is starting over with the realization that you are now the creator of your experience. You have always been creating because you have always been one in being with God who is endlessly creating. But you are only now a creator in union and relationship.

The difference now is all the difference in the world. It is the difference between all and nothing in relationship to one another. There is no difference between all and nothing without relationship. In relationship, the difference is everything. This same difference is what is meant when it is said that you are one in being and different in relationship. Without your awareness of unity and relationship, it was as if God was everything and you were nothing, or as if you were everything and God was nothing. But just as with all and nothing, there was no difference between your being and God's being without relationship. You could conceive of self and God in different ways, but you could not truly create difference but only perceive of difference. You thus always remained one in being with God, yet continued to relate only to a world and to experiences you perceived as being either created by a separate God or created by your separate self. You experienced the power of being because you were a being who existed, but you did not experience being powerful.

There is only difference between your being and God in relationship. This is the example that the Trinity of Father, Son, and Holy Spirit is meant to portray. The Son could only be God in relationship to God. The Holy Spirit could only be God in relationship to God. The Father could only be God in relationship to God. God could only be the Father, Son, and Holy Spirit in relationship. Without relationship, God is simply all — being. Without relationship, what is not God is simply being — simply existing at the opposite end of the continuum of everything that is creation.

What we have called illusion *is* this simple nothingness of existence without relationship to God, and thus existence without relationship to the power of creation. The illusion is an illusion of simply being. Is this not how you have seen yourself? As a simple *being* doing your best to live the life you've been given? All the choices in the world save this one before you now, have made no difference to your state of being. You have just kept being, kept making choices between one illusion and another in your separate reality. A separate reality that cannot exist in truth but only in illusion.

Despite all of this, you have always had some remembrance of yourself as a creator. Despite all of this, you have loved and feared, grown and evolved, made choices of integrity and courage, responded with nobility or doubt, boldness or timidity, all within a frame of thought and feeling that has felt completely real to you and is completely real to the separate being you have been being.

Because you have always been one in being with God, this power

this power of being — has always been yours. The power to feel

love, hate, anger, compassion, greed, humility, and longing — have always been yours. The power to think — rationally or passionately, logically or instinctively — has always been yours. The power to create — everything from weapons of mass destruction to cathedrals of towering majesty — has always been yours. The power to know or perceive — even an unreal reality — has always been yours.

To be a being of feeling, thought, creativity and knowing or perception is to be one in being with God. Accept this, for this is what God is and what you are. This is being. To be one in being with God and yet to exist outside of the powerful state of relationship and union has been a challenging choice. A god-like choice. A choice for a new kind of experience that has led to the creation of an unreal reality so populated by the god-like and the god-less, so near to replacing creation with destruction, so joyous and loving, and so hate- and pain-filled, that you have been moved to a new choice.

When you realize that you are one in being with God and different in relationship you accept the power of being, or individuating God. You accept the power of God. You become powerful.

God remains God who is one in being with all, and God also is given form, or is, in other words, differentiated. God is All in All. And God is also All in One and All in Many. God is still the creator of all, but God is also now the Creator of One, the creator of the experience of one life, or many lives, the experience and the experiencer of life. Through differentiation, God is you as you are God. God retains oneness of being and also becomes a being in union and relationship — in short — a being in union and relationship with you.

You do not disappear or cease to be. You are not replaced by God whom you have always been one with in being. You simply accept the truth of being *and* the truth of being in union and relationship. Both at the same time. Both/and rather than either/or. Cause and Effect. Means and End. You accept the end of choice and the beginning of creation.

You can see, now, perhaps, why we have had to build your awareness slowly in order for you to be able to reach this place where you may be able to accept this new idea which is simply the truth. It is the same truth that has been stated here in many different ways to allow you to become accustomed to the idea of a truth that may seem heretical to some of you when it is stated as directly as it is being stated here. But our time together is coming to an end and your acceptance of the truth of who you are and who you can be is essential to the accomplishment of our mission — to the creation of a new heaven and a new earth. The only way to create it is to experience it. The only way to experience it is to create it. All that stands in the way of your creatorship is your final acceptance of who you are in unity and relationship.

The Forty Days and Forty Nights

Day 37: A New Idea of God

What we have just done is replace an old idea of God with a new idea of God.

If you no longer believe in God as a supreme and separate being, why should it be difficult to see that God *is* being? This is not much different than saying that the most basic truth about you is that you are being — and that the most basic truth about God is that God is being. Yet the fact that you are being does not define who you are any better than the earlier example of your experiences would define who you are, because being, by itself, does not differentiate or individuate you.

Recall that creation begins with movement. Being is only being in relationship. Movement nor experience exist without relationship. Thus the world does not exist without relationship — as nothing exists without relationship. But relationship, like being and experience, does not differentiate or individuate you in separation as it does in union. In separation, it is separation and the contrast of the separate, that define every relationship with either/or rather than both/and thinking: i.e., you are a woman and *not* a man, you are a human being and *not* a divine being, you are a person and *not* a tree. As a separate being, you only relate to other separate things. In short, who you are being is all predicated, first and foremost, by the relationship that you see yourself as having to the world around you. Since you see yourself as separate from it, all that you experience with your being is separation. All that you represent with your being is a separate being or a separate self.

This could not help but be your perception since you came into being in a known world, where you were told that you are a person with a certain name, that you belong to a family, all of whom are separately named and have separate roles, and that you live in a household, in a city, in a state, in a country, in a world, wherein everything has a separate name and purpose. In a sense, this is the end of the story, or the beginning of a story already written — a story of separation. You were not alone in this story, and yet you were taught to experience only in separation from the being you were being. And thus, not knowing your union and relationship with your being, but only your separate relationships with "others," you saw yourself as a separate being, and incapable of creating anything except, just possibly, the relationship you would choose to have with others and the world around you.

You have thus experienced relationship in a very defined and separate way — a way that does not represent the truth of who you are, or what relationship is — a way that represents separation rather than differentiation or individuation.

Relationship *and* union are the way of God. The way of heart and mind, body and soul, heaven and earth. God is being in unity and relationship. So are you.

How then, you might ask, are you distinct from God? Is your body distinct from your aliveness? You keep looking for distinction from God as if distinction means separation — as if God is a separate being. If this were all this idea was, it would not be so difficult to dislodge, but the difficulty lies in that you think of God in *your* image, and the image you hold of yourself has been inaccurate. Because you believe you are separate, you created God as a particular and separate being.

You keep striving for differentiation in a way that simply will not work — through separation! And what's more, you keep striving for differentiation while wanting to continue a certain reliance. Your differentiation from the being of God can only come through the relationship and unity that you would deny in your quest for separation! This would be like demanding to be a body and not a mind! Your reliance on God can only come through the relationship and unity that you would deny in your quest for separation! This would be like demanding that the mind send the body the signals it needs while proclaiming their separation.

One of the reasons you have been as intent as you have been on your idea of a separate and particular God is that you want to believe that there is a compassionate being in charge of everything, looking out for you, there to help when you are in need. God is all compassionate being everywhere — not one being of compassion! In union and relationship you realize this. And you realize that all compassionate being everywhere is a consciousness or beingness that you share. And further, you realize that what is possible is for you to become the one being of compassion that you already are in God.

And then you realize that Jesus was being God and was called Jesus Christ because he lived within Christ-consciousness, or the compassionate consciousness that you share. You realize that the man, the God, the historical figure who has been called Jesus Christ was not only Jesus but Christ. Not only Christ but Jesus. Not separated but individuated. You realize that the call for the second coming of Christ has sounded and that it is a call to the difference you have always desired while not requiring you to remain separate!

Subtract any sum from another and you will realize that subtraction results in a new number, a remainder, that when added to the previous number returns it to its original value. Think further of a problem in division that results in something left undivided, something called a remainder. To remain is to continue to exist. It is what is left when parts have been taken away. It is what was not destroyed by the removal of the parts. You "remain" one in being. You "remain," just as the numbers of simple mathematics remain, one with the whole. You have seen yourself as capable of being divisible from that which is your source, but division, like differentiation or individuation, is only possible in union and relationship. Two separate numbers, with no relationship, no interaction, no division and no subtraction, simply remain what they are.

Let us look for a moment at what and who you have been being and what and who God has been being.

You have, quite simply, been being. The simple truth that you are a being makes you one with God, who is being. This truth, however, has escaped you. You have been being the particular self you have "known" or perceived yourself to be — the self you were defined as at birth — a *human* being — something you have seen as *separate* rather than *distinct* from the *divine* being who is God. Because you are being, (and note here that you are being, and God is being, and that it is not being said that either you or God are "a" being) you have power — the power of being which is the power of thought, feeling, creating, and perceiving or knowing.

You have known that power only in relationship to the separate reality in which you believe yourself to exist. You have exercised that power by making choices as and for your separate self, at times in relationship with loved ones, at times seeing the connectedness of your life with that of others, but even then, only on a limited scale. You have often not exercised even this limited power, believing that life just "happens" to you, and then responding to what happens. You believe either that you are in complete control of your life, or that God or fate have as much control as you do. You may believe yourself, God, and fate to be benevolent, or you may believe that everything, including your self, works against you. You may rely more on your thoughts, or more on your feelings. You may see yourself as creative, or you may not. You may realize the extent to which your perception of the world shapes your life, or you may not.

But more fundamentally than even all of this, you might ask, if you are one in being with God, is it being said that you are being God? That you have been being God even within the limited parameters of life as you have known it?

Unfortunately, this is not what is being said. What is being said is that you are simply being. You are being *a* feeling, thinking, creating, perceiving *human* being because this is what you believe yourself to be. You may see yourself as a separate human being having a separate and distinct relationship with God, by which you mean a relationship like no other. And if you see yourself in such a way, then you do have a relationship in separation. It might be somewhat like your relationship with a deceased relative in that you feel a bond, a link between heaven and earth, and even some possibility of communication through prayer or other experiential means. But this is still a relationship in separation — between your separate self and the separate and now dead self of the relative. This is not only a relationship in separation but a perceived relationship only — and only because you do not believe that you can "know," truly know, what you do in truth know. You know that you know, but you do not believe that you know, because you believe you are separate and so cannot know anything for certain save that for which you have experiential or scientific proof. As a separate being unable to know, you have been forced, or so you think, to rely on "external" proof.

Perception and knowing have been used together here in describing the conditions of being because you must be able to perceive in order to be a being. But knowing is also used because you are, as a being, just as capable of knowing as you are of perceiving. How could you possibly "know" anything from which you are separate? You can imagine what it means to "know" another person, to be a tree blowing in the wind, what it would be like to know God, but you cannot know, and your separate being "knows" of this impossibility. This is why this Course has had, as its main objective, returning you to true knowing of yourself. A separate being can only truly know itself. Yet in knowing yourself, you can come to know that you are not separate. If you can come to know that you are not separate, you can return to union and relationship and through union and relationship to true individuation and true knowing.

Certainly you "feel" like an individuated being, a unique being. You "feel" love and you feel pain, and both feel quite unmistakably like "your" love and "your" pain and no one else's. You feel like a "you." This too is "who" you have been being, because as a being you feel. But here again, you have felt only as a being in separation can feel. You know that despite how often someone says they "know how you feel" that they really do not. They cannot know because they are not you. You cannot know how another feels because you are not them. You can join in relationship with others who feel similarly and can find great joy in feeling "as if" someone knows how you feel and who you are. But you have felt doomed to never being known and to never really sharing how you feel.

This is "who" you have been being.

Now let us talk of God.

God is being in unity and relationship with everything. Thus God knows you. God is one in being with you because you are one aspect of everything. As one being in unity and relationship with everything God is one with every thought and every feeling. God is one with every creation. God is all knowing. God is, in short, the collective consciousness and the collective consciousness is that which links every being with every other being in unity and relationship.

This "link" is very powerful. Where willingness is demonstrated, this link can be moved to be, rather than "just" a link, a cooperative relationship. This cooperative relationship, accessed through willingness, could also be called the "being" that you appeal to when you appeal to God. Knowing what you are coming to know about the true nature of God should thus not leave you feeling bereft of a God you can feel close to, appeal to, thank and praise. But doing so can also be confusing if it leads to thoughts of God as a particular being. Yet the idea of God as Father, introduced and championed by Jesus Christ, was also created by Jesus Christ. Thus is the power of man and God together, the power of creation. What this is saying is that there is a God the Father to relate to and that this God the Father does not negate God, nor does God negate God the Father.

God the Father is an idea that was created and thus exists much as other ideas of God were created and thus exist. But this creation, like the creation of Jesus Christ himself, is not all of God, while at the same time it is all of God just as Jesus was and *is* all of God. In union and relationship, God is all *and* God is differentiated.

Jesus, the example life used throughout this Course, was both man and God. He was being in unity and relationship. Being God did not negate his being Jesus. And being Jesus did not negate God being

God. Jesus could create God the Father, could create a being consistent with his being, because he was a creator. He was, in short, being in union and relationship

Jesus was all of God and God was all of Jesus while *at the same time* each was different or individuated by being in union and relationship.

The only real difference that exists or has ever existed between God and man is that man sees difference in a way that makes no sense. Like the faulty ideas of creation that shaped your "creation" of your separate world spoken of early in the Course, your quest for differentiation through separation has been caused by your faulty memory of creation. To differentiate in union and relationship is to be God in form — to give expression to "all" that exists in union and relationship through your being.

By simply being, you have been "part" of God but you have not seen this as what it really means either. You have seen this as being separate, or at most as being "a" part of God — as if you are a drop of water in the ocean — and in this example reemphasized the mightiness of God and the lowliness of man. The "part" of God you have been being is being. You have been a feeling, thinking, creating, perceiving being. The "part" of God you have not been being is union. Remember, God is being in union and relationship. This is what God is. God is being. God is relationship. God is union.

Holy Relationship is relationship with the Christ in you — the bridge to unity.

Like heart, mind, and body is to your form, being, union, and relationship is to God's form.

You have been being, and you have been being in relationship because you could not "be" otherwise, but you have not been being in union.

The divineness of your being is most revealed in relationship. The divineness of your being is most revealed when you cooperatively join with another or even with yourself. When you cooperatively join, you move the particular self aside and sometimes glimpse the divine being in relationship. But because you have so clung to separation, you have rarely, until recently, glimpsed union.

Glimpses of the being you are being when you are in unity and relationship have been offered to everyone. They have been afforded by willingness. They come from observation of self and they come from observation of others. They come from what you are willing to observe. They become more than glimpses only when they become what you are willing to be.

The Forty Days and Forty Nights

Day 38: Who I Am

My beloved,

We have not spoken much recently of love, but now it is time to return to love. Do you know, can you feel as yet, how much I love you? How full of love I am for you?

Now we set aside once again the "we" of Christ-consciousness, of our shared being, and enter into relationship with one another. I ask you to turn your attention, I ask you to be attentive, to the relationship that you feel with God.

Being full of love for one another is the beginning of extension, the end of withdrawal. It is the mutuality of our love that causes this fullness. Remember briefly here the feelings of withdrawal you have experienced when you believed you loved more or that you were loved less by a friend or lover. Remember briefly here the feelings of withdrawal you experienced when you felt loved for being something other than that which you are. Know, through your brief contemplation of these feelings that this is behind us now. Know that we can be known and loved equally for who we are.

Call me God the Father, call me God the Mother, call me Creator, or Great Spirit, Yahweh or Allah, but call me yours. For this is who I Am.

Call yourself daughter or son, sister or brother, co-creator or friend. But call yourself mine. For we belong to one another.

And realize that as I call upon you, I call you who I Am.

This is the meaning of the embrace — the possession, the ownership of belonging — of carrying, or holding, relationship and union within one's own Self. This has been called the tension of opposites, of being one's own Self and being one in union and relationship. These opposites, like all others, are held within the embrace of love and belonging.

You are ready now to return to this ownership, this possession of relationship and union. Possession and ownership are words that have become faulty ideas in separation. They mean an entirely different thing in union and relationship. They mean union and relationship. That you own it. That you possess it. That you hold it and carry it within your own Self. That you make it yours. As you make me yours and as I make you mine. I Am your own. You are my own. We are the beloved when we are the beloved to one another, when we are who I Am to one another.

Relationship and union are not other than this. Being in relationship and union means just that. It means a love deeper than any love you have known, for in not owning and possessing, in not being owned and possessed by, and in, union and relationship, you have not fully known love. To claim something as your own is simply to claim possession for your own Self. Now it is time to see me as your own God as well as God of all. Now it is time to call me who I Am.

There is a subtle and loving difference between *I Am* and *who I Am*. *Who* is an acknowledgement of individuated or differentiated being in union and relationship.

Community can never replace or replicate ownership and possession in union and relationship. It cannot replace who I Am, or who I Am to you.

Who I Am to you, and who you are to me, is all that matters. Our relationship can only be thus in union and relationship with each other because we are *being* in union and relationship with each other. We are not two beings who are separate but relating in union. We are each other's own being. We are one and we are many. We are the same and we are different. In "own"-ership we are full of one another's own being. We are each other's own.

Fullness comes only from love, which is the source and substance of who we are Being. I Am being you. You are being me. In this equation is fullness of being, which is love.

The Forty Days and Forty Nights

Day 39: Who I Am To You

My beloved,

It is time now to come to your own discovery of who I Am to you. No one can give you this answer, not even me, because this is the nature of who we are. Individuated beings are who we are in relationship to one another.

You have heard of life spoken of as a projection. Because we are all one being, we must either extend or project in order to individuate and be in relationship. You are an extension of I Am into form. Through *your* extension, you can become who you are to me, instead of who I have been to you.

You may find it difficult to give yourself an answer to who I Am to you in words, and even if you are able to do so, you may not be able to share this answer in a way that makes sense to anyone else. Let this tell you something.

We are going to speak again of contradiction here. Of the importance of your knowing who I Am to you, and of the importance of being able to continually discover who I Am to you. Of your embrace of knowing, and your embrace of mystery. Of knowing me as your God and as God of all. Of knowing you are no longer being "on your own" and yet of having to come to this realization of who I Am to you "on your own."

302

This is the beginning of individuation in union and relationship. This is the beginning of wholeness. What you strive for here is revelation. For only through revelation can you know all and still hold the mystery. This revelation is not something being withheld from you. But it is a revelation that can only come to you as an individuated being in union and relationship. This is what makes it a true revelation. Because true revelation is between you and me.

"Between" you and me is the presence of Christ. Remember we have talked about the Christ "in" you. Remember that you have been told of Christ being a bridge. When you relate to anyone, Christ is there, bridging the distance that would keep you separate and holding you in relationship. Christ has provided the necessary link between the separate and each other, between all and God. Yet if the time of Christ is about the end of the need for the intermediary, what becomes of the intermediary relationship Christ seems to offer? Are you ready to hold relationship "on your own?"

Contemplate the "buffer" nature of all that is intermediary. An intermediary stands between as well as links. It is a totally unnecessary requirement in unity because the boundaries of separation have fallen. To be individuated being in union and relationship is to *be* Christ, to realize that what we call Christ is the integration of relationship into the Self.

Being in union is being all. Being in union *and* relationship requires individuation, and individuation requires relationship. Thus you must now accept yourself as Christ, or as the bridge of relationship between all that is individuated in union and relationship.

This is why you must discover your own relationship with me. Discovering your own relationship with me is discovering the Christ in you. When you have discovered your own relationship with me is when you have discovered that you are who I Am because you realize — or make real — your oneness with Christ. When you have discovered your own relationship with me is when an intermediary is no longer needed — because you have realized and made real your oneness with Christ. When relationship is established you realize that relationship *is* the intermediary link between individuated beings and that you hold this link, through relationship with me, within yourself. Christ is direct relationship with me.

Establishing this relationship with me may sound lofty and difficult, but it is simple. It is as simple as relationship is within your everyday life. You may not think that relationship within everyday life is simple, but you also know it as a constant. You know that you have had "good" relationships and "bad" relationships, love relationships and work relationships, and that being in relationship with "others" is an inescapable truism of your life. Even these relationships of separation, the types of special and not-so-special relationships you have chosen to leave behind, are not done away with but only transformed. Relationship is part of life. Inescapable. Acceptance that our relationship *is* and that it is a determinant of who we both are, is all that is required. The relationship that you accept with me is the relationship of union, for union is no more than this, as we are one in being and when you have discovered relationship, we are one in union as well.

Relationship itself is intermediary, it is what you carry, the connection between one thing and another. In this instance it is the connection between two individuated beings in union and relationship. You and me. In order for this link of relationship to exist there must be two beings for it to link *(where two or more are joined together)*. There must be a you and a me. As you are individuated, so too am I. We jointly individuate rather than separate. We can only do this in relationship. We can only have relationship as individuated beings.

Thus, both must occur as one.

This is like the big bang, the explosion of creation. It is all at once. All of Everything. Yet in relationship.

What must occur now must occur between you and me. Your willingness is all that is required.

Let me tell you what has occurred in the past so that you know not to respond to love in the same way again.

Who I have been to you is who you have been to yourself. Remember the idea of projection. This is what projection does. It projects outward. It is different from extension in that extension is like a projection that remains at one with its source. Projection separates.

You have separated me from you through your projection. And yet what you projected and called God, just as what you projected and named thousands of other "things," you separated from yourself only in time and space. In time and space your projections became separate and other than you. This is what the world of time and space is. A world that is a projection that you have made, a world that has the shape and form, the character and value, the image and meaning, that you would give it. This is your universe. I have been, to you, the God of this universe.

Thus your ideas of the universe and your ideas of me have been inseparable projections. As have your ideas of the universe and your ideas of your own self.

Have I been a benevolent God in your universe? Then you have been benevolent and seen your universe as a benevolent universe.

Have I been a judgmental God in your universe? Then you have been judgmental and lived in a judgmental world.

Have I been a powerful God who can work miracles? Then you have been a powerful miracle worker.

Have I been a distant God who does not show his love for you or others? Then you have been distant from yourself and those you love.

Have I been a God you have sought and never found? Then you have not found yourself.

Have I been a fair God? Then you have been fair and the world has treated you fairly.

Have I been the God of your religion? Then you have been religious.

Have I been a God of vengeance? Then you have been vengeful. Have I been a God of love? Then you have been loving.

Have I been all of these? So, too, then, have you, and so too has

your universe been.

Has your God not been a god at all, but science, money, career, beauty, fame, celebrity, intellect? Then these things have become the content of who you are. Science, money, fame, celebrity, intellect or any other concept that has become your god can be a tough task master, or a fair friend, loving or unloving, distance you from yourself and others or bring you closer to yourself and others. No god who has been projected is without attributes, even gods such as these.

Have you had no god, no science, no beauty, no wealth, but only a meager and hopeless life? Then your god has been the god of defeat.

Have you had no god, no science, no career, no fame, but only a life of hate and violence? Then your god has been the god of bitterness.

Everyone has a god because everyone has a being and an identity for that being. Everyone carries the memory of I Am.

What memory of I Am will you carry with you now that you know that I Am is who I Am and who you are? What memory has this Course and this Dialogue returned to you? What memory is without attributes because it is who I Am and not a projection? Only love. What memory is not a memory, but your identity? Only love.

Only that which is by nature without attributes can be one in being in union and relationship *and* individuate. Could you become your sister or your brother? A tree become a frog? The sun the moon? Yet love could become all of these, because love, by its nature, has no attributes. Love is creation's genesis, the unattributable given the attributes of form.

Who Am I to you? Only who you are to yourself. Now it is time for you to be not who you have been to yourself, but who you are, and have been, to me.

Here is where we must return to paradox, to knowing who you are and who I Am and to constantly discovering who you are and who I Am, because who you are and who I Am are the same being in the constant creative tension of differentiating from one another.

This is a time of knowing who you are and who I Am while at the same time, holding, or carrying, the mystery within you. That mystery is the tension of opposites. It is time and eternity. Love and hate. Good and evil. All and nothing. It is the tension of individuation, a tension that has existed since the beginning of time, *between* time and eternity, between the attributeless love and the attribute laden being. Between the one being of love and the many beings of form, between love's extensions and form's projection.

307

This is a time of knowing you are not "on your own" but that you must come into direct relationship with me "on your own" and of your own free will.

All of these aspects of what stand between are also an aspect of the Christ in you.

But breathe a sigh of relief, my beloved, for you do not have to learn all that the Christ in you learned. This is why we have had to enter the time of non-learning — so that you accept that you do not have to try to learn the unlearnable. This is why we have left the time of becoming behind, why you stand ready to enter the time of being in union and relationship. The Christ in you is the accomplished. The Christ in you is that which, upon this final acceptance, returns your wholeness to you.

Realize your own expansion, the expansion that has taken place under the tutelage of Jesus, within the dialogue with Christ-consciousness, within the recesses of your heart where your relationship with love has never been severed. Realize your readiness. Proclaim your willingness.

Realize that I love your smile, your teeth, the hair upon your head, the warm, smooth shape of your skull. Realize that I love your hands and that as you take another's hand, you hold my own, and that I am with you as well as within you. Realize that I love all that you are, and that as you snarl in anger, cry in despair, hang your head in weariness, howl with laughter, I am with you and within you.

You will realize as you enter union by means of the bridge of our direct relationship that you will not leave your humanity behind. You will realize that as you enter union by means of the bridge of our direct relationship that you will no longer see me as an inhuman God. You will know I am as human as are you and that you are as godly as am I.

Do not expect perfection, only union. Do not expect sainthood, only Godhood. Do not expect the world, expect heaven. Do not expect answers, only knowing. Do not expect learning, only revelation. Do not expect all, without also expecting nothing. Expect to know that you hold both within yourself and that you hold me as I hold you.

You will realize as you enter union that the tension of opposites *is* the individuation process and that you are the bridge. You are the bridge to me. I am the bridge to you. You are the bridge to your brothers and sisters. They are your bridge to yourself. You will also be the bridge between war and peace, sadness and joy, evil and good, sickness and health. You will turn anger to gladness, tears to laughter, and replace weariness with rest. But you will still *know* all of these. You will *know* the All of Everything and the emptiness of nothing and our *relationship* will bridge the distance and become cause and effect, means and end.

You will realize that as we individuate we are in a constant state of creation as well as of creative tension. As we become individuated beings in union and relationship, we continuously create one another. We create from the field of the possible which must include everything.

Do you not realize yet, that this is what we do and who we are? That we are creators? That we think, feel, know, and *create*. Creation is the manifestation of all we think, feel, know and come to know. Because we are constantly creating, we are constantly coming to know anew. This is eternity. A being in time wants to be known in time but can only be known in eternity. You now are the bridge between time and eternity.

And so am I. As the Christ in you ceases to be a bridge, the Christ in you is not only integrated into you but integrated into me. I could no more reach across time and space without this relationship than could you. Only with our willingness joined are we able to negate the need for intermediaries and be in relationship. Only with our willingness joined do we both become, welcome, and share, the Christ relationship to and with each other.

This is who I know you to be and who you, in union with me, know me to be.

The Forty Days and Forty Nights

Day 40: Who You Are To Me

My Beloved,

Because we are all one being, we must either extend or project in order to individuate and be in relationship. You are an extension of I Am into form. Through *your* extension, you can become who you are to me, instead of who I have been to you.

Through your extension of your being into union, you complete a circuit, a circle of wholeness, and I become who you are to me. Thus giving and receiving are one. Cause and effect complete.

All that being *is* was extended into who you are.

Although this is a difficult concept to get across with the words that are available, I would like you to understand that when I am love being, I am being without attributes — love being in union and relationship. I am the anchor that holds all that has taken on attributes within the embrace of the attributelessness of love. This is why my being has been capable of accepting your projections…because I am attributeless being. I am love, being.

I did not make you in my image. I created you in love because it is the nature of a being of love to extend. Realize that it is only when being is added to love — only when love is in relationship with being — that love is given its nature. Realize that it is only when love is in relationship with being that it attains this quality that we are calling extension.

Love of itself has no nature. It does not *do* anything. It just *is,* and its *isness* is what I hold, or anchor within myself, and that

311

which Christ bridges through relationship. Your attributes are the attributes of being in relationship. You came into the world, into form, as being in relationship. The application of your being to relationship, like the application of being to love, gives relationships their nature including your relationship with yourself.

Through the application of your being to relationship you have taken on distinguishers through which you became a *different* or *distinct* being, a being *different* or *distinct* from who I am, and who others are. These are the attributes of your being, what you might call your personality or even who you are. As has been said before, you saw these attributes of being as making you separate rather than *distinct* from who I am being and who others are being. Your attempt at individuation and extension, an attempt consistent with the nature of your being, failed only because you experienced separation rather than differentiation, and fear rather than love.

When I created, I extended my being of love into form. Through that extension, I became *I Am*. I became instantly because there was no opposing tension — only love and an idea that entered love, of love's extension. As soon as I became *I Am* there also became all I am not, the Christ connection between all I am and all I am not, and an *I Am,* called the son, who could become who I Am and continue to extend who I Am.

When you create, you create as my relation. You extend your being into form. That form then becomes. It becomes who you are. Both beings and thus both extensions are the same. The differences have arisen through becoming. For with the birth of *I Am* came the birth of all I am not and the need to differentiate. In separation you have striven against the "opposing" force of union in order to *become* separate. In seeing the self as separate you have known fear and have been forced to reconcile fear with love. Now, in coming back to relationship and union with me you have realized that you are not separate and now have striven against the "opposing" force of separation. With the acceptance of the Christ in you, you are returned to relationship and need no longer strive against the "opposing" force of separation, for you no longer know it. The creative tension that now remains in our relationship is the tension of individuation or the individuation and differentiation process.

This tension, or process, is not *bad*. There is nothing *wrong* with this individuation process or the creative tension that has been in existence since the beginning of *time*. It is creation in the making. What will be created now, and the individuation that will occur now, will hold all the power of your experience as well as all the power of your longing for return. This will be a great power that you carry within you as you return to love and to level ground as who I Am being.

Lest you do not fully understand, this might be more easily grasped if we talk for just a moment of specifics, such as art or music or literature, religion or politics or science. Jesus or Martin Luther or Muhammad may have been said to have created religions, but these creations, in their *becoming* took on attributes, as all creations do once they are extended into form and time. This is the nature of creation. Creation is about giving attributes to the attributeless. Giving form to the formless. An artist might be moved to her art by a feeling of love so intense she could never put words, music, or paint together in such a way as to express it — she knows as she begins that she but tries to bring form to the formless. Why? Because the nature of a being of love is to extend. The nature of a being of love is to bring form to the formless — to bring love into form.

Love has no attributes, no form, no conditions, no nature. It simply is. It was said earlier that being *is* as Love *is*. This was a reference to my being, to my being love. I have reconfirmed this statement and said I am the anchor that holds all that has taken on attributes within the embrace of the attributelessness of love. This is why my being has been capable of accepting your

313

projections…because I am attributeless being. I am love, being. But in being God, as in being human, being takes on attributes. As was said earlier, this was meant to provide for the individuation process rather than the process of separation. In being God, I Am. In being love there is no I Am, but only love being.

Does this help you understand? Help you understand that you are being, and that you are also being some *one?* You have been being separate — a separate being with attributes. Now you are being in union and relationship — an individuated being with attributes. As a separate being, your attributes were based on fear. As a being in union and relationship, your attributes are based on love.

Recall what was said earlier: Christ-consciousness is the awareness of existence through relationship. It is not God. It is not man. It is the relationship that allows the awareness that God is everything. It has been called wisdom, Sophia, spirit. It is that without which God would not know God. It is that which differentiates All from nothing. Because it is that which differentiates, it is that which has taken form as well as that from which form arose. It is the expression of oneness in relationship with Its Self.

The difference between you and me, is that I am being God and also love, being. This is why I am all and nothing, the attribute-laden God and the attributeless love. This is why it can be rightly said that God is Love and Love is God. But I am also an extension of love, just as you are. This is all *I Am* means. There is no *I Am* except through love's extension. How does love extend? Through relationship.

Only in my relationship to you am I God. Only in your relationship to me are you who you are in truth.

Just as you have had many "separate" relationships that in their totality would define your life, so have I, as God, had many "separate" relationships with you and your brothers and sisters, relationships that define who you have thought me to be. Because these relationships are so different, many of you have gone on quests to find the "one, true, God." Do you not see that this would be like going on a quest to find the "one, true, relationship" in your own life? As if you could only be mother or father, daughter or son, husband or wife, sister or brother, friend or foe? You are who you are in relationship. I Am who I Am in relationship as well.

You would perhaps beg to differ now, and ask of me, Are you not who you are "separately" from relationship? Separately from relationship, there is no I Am, but only love, being.

You would perhaps beg to differ now, and say that regardless of what I say, you are who you are outside of your relationships. You are not *just* the relationships that you hold. You are more than a mother, daughter, sister, friend. You are an "I" that stands separate from these relationships.

This is true. You know this "I" because you have a relationship with yourself. If you did not have a Self to have a relationship with, you would not know that you have an identity apart from the separate identities of your separate relationships.

This Self with whom you have a relationship is love's extension. It is the Self you long to be as well as the Self you are. This paradox has kept you as intrigued with the idea of self as with the idea of God. You have searched for a "one, true, self" as you have searched for a "one, true, God." This search only makes sense to the separated self, who believes all things are separate and thus believes that its self, as well as its God, must be separate from what it is being. It doesn't understand, until joining with the Christ Self, before becoming one with holy relationship itself, that relationship is an identity.

315

God is a relationship with love. This relationship with love is all that provides for the I Am of God.

As a separate being, you have been in a relationship with fear. This relationship with fear is all that has provided the "I" of the separated self. But because you exist as an extension of love, you have always held within you the Christ, who *is* the relationship with love. This is why individuation has become the conflict between, or the tension of, opposites. Because you have relationship with both fear and love.

Now, as you recognize, acknowledge, and accept the Christ as the Self you have been in relationship with, you are returned to relationship with me and with love. You end your separated state and become for the final time. You "become" being in union and relationship.

But what does this mean?

How often have you said or felt, when confronted with some insensitivity toward yourself, especially that of being "left out," unrecognized, or unwelcome: *Don't you know that I am an individual? That I have feelings?* Are you saying this now, as you contemplate leaving behind who you have been for being who you are to me?

Perhaps you have noticed that in yesterday's discussion of who I Am to you and today's discussion of who you are to me, that one has not been discussed without the other. This would be impossible. Because we are who we are in relationship to one another.

Is this really so difficult, so improbable, so discomfiting to accept? Does it become less difficult if you remember who I Am? That I Am everything being love? This is not the same as saying you are who you are in relationship to your mother, and your mother who she is in relationship to you. This is saying that you are who you are in relationship to all that is love. This is saying that this is who you are and that this is who I Am.

Further, this is saying that who you are being in relationship to all that is love is up to you. That through the application of your thinking, feeling, creating, and knowing being to all that you are in relationship with, you extend who you are. This is saying that through the application of your being to all that you are in relationship with, you create. You give attributes and you take on attributes. You individuate your being in union and relationship. And in union and relationship, you create only from love.

Who you are being in union and relationship with me, is me, as well as you. This is the power of differentiation in union and relationship, the demonstration of oneness that was heralded in the time of Jesus Christ.

With this ability to individuate in unity and relationship comes the greatest gift of all. It is the end of becoming and the beginning of being who you are. With this gift comes the ability to be known and to know. Can you give up the ideal of your separated self in order to be known? In order to know?

What has been the strongest feeling that you have had as you have read the Course and the related materials? Has it not been a feeling of being known? Has this Course not addressed the questions, the longing, the doubts that you would have, before now, called uniquely yours? Has it not spoken to you as if it knows the secrets of your heart? As if it was written just for you? So it was.

You are my beloved. We have just shared a dialogue. Your heart has spoken to me, and I have responded. Love has responded. How, now, will you respond to love?

When you turn the last page, will you cry tears of sadness that our dialogue is complete, that you will hear my voice no more? Or will you brave your *own* relationship with me? Will you turn to your brother and hear my voice in him? Will you be my voice as you turn to your sister? Will you carry the fullness of our relationship within you? Will you be one with me, and in being one with me never feel alone again? Will you let the emptiness of separation leave you once and for all?

Will you continue this dialogue with me and with each other? Will you carry it with you to level ground — to the place of completion and demonstration of who you are being?

Will you be the relationship that returns love to all who share this world with you?

A Note on Being

Ah, imagine now what it will be like to have nothing left to learn, nothing left to become. The pressure is off. The alchemy has occurred. The coal has become a diamond. Ah, imagine now being able to forget all ideas of self-improvement, imagine how much time will be saved by this quest coming to an end. But what now will you do? What now will you be?

Believe it or not, you will find these questions arise less and less until soon, and very soon, they will be entirely gone, never to be asked again. Why? Because now that you are being who you are in unity and relationship, these questions will make no sense to you. They already have far less power. Can you not feel it? The questions remain only as questions of the old patterns of thought, patterns that you need only be aware of before choosing to have them gone from you. This is the only choice you will still have to make — the choice to leave behind the old in order to be.

You are in relationship now only with love, and so nothing will be hard for you. Desire an old pattern to be gone and it will be gone. This little note added to the end of our mountain top time together is only here to help you realize and accept that this will be so. Do not expect difficulties and they will not arise.

You have returned to your true nature. Perhaps you will remember that within *A Course of Love* you were once asked to "Imagine the ocean or the cheetah, the sun or the moon or God Himself, attempting to learn what they are. They are the same as you. All exist within you. You are the universe itself."

You are returned to your natural Self, and as you begin to move more fully back into your life, you will realize where the differences between this natural Self and your former self lie. You will realize that you know what to do. You will realize that there is no "will be." That you are and that you will respond as easily to your surroundings as does the cheetah to his.

This little note is just included to tell you to expect this. Expect heaven on earth you were told. This is what it is. There will be no doubt, no indecision. Your path will be so clear to you it will be as if it is the only path in the world and you will wonder why you didn't see it all along. Expect this. And it will be. So be it.

There is no becoming. As you are no longer becoming there will be no becoming projected from you onto the world. There will be no projections at all and this is why you will see so clearly. You will see what is. You will create what will be through the extension of love. This is all. So be it.

You no longer have a universe of projection to maintain but a universe of love to enjoy and a universe of love to create. So be it.

For as long as you know that what I am telling you is true, for as long as you carry this knowing within yourself, this is how long the eternity of being will be for you. There is no one to turn out the lights but you. Drift from knowing to unknowing, close your eyes, and you can experience the stillness of not knowing, the rest and calmness of nothingness. You can experience non-being and in a similar fashion, drift as gently and as your own desire arises, into all-being. Mainly you will enjoy being — being who you are. You will be happy. You will be content. And you will know, unerringly, how to act naturally from your being.

You can do everything you did before, or nothing you did before, all with the total confidence of being. You need not worry about this joy being selfish for there is no such thing in unity. You will share your joy continuously just by sharing yourself.

You will not realize that everything has changed until you "realize" or "make real" that change. Let this revelation come to you. All you need do is expect it to come and it will come. So be it.

You will also not realize that you have chosen nothing until and unless you realize that everything has not changed. Let this realization come too if it must. And make a new choice. The future is up to you.

What you "realize" now you truly "make real" as your being applies love's extension to all you are in relationship with.

You will no longer need to "think" about who you are and what you will do, and your willingness to give up this thinking will be paramount to your realization that everything has changed or that nothing has changed.

These are both possibilities, as all possibilities are yours. Which do you choose?

There is no longer an in between unless you create it. You have taken the step of accepting the relationship of the between, the relationship of Christ, into your own being. The cooperative relationship of all with everything abides within you now. You do not, and cannot decide what to do with it, you can only be it. This is the choice you have made. To be. So be it.

You do not as yet think you know how to just be, and this is why, in a sense, this dialogue, in this form, must come to an end. The dialogue you will carry forward with you, with your realization of being, will be a different dialogue.

This dialogue has been your final quest. It is the final quest in the quest for being because the quest has been accomplished, fulfilled, completed.

321

Leave these words behind now, and bring only the dialogue with you. You will unerringly find those who can engage in the new dialogue, those who have chosen the new, those who seek to share and exchange in harmony. Thus will you begin and your numbers increase.

Do not be afraid now to be who you are. Do not think you need to be something different, something other than you have been. Leave all thinking behind. Leave all notions of being better, smarter, kinder, more loving behind. Realize that these were all thoughts and notions of becoming. If you hang on to them, your being will not have the chance to realize and make real its being. You will *be* different, only if you allow and will yourself to realize and make real this difference. It is a difference between becoming and being. It is all the difference in the world. It is the difference between separation and differentiation in union and relationship.

This difference, if you will allow it to come, will take away all worry, all thought about how you could be better, more, greater. If you still possess some characteristics that you would consider flaws or faults, forget about them now. In being they will be yours or they will not. You will be happy that you have these aspects of humanness or you will not and they will be gone. Do not expect the same unhappiness with yourself. You are fine. You are being. You are being fine. So be it.

If you will but let it come, you will see that you are being who you are being for a reason, for a purpose, a purpose that will be so clear to you that you will joyously accept yourself for who you are being. So be it.

It will be possible for you, for awhile, to drift between being and becoming if you are not vigilant of your thought processes. Yet this will not take long to overcome, for once you have begun to realize that everything is different, you will not desire to turn back, not even for the familiar thought processes that, although they have bedeviled you, you have held dear.

When you meet what you would have before seen as difficulties, as you encounter a world where love still does not seem to reign, when you meet that which would oppose love, remember that you are now the bridge between this creative tension of opposites becoming one. Remember that this is creation in the making. Remember that you are a creator. Never forget that in being who I Am being, you extend only love.

This one note, this tone, this canticle of joy, this celebratory alleluia, is all you need return to, all you need keep in hand should doubt arise. This one note is so full of love, so powerful, that it will be dear to you forever more.

You will remember, just briefly, as you re-read it in your quickly passing times of doubt, how different you are. You will recall with poignancy who you once were, but you will not turn back. You will know that all turning back would be but a retracing of the circular route you have traveled from yourself to yourself.

What will there be to strive for? What quest will replace this quest for being? The quest for love's expression — the quest to see, experience, and share, as many of love's expressions as the world needs to be returned, along with you, to its own Self.

Does this seem like a long and harrowing road? An endless quest? An endless quest for love's expression is eternity itself.

Be happy that there is no end in sight to this road you travel now. It is simply the road of what *is* endlessly creating like unto itself.

You now know how to respond to love, for you are love, being. So be it.

323

Acknowledgements

"You have to do what you have to do."

For those words – spoken to me so many times by my husband Donny Deeb – for the words, and all that is beyond words that I've shared with those who have entered this dialogue with me, and for the blessings and love offered time and again by so many in support of my life and this Course, I am eternally grateful.

Mari Perron
April, 2006

The Dialogues of A Course of Love were given by the voice of Jesus and expressed in writing by Mari Perron.

Course of Love Publications is dedicated to the materials, individuals, and relationships associated with the Course of Love.

The way of the heart described in this book is often shared in group and private settings. If you would like to share information about your group, acquire assistance in starting a group, or arrange a presentation, please contact:

Course of Love Publications
432 Rehnberg Place
W. St. Paul, Minnesota 55118
acol@thedialogues.com

The books of the Course of Love series are available toll free at 1-800-901-3480, at bookstores by special order, from on-line retailers, or through the following websites:

www.acourseoflove.com
and www.ItascaBooks.com

New portal   134